Memories of
Men and Women

Memories of
Men and Women

A. L. Rowse

EYRE METHUEN   LONDON

First published in 1980 by
Eyre Methuen Ltd
11 New Fetter Lane, London EC4P 4EE

Copyright © A. L. Rowse, 1980

Filmset, printed and bound in Great Britain
by Hazell Watson & Viney Ltd,
Aylesbury, Bucks

British Library Cataloguing in Publication Data
Rowse, Alfred Leslie
Memories of men and women.
1. Biography – 20th century
2. Great Britain – Biography
        I. Title
920′.041   DA28
ISBN 0-413-47700-2

Contents

Preface

It has been suggested to me that a word of preface might be in order, threading these ten studies together along the line of what they had in common. What indeed had they in common? Some of them knew each other quite well, for all of them were public figures who had made notable contributions to the life of their time.

Looking back over them all, I note that all of them were writers, even the politicians (except for Nancy Astor, who was rather more than a politician). I note too that they represent the two sides of my own interests, public and private: history and politics, literature, in particular poetry.

The earliest friendship here recorded is that with the poet Auden, going back to his undergraduate days, when I was hardly more than an undergraduate myself. My acquaintance with Maurois went back to those early days, when he devoted a couple of pages to my first essay, *On History*, in his *Aspects of Biography*. For the rest, I came to know them in the years after those recorded in my own autobiography, years beyond which I do not intend to go. Hence these portraits of others – I feel signally honoured to have had their friendship, and how much poorer the world since they have gone. And how much I miss them from it!

A.L.R.

I

My Acquaintance with Churchill

My acquaintance with Churchill was brief, but not without significance. Hundreds of people knew him politically, and scores of people have written about him as such; my acquaintance with him was something different – over history, the family history of the Churchills which I was writing and in which he took a close interest, and his own *History of the English-Speaking Peoples*, of which he asked me to vet the Tudor volume.

Plenty of jackals have rushed in to attack the dead lion, in the usual way; my acquaintance with him was wholly pleasurable – I was interested in him as an historical phenomenon. Even all that he told me about himself and the war was a contribution to history – and I wrote down everything. He was generosity itself – not like a cagey politician, as it might be with Clem Attlee or John Simon, all shut up and unwilling to divulge anything, or Harold Wilson, bent on putting something across (understandable enough in a politician, but whom does he think he is taking in?).

Churchill was not like a politician – as a matter of fact, he was not a good politician, but he graduated – in his sixties and seventies! – into a statesman. He was completely open and honest, not shut up like a clam; I remembered in talking to him that he had started as a soldier and war correspondent, that he had earned his living, as he said, by his pen and his tongue, and that in addition he was an artist, with the temperament of an artist, the ups and down – like the ups and down of his career. A combination of soldier plus artist – that

was what struck me in facing him and in my dealings with
him.

Though he had the courage of a lion and a rock-like endurance – I don't think he ever knew what fear was – he had a
rather feminine temperament. This may surprise people, but
his close and early friend, Birkenhead, knew it. The disasters
of war, like the sinking of the *Hood*, plunged his spirits into
depression. This is where Beaverbrook came in – people have
wondered what their relationship was and why the Beaver
should have had such a hold. Beaverbrook would arrive, give
Winston an injection of his primitive vitality and rattling
spirits, they would spend an evening together, and next day
Winston would feel better, able to take up the intolerable
burden, the inhuman task. (Winston to me: 'When the war
was over, I couldn't walk upstairs.')

Historically I owe him a great debt. In deciding to write
the family history of the Churchills, who were West Country
in origin (instead of the Cecils, which my pupil, Dicky Cecil
– killed in the war – wanted me to write), I took a risk. The
first volume, *The Early Churchills*, was plain sailing: all the
materials were in printed sources or otherwise accessible. But
the second volume, *The Later Churchills*, could not be written
without access to the archives at Blenheim Palace – and those
had been closed to G. M. Trevelyan when writing his *England in the Age of Queen Anne*. I decided to make Winston's
acquaintance, the only man I have ever gone out of my way
to know. Goodness, how it paid! He was extremely interested
in his family history, the generous side came uppermost: the
Blenheim archives were opened to me, and I could complete
the book. How lucky this was – and, as a bonus, he was ready
and willing to tell me everything else I wanted to know.

I recall with pleasure those daily excursions out from
Oxford to delightful Woodstock, the pass I had in at the grand
gate Duchess Sarah built to the Duke's memory, and where
Winston's father, Lord Randolph, had paused to impress his
bride, Jenny Jerome of New York. It is indeed spectacular –
the splendid park, the monumental bridge over an arm of the
lake, the outspread wings of the Palace on the skyline – I have
always thought that not for nothing was the architect Van-

brugh also a dramatist: it all presents itself like a grand stage-set.

Thence I would make my way, skirting the lake, to the military-looking gate, pillars resting on stone cannon-balls, into the side-court where the archives were kept. 'This Way to the Tomb' I used to think, after Ronald Duncan's play, as I settled down to the dank inspissated gloom within. I have never known gloomier surroundings for historical research, not even the prison of the Public Record Office. However, I was grateful to be there, alone with the letters and missives of Marlborough and his Duchess, and their great friend Godolphin.

Even so, the archives came to an end in 1815 – I can well understand why, from the family doings in Regency days. The Duke (Consuelo's son) to me one day at dinner: 'You didn't spare us in your book.' I said, 'Look, I was careful there to say what was already in print, though I knew a good deal more!' I believe that, since his death, with death-duties and what not, the archives have now been moved from Blenheim to the British Library.

When my first volume was written and Winston wanted to see it, it was to Chartwell down in Kent that I was bidden.

He was then eighty-three, still at work on his own *History of the English-Speaking Peoples*. I have often been asked, especially in America, whether he wrote his own books, or whether they were written for him. I can assure people that he wrote, or dictated, his own books, as he painted his own paintings (disconsidered by the critics, simply because painted by him). He did employ research assistants to gather materials for him, like my friend Maurice Ashley who did a lot of work for the big biography of Marlborough. But Churchill shaped up the masses of material and wrote every word of his books himself. (Unlike his friend Lord Birkenhead, or his rival, Lord Baldwin.) Churchill was a conscientious artist as a writer – if, naturally, somewhat too rhetorical, for, like Henry James, he dictated his later works. I had experience of the thought he put into the choice of words, the artist seeking for the right expression, his strong likes and dislikes (which I did not always agree with). It was fascinating to observe him at work, the intensity of concentration, the irritability, the bursts of naughty humour.

Other people have thought that I did some of his research for him. Not so: each volume of his *History* he conscientiously submitted to a recognized authority in the field to be vetted, and I was honoured by his submitting the sixteenth-century volume to me. His galleys had exceptionally wide margins, for corrections and comments; it was rather fun getting some of my own back, after his comments on the typescript of *The Early Churchills*. I found few corrections to be made, but was amused to see that where I had commented, 'Sentence much too long: please divide', it was conscientiously divided in the published work.

What fun co-operating with so idiosyncratic, outsize a man, who knew his own mind – as I knew mine! The day at Chartwell which we spent in part over my book was quite the most wonderful day I have ever known; perhaps the immediacy of it may best be recovered by resorting to my Journals.

'11 July 1955. While waiting for Churchill's car to pick me up at the English-Speaking Union, I spent half an hour at Lancaster House looking at the portraits of Churchill women, Henrietta and her sisters. Henrietta was the eldest, second Duke in her own right, married to Godolphin's son and heir; so that, if their boy hadn't died, the Churchill family would have been Godolphins, instead of Spencers. When the car appeared, it turned out a very grand affair flying Churchill's standard as Lord Warden of the Cinque Ports. Evidently everything was to be done in style.

'As we sped down into Kent I reflected that I had never seen him in private. I had missed my opportunity of a whole weekend when he came down to stay at All Souls in the thirties. I was away, but heard some echoes of the talk, of his onslaught on Baldwin as a "corpse", who would not wake up and take notice. (When foreign affairs came up in Cabinet, he would say, "Wake me up when that's over.") I had had an unforgettable glimpse of Churchill on VE day 1945, when I saw him stepping out with Attlee, chin up, leading the mem-

bers of the House of Commons across Parliament Square to
give thanks for victory (survival rather) in St Margaret's,
Westminster. Now, at last, I was to meet the man of that
hour, of those heroic years.

'Arriving at Chartwell I was surprised by the beauty of the
place. I should have reflected that he was an artist, and this
was his creation. He had added on to a small Elizabethan
redbrick house to make it pretty considerable, walled terraces
defining the situation: confronting an open valley which he
had improved with a lake in the hollow, a sickle-shaped ridge
of wood down the opposite side, looking sideways away to
the South Downs in the distance.

'Within, I was struck by the hum of activity – evidently
there was a dynamo at work somewhere in the house. First,
turned up a waxed-moustached ex-Guardsman of a valet, a
Scot of ferocious aspect and whisky complexion: I suppose
the famous Sawyers of the story of Winston, squeezing himself into a tight bunk on a plane somewhere in the war, right
on top of his hotwater bottle. Sawyers remonstrated: "Do
you think that a good idea?" Winston already half-asleep:
"It's not an idea, Sawyers, it's just a coincidence." Then
appeared the private detective, with fine eyes that took in
everything, Sergeant Pride, who accompanied us in the garden most of the afternoon, to see that the visiting professor
was not tempted to win fame by bumping off the most celebrated man in the world – at that moment. Next came the
housekeeper, devoted to Clementina's exquisite Siamese cat,
Gabriel, and a pretty young secretary. Workmen were changing rooms about, moving books to and fro, those upstairs
being brought down, others from downstairs being carried
up. Evidently at the behest of the unseen genie of the house.

'The downstairs library, into which I was shown, gave a
fair indication – as libraries do – of the Man. Above the
chimneypiece a vivid Frank Salisbury portrait of the war-time
Prime Minister, in familiar zip-suit of RAF blue-grey. Opposite, a big diagram of Port Arromanches – the floating harbour that so surprised the Germans, with all the ships, tracks,
quays, etc. marked. On a table, a new biography of Anthony
Eden uppermost. The books revealed the man: modern pol-

itical history, biography, memoirs dominant. In one corner the original Correspondence of Lord Randolph Spencer-Churchill, two shelves of folios, upon which Winston based his biography. (The copy of the published work in two volumes which he had presented to the Kaiser, at the German Military Manoeuvres of 1909, I had seen in the Kaiser's study in the Berlin Schloss before its utter destruction in the second German war.) There were some eight or ten volumes of Marlborough's Letters, I suppose from Blenheim. In addition, shelves of English classics and historians, complete sets of Scott, Johnson, Macaulay, etc.

'Before lunch I was summoned up to his bedroom, and there, at last, was the so familiar face, much aged: that of an old man who had gone back to his baby looks. The eyes a cloudy blue, a little bloodshot, spectacles on snub nose, a large cigar rolled round in his mouth. He had been at work – "I like work" (unlike ordinary workpeople today, who have no other *raison d'être*. What else are they for?) Beside the bed a small aluminium pail for cigar-ash; before him, stretching right across the bed, a tray-desk (*that* was a good idea!), on which were the long galleys of his *History of the English-Speaking Peoples*.

'He welcomed me with a touch of old-fashioned exaggerated courtesy, as if the honour were his that the professional historian had come to see him. I returned the compliment, sincerely meant, that he had beaten the professionals at their own game, that his *Marlborough* was an historical masterpiece along with Trevelyan's *Age of Queen Anne*. He said that, now that he had some time, he was rereading the *History* he had written before the war, but he wasn't satisfied with it. However, there were people who would read it on account of his "notoriety". Pause. I was evidently expected to say *something*; so I said, "Just as in the emotion of love there is an element of volition, so in great fame there is an element of merit."

'He was pleased at this sally – something was called for, and I had passed the test. I was relieved, for I knew that he was apt to be bored at meeting a stranger. After this we were on easy terms, and shortly he sent me off to read his chapters about Henry VII and Henry VIII, while he got up and was dressed.

'This process took some half an hour, before I was alerted to the dining-room, with its Orpen portrait of the young Parliamentarian. The corridors, I noticed, were filled with his own paintings, in themselves a revelation of the hidden side of his character – the gentler and more feminine: I do not underestimate them, but they gave no evidence of power (unlike his speeches and writing), they were impressionistic and descriptive, expressions of his delight in the appearances of things (like his pleasure in costume) and of his joy in life.

'The figure all the world knew then entered: striped blue zip-suit, blue velvet slippers with WSC worked in gold braid, outwards, in case anybody didn't know who was approaching. He led me to the window to look at his beautiful mare cropping with her foal below – I think, Hyperion, out of whom by someone I didn't take in. He soon saw that I hadn't come to talk horses, even if I could; we looked away down the valley, "up which the planes came", he said. The memory of 1940, when the Germans had everything their own way, was still vivid.

'I knew his dislike of making the acquaintance of somebody new at his age, so I shifted the conversation away from history, which was beginning to stick, on to the war. There were so many things I wanted to know. He was at once all interest, told me everything I asked for, uninhibited and generously.

'The first thing I wanted to know was what he thought Hitler thought of him. He considered that Hitler thought him representative of a minority in Britain, and that if Hitler pushed hard enough he could topple him over. I said that Hitler understood evil to his fingertips, but had no understanding of the power of the good in men. I reflected, but did not say, that perhaps all those idiotic Appeasers who had gone to the footstool at Berlin or Munich – Philip Lothian, Tom Jones, Clifford Allen, Arnold Wilson, etc. – had served a useful purpose after all: they had served to mislead the autodidact of genius as to the real character of Britain. But suppose if he had been an educated man, and knew what the

situation really was and the latent forces he was up against –
how even more dangerous that would have been! (Of course,
if he had been really educated – particularly, morally educated, he wouldn't have tried it all over again as in 1914–1918.
The Kaiser on the subject: "I hope the machine won't run
away with him, as it did with me!" – i.e. the German military
machine, responsible for it all.)

'Stalin had a revealing exchange with Eden on his last visit
to Moscow. He said to Eden, "You know Hitler was a
remarkable man – only he had no sense of moderation." He
caught Eden's expression, and said: "I see that you think I
have no sense of moderation. That's where you are wrong."
And, for all his enormities and mass-murders, Stalin did
know where to draw the line – when he came up against
superior force. He was not a Hitler, but a Bismarck, an utter
realist, with not a spark of idealism in him – and, of course,
immeasurably more brutal, for Bismarck belonged to a civilized world; where Stalin was in keeping with the emergent
people, with their lack of civilized standards or any cultiva-
tion. Where now are the idealist illusions of 1917, of our
fellow-travellers, the parlour Communists of the thirties? *Où
sont les neiges d'antan?*

'Churchill added that, since Britain was anti-Communist,
Hitler thought she should go along with him. I said that he
had behaved too criminally for that ever to be possible (quite
apart from the question of power: we should have been at his
mercy). What a providence it was that he didn't really know
England!

'The next thing I asked was even more crucial: did he think
that this country could have been invaded and overthrown in
1940?

'No, he said firmly. We should have put everything into it:
the whole of the Navy and Air Force. They couldn't have got
across – and he made the gesture familiar to us at the time, of
their swimming in the Channel in vain.

'This was a piece of information of the first historical
importance; for it meant that Churchill's resistance in 1940
had not been mere bravado, but rested on a firm estimation
of Britain's capacity to resist. This was what he was able to

assure President Roosevelt of, and convince him with; and upon this Roosevelt made his decision to back Britain.

'At this point Churchill added subsidiary bits of information. If any of the Germans had got across, he had a slogan ready: "You Can Always Take One With You". I think that would have appealed in the circumstances of 1940, after Dunkirk and what we had had to put up with for so long. If the Germans *had* invaded the country and government had to scatter, he had it in mind to form a triumvirate with Ernest Bevin and Beaverbrook. But the Germans weren't prepared with ways and means of crossing the water.

'(They would have been by 1943, with all Europe under their heel – by which time Hitler meant his show-down with Britain: not in 1939, which was inconveniently early for him. The Foreign Office stole a march on him there, with the assurance to Poland, which could not be waved away, like his own assurances to so many others. The liar was caught in the net at last – not by Chamberlain, but by the Foreign Office, which knew better.)

'I drew him on the subject of Chamberlain. He wouldn't say anything unkind, but didn't approve. It wasn't straight, that interview with his own Foreign Secretary (Eden) in the presence of Grandi; and saying one thing to one, another to another. And he knew another thing. At the end of Mr Baldwin's premiership, when he wanted to go and various people said he couldn't, there was a test by-election in a safe Tory seat in Westminster, completely blue. Moore-Brabazon said he wouldn't fight it so long as Baldwin remained PM. "That settles me," said Baldwin. Duff Cooper was prepared to fight it, and went to Chamberlain, who was head of the Party Office. [Duff Cooper was with Churchill and Eden against Appeasement.] Chamberlain told Duff Cooper that there would be no funds for him to fight the seat. "Not straight. Take your chance" – said the old sportsman.

'That was just like Neville Chamberlain, with his small-minded personal resentments. His main motive for returning to politics was his detestation of Lloyd George, whom he succeeded in keeping out at the height of LG's powers, a man of genius – to the country's loss. And Chamberlain kept him out on Churchill's formation of his government in 1940 – made it a choice even at that moment of crisis between himself and Lloyd George, whose name would have been a legion in itself.

'Winston spoke with gallantry of Mrs Chamberlain – "wonderful woman: twenty years, and she's quite unchanged". I responded that I was glad he had asked her to his Farewell Dinner at 10 Downing Street, and delighted that he had asked the Attlees and Morrisons. "That was not much after five years of comradeship in war," he said feelingly. He added that the new Mrs Herbert Morrison was a strong Tory, though they were not advertising the fact.

'A third thing I much wanted to know was how it came about that Attlee made Bevin Foreign Secretary at the last moment, when he expected and wanted the Exchequer, to which Hugh Dalton was appointed – who had expected to go to the Foreign Office, for which he was well qualified. It seems now that Churchill was not informed about this, for he told me that it was the King who did not want Dalton at the Foreign Office. It does not now appear that the King had any part in it – that Attlee, above all shrewd, realized that it would not do to have Bevin and Morrison, who detested each other, both dealing with Home Affairs. Attlee effectively divided them by sending Bevin to the Foreign Office – where he made a great Foreign Secretary – and making Morrison Leader of the House of Commons, where he did equally well, for he was an efficient Parliamentarian.

'The change of government was a great surprise to Stalin, who could not make out what the British were up to. When Churchill had warned him in Moscow that in Britain there were two parties and he might be defeated at the election of 1945, Uncle Joe was able to assure him that "One Party is much better". As for Molotov, he obviously preferred dealing with Churchill – Bevin knew only too intimately, from a life-time's experience, the nefarious ways of Communists and how to deal with them.

'Winston spoke kindly of Dalton, and said that of all the letters he had received on leaving office in 1945, his was the nicest. I told him of Dalton's admiration for the weekly talks he used to give the Cabinet, to strengthen morale in the worst days of 1940, and that Dalton used to go away and write them down. Winston didn't know that. Of Eden he said that he and "Anthony saw very much eye to eye: if you presented us both with a set of papers we should take very much the same line." I said politely (I was still paying my subscription to the Labour Party up to Suez, though not subscribing intellectually) that the handover had taken place in the right way at the right time. He replied, with *politesse*, that he had been very lucky: he hadn't done anything, it was the people – he but gave the *Roar* – and he emitted the roar for my benefit.

'(He was indeed lucky to be out before Suez, which would never have occurred if shrewd Clem Attlee had been there. Almost the last thing, he went into 10 Downing Street and said: "Now, Anthony, no getting caught out on a limb with the French." Which was exactly what happened.)

'Winston told me quite candidly of the severe stroke he had, said that he couldn't feed himself – and yet managed to hold on to office (for Eden too was ill at the time. They had all of them been exhausted by the war – hence, in part, Britain's poor showing after it). He talked about the Labour Party, with no animus or opposition: all that had drossed away with the years. He did not speak like a party-man, indeed he never had been a mere party-politician, had sat loosely to party-ties. I noticed that he referred to the Tories, not as "we" but as "they" – as if he sat on some Olympus above the party struggle, as indeed he did. He had made that most difficult walk in life, crossing the floor of the House of Commons, not once but twice – "I have never had any objection to the rat, as such". When Jowett awkwardly left the Liberal Party to become Labour's Lord Chancellor, Winston with a twinkle: "He has disgraced the name of rat." He asked me what would happen to Labour now that they were finding out that nationalization wasn't a solution. I suggested that it should mean that Labour would take the place of the old Liberal Party. He agreed, and went on to say that you don't create wealth by just taking it away from other people.

There should be minimum standards beyond which people should not be allowed to fall – and beyond that, *Free Run!*

'There was the old sportsman again, but I did not forget that earlier he had had a great part in creating those minimum standards, laying the foundations of the Welfare State. Of course, he was quite right in maintaining the crucial importance of incentive: when that is damaged, as it is under the social revolution, whether in Soviet Russia or Britain, it eats like a cancer at the vitals of society. Witness Britain, twenty years later: not a democracy so much as a trade-union bureaucracy, a squalid kind of society, a second-rate country. He was indeed lucky not to live to see it. I was in California when he died, and had to give an obituary address at a memorial service at Occidental College. A friend at All Souls went out into the High as Churchill's funeral train passed through Oxford on the way to his resting-place at Bladon – the western sky filled with the lurid glow of winter sunset, the sun setting upon the British Empire.'

We went back to the war; I told him how much I admired his chapter on the sinking of the *Bismarck* (as I had years before that on the battle of Jutland in his First War memoirs). He said how bad it was to wake up in the morning to receive the news of the sinking of some great ship. He asked what was the name – he couldn't remember. The *Hood*, I supplied, she was manned from Devonport; we were all miserable in the West Country at her sinking. 'Yes, the *Hood*,' he said, tears in his eyes, remembering. Then, perking up, 'We *had* to get the *Bismarck*: the nation expected it.' One admiral said his ship hadn't enough oil to get to the spot and back again. 'I sent the telegram: "You get there and we'll tow you back." '

His mind went back to the First World War and combined operations, on which he obviously felt that he had made a contribution to the art (or science) of war. While Lloyd George was working to reduce Tory prejudice against him, before his return to office in 1917, he had written a private paper for LG advocating our seizure of the island of Borkum, as a base to bring the blockade nearer to Germany, to alleviate the strain of maintaining it hundreds of miles out at sea.

In this he had put forward in embryo form the idea of landing tanks, and the later developments of landing-craft. By the mercy of Providence he hadn't published this paper in *The World Crisis*, when he might well have done so – nothing against it; and the German General Staff scrutinized everything he wrote. When the second war came, the Germans had nothing of the sort: they hadn't thought of it. He himself gave orders for building landing-craft immediately after Dunkirk. Yet it was three years before we had enough to invade.

Unqualified to assess that, I leave the pros and cons to the military historian. One knows, however, as a non-military historian how anxious Churchill was to shine in the expertise of war, worthy of his ancestor Marlborough.

I recall now a most significant remark he dropped, almost casually, without following it up. 'If only I had had more time . . . to make peace . . .' I saw at once what he meant. He was very self-conscious about the accusation that had been cast at him all through his life that he was a 'war-monger'. (After all, he was a soldier by origin and training, and he *understood* war, as pacific politicians like Asquith and Neville Chamberlain did not.)

Now, enormously ambitious as he was about his place in history, having won the war, he had longed to be the man to end the Cold War with Russia. I believe that he hung on and on to office in the hope of outliving Stalin, or at least of a change of mind in Moscow. Harold Macmillan told me that in the end the old man was more friendly disposed to Soviet Russia than Anthony Eden, with his more rigid mind, was.

Lunch was coming to an end, but well after three o'clock! It had been a good one: fried fish, then lamb cutlets and peas, ice-cream and fruit. I am really a teetotaller: I did not dare to confess that with Winston: he would not have been able to support so dire a confession. I had had some Bristol Milk in the library, as ordered, while waiting for him; an excellent hock accompanied the meal. When it came to cheese, I wasn't going to have any – let alone port with it. Port in the middle of the day! or indeed at any time. I was forced to compromise with a bit of cheese. Then – 'Some brandy?' A lifelong mem-

ber of the Duodenal Club, I drew the line at brandy. 'Then
have some Cointreau with your coffee! It's very soothing.' It
was very soothing.

He tottered out on his stick; I tottered out, wondering
whether I was not a little sozzled. 'Like to go round the
corner? Or are you like those people coming to lunch who,
asked if they would like to wash, said, "Thank you, we did
that at the gate." '

Upstairs we went, to the big study next his bedroom –
over the fireplace a large eighteenth-century landscape of
Blenheim – for our work-session at my typescript.

It was like taking one's essay up to the headmaster. Making
after-lunch noises, he is going to fall asleep over my book, I
thought. Not a bit of it: he was all attention, to points of
detail and style – here was the conscientious artist – as well as
content. *A propos* of Charles I, he made an impressive point.
I had written him down as an inept politician, in the usual
academic manner (the 'Whig Interpretation of History').
Churchill didn't agree: he said that we did not sufficiently
consider how much more difficult things were for these
people in the past, that they had far less efficient instruments
and had to cope with everything themselves. Things were so
much easier for us, with specialists to advise, a machine upon
which things move and are handed up to us for decision.
Even at the time I registered how generous a judgment this
was, and salutary coming from a man of action who knew
how things are done and the difficulties in getting them done.
Actually I did not agree about Charles I, and I kept to my
own opinion of him, though I did not say so. Now I am
inclined to think that I was wrong and Churchill more nearly
right: Charles I had a well-nigh impossible situation to cope
with, a revolution on his hands, the fatal Puritan Revolution.
Either Stalin or Hitler would have known better how to cope
with such people.

Winston was particularly attentive to words. He did not
like my describing the days of the Restoration – when everybody claimed to have been descended from the Conqueror,
including the Churchills (who had no such Norman descent)

– as 'snobbish'. 'Why do you say "snobbish"?' I explained why. 'But I don't like the word "snobbish".' So, in deference to the great man, the printed text reads, 'in the grand days of the Restoration' (however, they were snobbish). He took exception to a phrase about the Civil War 'degenerating' at the end, and asked what it meant. I explained about the low-ering of standards, the increasing inhumanity of it. 'But I don't like the word. Now [engagingly] – why don't you say "spiteful"? I like the word "spiteful".' Well, I didn't, so I kept to my own text. When I used the phrase 'pooh-poohed' in conversation, 'I hope you don't say that,' he said mocking. We both laughed. And so it went on.

He sat in an armchair, back to his bedroom; a chair had been placed for me opposite him. A photograph of Roosevelt faced me, and high up on the wall behind, the black-and-white caricature of the Bull-dog Winston. Before going down, he showed me everything with old-fashioned cour-tesy. Everything had been laid on for me – I suspect that he knew I would record it all. A fine George I card-table had been given him by some section of Conservatives; a curious upright desk by his children – upon it the proofs of his *His-tory*, some of which I was to work at later, were laid out.

Somewhat recovered, we went down into the broiling rose-garden, to go on with our task – he was clearly inter-ested – sitting in a deep seat together. The detective walked round behind the rose-bushes unobtrusively, never leaving him out of eyesight, unless sent off for something – to get the gardener to put up a sunshade, or the secretary to send out *Marlborough* vol. I, or to fetch the stuff for feeding the gold-fish. Drinks were sent for – whisky and soda for him, oran-geade for me, though this was the tea-hour and I would have given anything for a pot of tea.

I could not believe that he would be so interested, until, partly out of self-deprecation, I chipped in to explain some-thing. And was at once ticked off. 'I can't read, if you inter-rupt,' he said firmly. I laughed at myself – just the way I am with people, I registered; and kept quiet, while *he* com-mented. 'Very good,' or 'Quite right,' he would say. 'Quite right about James I's execution of Ralegh: I have always thought that one of the worst blots against that' – he paused for a word, or for effect – 'that extravagant . . . sodomite'. Actually, I have changed my mind since then, and now think that there was more to be said for James I than for Ralegh. Then, the old gentleman rippled over with amusement at my description of handsome young John Churchill returning from service of arms in the Mediterranean to those other arms awaiting him at Court of – who but the beautiful Lady Castlemaine? 'Very good,' he twinkled, 'to have been seduced by the King's mistress at sixteen [actually rather older] must have been interesting – and valuable experience.'

Reading my typescript reawakened his interest in his own *Marlborough*, which he sent in for. It was Lord Rosebery who suggested that he should write it. Winston objected that he had never liked the Camaret Bay affair, in which Marlborough had been charged with giving treasonable information to the enemy (apparently he told them only what they knew already). Rosebery said, 'But you have never read Paget's *New Examen*' – which cleared the matter up and exonerated Marlborough. Winston had never heard of the book; Rosebery lent it to him and that settled it. He called Macaulay, roundly, a liar.

I don't think that was quite right, but Macaulay certainly saw only one side of a case at the time; he had the boring 'either-or' mentality of the Parliamentary orator. Often 'both' is better, the subtlety of ambivalence; there was no subtlety in Macaulay.

Once Winston's own book was fetched he became immersed in it, read some of it with approbation and tears of appreciation as he turned over the pages. It was a little the mood of Swift's 'What a genius had I then!'; or the stricken Marlborough catching sight of an earlier Kneller portrait of himself and saying, 'There was a man.' He had been to see all his ancestor's great battlefields: Blenheim, Ramillies, Oudenarde, Malplaquet. Down there on the terrace was the Marlborough pavilion his nephew had decorated for him with a frieze in relief, roundels of Queen Anne, John and Sarah.

The afternoon wore on, the time had come to feed the

goldfish. On the way he showed me round his creation: the little ponds, the stream and cascade, looking down to the swimming pool, inviting in the heat. The hay was all cut and lying in bundles pretty thick along the upper valley. The Churchill flag was flying from the flagstaff over all. Up the slope we went, where I remarked on a sickle-shaped swathe of blue anchusa and white foxgloves – splendid. 'Yes. That's Clemmie – now with regard to the battle of Blenheim . . .' I saw something of what Clemmie had had to put up with. She was in London, much preferring London life; surprisingly, Winston preferred the country. And, after all, this place was his creation – he had even done brick-laying on the walls himself.

I had at various times made motions of taking my leave. No notice was taken: he had evidently allotted the whole day to me. When we at last went in, he took me into yet another study, plainer and simpler, full of mementoes of the first German war, signed photographs of Foch, Pétain, Pershing and so on. Above them better photographs from the Second War – Eisenhower, Montgomery, Tedder, and the rest. At the end he drew my attention to the Notice from the South African war, advertising in Afrikaans £25 reward for the escaped Prisioner [sic] Churchill, dead or alive. What a space in history he covered! 'Twenty-Five Pounds,' he said with emphasis; 'that is all I am worth.' He sank into a chair dejectedly, acting the part for me – I thought, more like a weary Titan.

We went out into the entrance hall, a big wooden bust of Roosevelt beside the door. Winston was now taking off his shoes, having some difficulty in putting on a slipper. I dared to help – but he would not be helped: the same self-willed, self-reliant, self-centred spirit from childhood, as his mother had written of him then.

Sun poured from the west into the front door, upon the flowers, the Roosevelt bust, the aged bulky figure waving goodbye in so friendly fashion. He would go off to bed for a couple of hours, for Beaverbrook was coming to dine, and no doubt they would make a night of it.

I was utterly tired out, by the fullest and richest day's

experience I had ever had. My Journal ends: 'It was infinitely sad and touching. One may never see or hear him again. At any moment the last stroke may come.'

But it did not, for – unbelievably – another ten years; I did see him again and spent an evening with him at Blenheim where he was born.

Thousands of people now will know the ground-floor room inside the entrance hall, which was as far as his mother, Lady Randolph Churchill, could get that November day in 1874 when she had been outside prancing about with the guns, and baby Winston arrived prematurely, he was so anxious to start on his public career. He was said to have been a seven-months child.

Blenheim meant much to him all through his life – clearly a formative influence in the career he shaped for himself, history as inspiration for the life of politics, as was characteristic in the aristocratic days now over, but with exceptional force in his case. He was an historian of eminence as well as a politician; history shaped his mind and gave him his understanding of Britain and the United States, of Europe and the world. From his aristocratic side he drew his political courage, his sense of and care for the well-being of the state, no matter what anybody else thought, popular or unpopular. From his American side he got his boyishness and zest, his optimism and generosity, his bounce.

In the intervening time we exchanged books: the two volumes of family history, *The Early Churchills* and *The Later Churchills*; and he sent me each volume of his four-volume *History of the English-Speaking Peoples* as it came out. I received several friendly, brief missives. Here are a couple relating to his *History*, from 28 Hyde Park Gate, 12 April 1956:

My dear Rowse,
   I am indeed obliged to you for your letter of April 7 and for all the trouble you have taken. Your comments are most valuable, and it is very good of you to have devoted so much time to my affairs.

Thank you also so much for sending me a copy of your review of Volume I. I am much complimented by what you say.

Yours vy sincerely,
Winston S. Churchill

Shortly after, on 4 May, he wrote: 'I am grateful to you for reading my chapters on the Tudors and for commenting on them. I hope you will also read my chapter on *The May-flower*, which is now being re-proofed. Your observations on it would be most valuable to me.'

I think he was pleased with my history of the family. He was taken by my account of his namesake, the original Sir Winston of the Civil War, the Cavalier Colonel, whom the Restoration Parliament always called the 'Colonel'. 'Oh, so they called him that, did they? I didn't know that.' There was a fine phrase in the old Colonel's *Divi Britannici*, forerunner of his descendant's *History*, referring to 'those far-distant regions, now become a part of us and growing apace to be the bigger part, in the sun-burnt America'. Winston was much taken with this: 'Would you mind if I made use of it?' 'Goodness, it's *your* ancestor's phrase, isn't it?'

Like other people, I did not expect him to survive yet more years. On the occasion of the launching of the *History*, St George's Day 1956, I was invited to the luncheon given by his publishers at the Royal College of Surgeons in Lincoln's Inn Fields. The Hall was packed with a curious company – none of his political associates but his connexions with the world of journalism and publishing and those who had helped him with the book.

The old journalist and war correspondent beamed with pleasure at the company, and made a short speech. I sat at the top table not far from him, but there was no chance of speaking with him there.

But I spent an evening in his company on Saturday, 28 June 1958, when he and Clemmie were stopping at Blenheim for the weekend, to celebrate some anniversary of their engagement; for it was there in the garden that they had got engaged so many years ago. It was a sentimental family occasion – I was rather touched to be included. Winston as a guest was as special a case as ever, as troublesome as a child, everything arranged to suit his convenience. The Duchess, Mary Marlborough, was wonderful at coping with him – not for nothing was she descended from the great Duke's Quartermaster-general, Cadogan. A good trooper, she would both humour Winston and give him his orders.

Much more successful with him than the high-minded Eleanor Roosevelt, hopelessly gone to the good: 'How anybody can *drink* so much – how anybody can *eat* so much – how anybody can *smoke* so much – and remain healthy! . . .' It is indeed astonishing that he survived, in spite of all Lord Moran's gloomy prognostications, to be over ninety. I did not expect him to live for much longer after that evening at Blenheim. Like so many great men in history – like Napoleon or, for that matter, Stalin – he was rather a small man, an advantage for longevity.

When staying at the White House he always upset Eleanor's domestic arrangements. The President liked to go to bed early – Winston kept him up late; he was the only person for whom Roosevelt would stay up at night. At their last meeting the survivors of those fateful encounters made it up; Winston, with his boyish smile: 'You never did like me, Eleanor, did you?' Rather irresistible.

I resort to my Journal for the occasion. I had dined out at Blenheim the previous Saturday, but was now 'bidden again specially to sit beside Winston. He could hear me, but could take no part in general conversation. It was two years since he had been at the so familiar place – he had spent some time there off and on during the war – and this fairly certainly would be his last. I arrived early, again the little girls, the Russell granddaughters, absorbed in television – one of them the image of her great-grandmother, Consuelo Vanderbilt, with that exquisite swan-neck.'

I had owed my introduction to her in New York to Winston; in her apartment in Sutton Place – Marie Antoinette's console-tables, Pissaros, Segonzacs ('a friend of ours') – we had a good deal of talk about Churchills, not wholly favourable on her part. She had a complex about her former husband, the ninth Duke, Winston's cousin, as being a sad, unhappy man: '*fin de race*', she described him. I did my best to *rapprocher les deux*, said what an historic job they had done together for Blenheim; without either of them it would not have been possible.

This reflection rather reconciled her. She was ready to admit to a mistake – that in the redecoration of the rooms they should have adhered to Vanbrugh, instead of the French taste. But 'Ev*err*ything *Frr*ench is best,' she said with her French accent, expecting a patriotic protest from me. 'But of course,' I agreed – and that took her aback, for a moment she didn't know how to go on. Mary Marlborough had told me that Consuelo was doing up the Grand Cabinet at Blenheim, which had been all rather overpowering red and gold; she had called in the best decorator from Paris, who had covered the walls with silvery grey silk. On a night when the Queen Mother was dining, I noticed how this background brought out the colour of the women's hair, particularly the Duchess's auburn.

I couldn't but think of the irony of things, Consuelo's breach with her husband, 'Sunny', as they called him, long dead, and she herself still going on, regularly back at Blenheim, her son in possession. 'But what about Winston?' said she; 'Where does he get his looks from?' All sorts of things used to be said of Winston's paternity in gay Edwardian days, that he had Gambetta's red hair, for example. I was able to tell her: he was exactly like his respectable old grandfather, the seventh Duke, the same pug-face and extraordinary eyes, with the red hair of the Spencers. (They are all Spencers; they resumed the Churchill name in 1815.)[1]

Winston remembered his grandfather, a curious outcrop of religiosity in their divagatory nineteenth-century story. He told me that, when a boy at Blenheim, he had the impression that things were distinctly 'tight' – this was after the great agricultural depression of the late 1870s; the Duchess used to collect left-overs and scraps from the meals, pack them into panniers to be carried round to the tenantry on the estate.

Here I was at Blenheim again. 'At last the circle assembled,

1. v. my *The Later Churchills*.

and Winston and Clemmie appeared, Clemmie all billowing gown and broadened out with age. I was shocked to see how much he had aged, much more feeble, another illness will puff him away – or possibly without. Unsteady on his feet he took a low seat, beaming happily, contentedly around, saying nothing, kissing the children goodnight. It was sad to see him: still the centre of all our attention, the embers of a great fire, all the force gone. Very deaf now and rather impenetrable, apparently he had asked for me to sit beside him at dinner, the ladies' talk being like "the twittering of birds" to him.

'We went into dinner, he on the Duchess's right, I next to him. She was very good at managing him, but we were reduced, as with the very old, to treating him like a child. He spent much of the time holding her miniature dachshund in his arms, at one point offering it some of the delicious lobster *mousse* on a fork: the expression of disgust was charming to see, little velvet paws hanging limply down, head drawn back, nose averted. "Darling," said the old man, always sentimental about animals.

'Not that he has become senile: he is still capable of a good phrase, an echo of his former power. Someone asked whether he would be attending church tomorrow. "At my age," he replied, "I think my devotions may be attended in private." I did not worry him any more about the past, though I should have liked to know more about the St George's by-election in 1923, which he said he had enjoyed more than any other, and when the Duchess had canvassed for him. If he had won it, might he have won the lead of all the anti-socialist forces, instead of everything falling into Baldwin's lap? I did not like to put the point too clearly, and he did not catch the drift of it. He commented vaguely, "it all seemed to work out very harmoniously", the kind of Parliamentary formula he must often have employed.

'He still could make single comments, rather than command an argument. He thought the failure of the new French constitution to provide for an interim dissolution of the Chamber a mistake. Similarly of the statutory limitation upon American Presidents to two terms of office. (He would!

Never say die, his motto.) This led to a long disquisition in the American manner by the Duke's son-in-law, the Duke obviously impatient, Winston all bland courtesy. (He couldn't hear it.)

'Indeed it was the most touching thing to observe – all force gone after these strokes, now all contentment and old-world courtesy. He was still *compos mentis*: he had won £21 off the Duchess at bezique that evening, and during the week-end had cleaned her out of £50 altogether. He takes his own cards, case and spectacles around with him, laid out ceremoniously upon a red velvet cloth. Upstairs in his bedroom he had brought his love-bird in a cage – boyish, troublesome, lovable as ever. To everyone's surprise he demanded water: "Oh, I drink a lot of water – the doctor tells me to – along with everything else."

'I took my leave fairly early, after a few words with the Duke, who had been helpful in letting me have the run of his archives. Once before, at dessert, he had asked *à propos* of my history of the family a blunt, direct question: "What did Lord Randolph [Winston's father] die of?" I felt that he knew that I knew, but wasn't going to say; I gave a noncommittal answer, from which he could be certain that I knew.

'Scaffolding was up all around the great hall under repair; I went down through those Vanbrugh corridors into the basement to the private entrance, a moon appearing above the forest of spars, shedding a strange unreal glimmer about that place of ghosts, the park, the bridge, the Victory column: the place where Winston was born, to which he was for a time the heir-presumptive (until Consuelo's son was born), the inspiration of so much of his life and work.'

It was historically appropriate that I should last see him there. Though my contact with him was cursory, in a way sketchy, it was different from anybody else's, and significant for both, since we cared for history more than anything – to him politics was history. This was why he spoke to me more than all the Baldwins and Chamberlains, or even the men of my own party whom I knew better, Attlee, Bevin, Morrison.

To me as an historian, my contacts with Churchill were contacts with history, direct and live.

2

Nancy Astor

Now that Nancy Astor – dear, gallant, golden-hearted woman – has vanished from the scene and is forgotten in the House of Commons, where she was a unique figure, and even at Plymouth, which she loved and for which she did so much, what was her importance in history? Most people would find it hard to say, but an historian should be able to define it.

She was an idiosyncratic character, a public figure, scintillating like a star, perhaps a meteor across a sombre firmament. More than that, she was a symbol of two historic themes: first, of the emancipation of women and their political rights; second, of the *rapprochement* between Britain and America, indispensable to Britain's survival in the two German wars of our century, and of Anglo-American friendship, a stabilizing factor in the upheaval of our time.

Besides that, she did a mass of good work, public and private, countless good deeds, for individuals even more than for institutions. In one way her life could be summed up quite simply – *doing good*; in another, it is not easy to get her quite right, for hers was a complex character, mercurial and contradictory, and few have been able to grasp it, let alone render it in words, do her justice. For she was at once overbearing and modest, censorious yet kind, fierce and direct yet sympathetic, tactless at the same time as sensitive, didactic and even minatory yet remarkably intuitive and willing to learn. Her general ideas were apt to be wrong and largely emotional prejudice. She hardly ever read a book, except the

Bible – in that so like a Southern Puritan, which she was, for all her Christian Science; but she was well read in the book of life: she was rarely mistaken in her judgment of people. For all her natural gifts, Nancy wasn't educated; but that is no disadvantage in a democracy.

She had the courage of a lion and a heart of gold – which may sound a little equivocal, for of course she had the gold of the Astors to work on and with.

Oddly enough, for all that I knew her intimately – and it was hardly possible to know her, if at all, *un*intimately – I cannot remember when I first met her. My first memory of Waldorf, her husband – whom I also came to know better than most – goes right back to when as a schoolboy I attended a Sunday evening meeting at my home town, St Austell. It was a Temperance affair, and I didn't take in anything of what was said – just like any other member of an audience. Later on, as a Labour man and (mistakenly) a political candidate for my home constituency, I did not hold with the Astors' grip on Plymouth, notwithstanding the good works they did there. After all, I belonged to the perpetual Opposition and thought that my working people should stand on their own feet. Caught in a dilemma as I was, a cleft stick of my own making, I would not allow, as a Marxist, that concrete good deeds were worth all the politicizing in the world.

So my acquaintance with the Astors did not come from the West Country, where we were politically on opposite sides, but from the All Souls end. They were very close to All Souls (their son and heir, Bill, even made the College his residuary legatee, he told me). They were close friends of Lionel Curtis, Geoffrey Dawson and most of the Round Table group. Lord Brand, married to Nancy's sister, was their brother-in-law. Waldorf was Chairman of Curtis's Royal Institution of International Affairs, one of Lionel's many brain-children. (I do not suppose that the Institution, Chatham House, served much purpose, except to provide jobs for several excellent people, Arnold Toynbee chief among them.) Philip Kerr, to become Lord Lothian, closest of all to Nancy, was constantly in and out of All Souls as of

Cliveden – he had, like a lot of other eminent persons, tried for the Fellowship but not been elected. It gave him, unlike some others, a friendly feeling for the place.

Hence, when I became a guest at Cliveden, for all its somewhat daunting grandeur – an Italianate palazzo with terrace and fountains from the Borghese villa ('loot,' I once remarked within hearing of some of the family) – I was not on wholly unfamiliar territory. The books in the library had been selected by a posse from All Souls, headed by Craster and Curtis. Arthur Salter had also been a *habitué* before his marriage to a rival American, not much liked by Nancy, for Ethel was a New England Bagge, a 'dam' Yankee', and Nancy was an unreconstructed Southerner, a Virginian first and last. For all her life lived in England, she never ceased to be a Virginian. When I told her of my visit to the National Cemetery at Arlington (where now the two Kennedys lie), she exclaimed, 'National Cemetery? – dam' Yankees – it's *Lee's* place, Arlington.'

In the entrance-hall at Cliveden was Sargent's portrait of her, slim, radiant, beautiful; he had intended to portray her carrying baby Bill pickaback, but it hadn't worked out, hence the original pose, back half-turned. Improbably in this strict household was a portrait of the wicked Countess of Shrewsbury, a previous owner, who was said to have held her lover's horse while he killed her husband. But that was an acquisition of Waldorf's father, the first Lord, a collector on the grand scale.

William, the first Lord, was a strange and fascinating character, creator of it all – dead, he loomed in the background, both here and at Hever Castle, the second son's, J.J.'s, place. But he is not my subject; I must confine myself to what Nancy told me – and, the soul of indiscretion, she told me a lot. The most placid and least quarrelsome of men, Waldorf had quarrelled with his father for taking a peerage. Waldorf considered that, already a member of the House of Commons, this ruined the prospects of a political career for him. He was thereupon excommunicated by unforgiving father. Things work out ironically in people's lives, which form the stuff of history; I doubt if Waldorf would have had much of a political career anyway. Paradoxically, and unexpectedly, Nancy had the political career; Waldorf took second place to her, was her chief of staff, content to remain in the background – though in the family, he had the last word: the gentlest and most considerate of men, he carried authority.

The older Astor background was strangely withdrawn and reserved, Waldorf's father shy to the point of incommunicativeness. This gay, unrepressed Virginian girl brought gales of laughter and fun into the conventional stuffiness of Cliveden under the first Lord: she was the light of Waldorf's eyes, she released his spirit and made the happiness of his life. She gave him five children, though herself as sexually cold as Elizabeth I, whom she resembled in some ways, looked a bit like her – though better looking. She told me that she had experienced sexual desire only once in her life – so I supposed that the children were conceived, like the British Empire, in a fit of absence of mind. The fabulous structure of their lives was based on Waldorf's consuming love for her. This corroborated her telling Curtis – though not all Nancy's *dicta* were to be taken literally – that he had pestered her to marry him; eventually she capitulated and – 'his possessions were magnificent'.

She held out some time before consenting, for she had had a disillusioning experience in her first marriage – to Robert Gould Shaw, who turned out an alcoholic. Unacquainted with the facts of life and a Puritan *enragée*, on her wedding night she had fought him like a wildcat. Once, when I remarked on the beauty of the turquoise bracelets she was wearing – the colour of her eyes – she said, 'Yes, I put them on the hotel bill, in Vienna, on our honeymoon; Waldorf wouldn't notice.' Then, sadly, 'I couldn't do that now.'

True or not, it was in keeping with her account of her one experience of desire. Everyone accepted that her relations with Philip Lothian were entirely platonic. Only once, in a bedroom, was she overcome by desire. Acknowledging this weakness of the flesh – though to Nancy and Philip as Christian Scientists matter wasn't real – they knelt on opposite sides of the bed until this cup passed away. Thereupon Philip said, 'Now, Nancy, you know what men have to put up with.' (I rather think that she gave him his Christian Science, of which he died, in the Embassy at Washington, without calling a doctor. Lionel Curtis on his friend's death, arch-advocate of Appeasement of Hitler: 'Philip died in the know-ledge that he had been wrong.') I dare say Waldorf was rather bored with Philip perpetually on a pedestal.

This lends point to the celebrated exchange with Lloyd George, whom Nancy admired most of public men – nor was she wrong: he was a man of genius. Because she was so censorious she was the last person in their circle to know that L.G. lived with his secretary, Frances Stevenson. The moment Nancy heard the rumour she went straight to the great little man: 'L.G., what is this I hear about you and Frances?' Lloyd George, not the least perturbed, retorted, 'And what about you and Philip?' Nancy replied hotly: 'Everybody knows that my relations with Philip are com-pletely innocent.' L.G., spectacles gleaming with mischief: 'Then you should be ashamed of yourself.' End of the inter-view.

Nancy exposed herself to being scored off like that by her interfering, head on, in other people's affairs. She really was innocent and never learned in this regard – perhaps because she almost always had the ace of trumps up her sleeve and got the last word. Only a Lloyd George or a Churchill could trump her: nobody else could. One of the well-known exchanges with Winston (whom she didn't like) was undoubtedly true: 'If I were your wife I would put poison in your coffee.' To which Winston replied, 'And if I were your husband I would drink it.' The imagination boggles at the thought of those two married: bull-dog confronting wildcat.

Her wit made her superb at dealing with hecklers: she always scored. A countryman in her constituency thought to floor her with 'Missus, how many toes have a pig got?' I'm sure Nancy wouldn't know, but what he got was: 'Take off your boot, man, and count them for yourself.' One thinks of her sudden inspirations – at a solemn Temperance meeting to raise funds in dreary Glasgow, when things weren't going well: 'It's hard enough to be a Christian when sober; it's impossible when drunk.' The meeting raised £7,000. She was a natural wit, to whom droll ideas came bubbling over: like 'those rich houses where the sheets are so fine that the blankets tickle the guests all night so that they wake up in the morning exhausted with laughing' – such an odd idea. 'Did I say that?' she said to me.

And to such a spontaneous natural comic odd happenings attached themselves, as to Bernard Shaw, a great friend. They had some things in common, as teetotallers, non-smokers, Puritans; to this Shaw added vegetarianism, so that at ninety-two or so he just couldn't die. Nancy sat with him at his death-bed. The old boy woke up suddenly from a coma and said, 'Nancy, did you ever hear the story of Patti's husband?' No, she did not go back so far as Adela Patti. It appears that the *prima donna* and her (foreign) husband arranged a country-house party after what they supposed to be the English fashion. The guests were assembled, the music struck up, when the husband appeared running down the staircase: 'You must all go away: I have found a man in bed with my wife.' Consternated, the guests hardly knew what to do and were preparing to leave when the husband appeared again: 'You must all come back. It is quite all right: he has apologized.' Apparently this was Shaw's last communication to the world: he thereupon relapsed into coma.

Sexually cold, Nancy could exploit her sex appeal shamelessly, like Elizabeth I, though more appealingly: both tremendous exhibitionists, for ever playing to the gallery. A Queen hardly enjoyed such opportunities as Nancy, who, accosting a young American sailor in the second German war outside the House of Commons, asked him if he would like to come in with her. He replied that she was just the sort of woman his mother had warned him against. That night she was able to tell Admiral Sims that he had one perfectly upright sailor under his command in the American Navy. And I have heard her tell similar salty yarns about her marine constituency at Plymouth, and the misunderstandings with which respectable couples were apt to be greeted at lodging house doors, with rates of prices for the night.

But there was a serious side to Nancy's capers and jests, her fishwife's haranguing and teasing, scolding and cheering people up, in Barbican style at Plymouth as everywhere she appeared. At Cliveden the Astors supported a hospital for wounded soldiers in the two German wars. In the first, 1914–18, 24,000 men passed through the hospital, 'so, if I have a sergeant-major's manners, no wonder'. During the second war Nancy took me along with her as she went through the ward, doing her turn – like her niece, Joyce Grenfell. Nancy's mother was Irish-American, so the Irish strain – the wit and warm-heartedness – accounted for something in her make-up. The ward woke up at once on her appearance, everybody galvanized to attention, jokes and answering her back. She carried a basket and marched up through like a fishwife on the Barbican. Then her demeanour completely changed, beside a bed where a young RAF officer was too ill to take part in the fun. His face had been fearfully smashed, and she got no reaction from him lying there passive and inert. Quietly and gently she coaxed him along, until he took a bite at the peach she held out to him. Coming back to me, she said, 'He'll recover.' I was reduced to tears by the spectacle.

Here was the splendid side of Nancy. I would forgive her anything she said – though she never came within a millimetre of infringing any of my too-exposed sensibilities – for the sake of the things she did. Only once did she indicate disapproval with a shrug – when she found that, after all I had had to put up with as a Labour candidate in Cornwall throughout the thirties, I had turned my back and wouldn't raise a finger for the place, or even speak there. *They* had had it all their own way for the whole decade – they could now get on with it, and without me.

During the Plymouth Blitz – it lasted the best part of a week, until the centre of the city was completely shattered – Nancy and Waldorf were there through it all in their house on the Hoe, damaged as it was, Nancy's maid, Rose, picking the glass out of her hair from the blown-in windows. From thirty miles away at St Austell we could see Plymouth burning; the little local fire-brigades went up from Cornwall and stood there in St Andrew's Square fighting the flames, until half of them were obliterated where they stood. Plymouth was stunned and demoralized after five nights of it, and the population streamed out into the countryside.

Waldorf told me that it was Nancy's own idea that helped to recover morale: she thought of public dancing on the Hoe, and led off with Menzies, Prime Minister of Australia, who was staying with them, RAF men and WAAFs, soldiers and sailors and WRENs, British and Americans, all joined in – and people began to come back to the city and recover their nerve. Nancy never said a word to me of what she had done – and that was like her, for underneath the public turns and playing to the gallery was a woman who was not just modest (modesty is an overrated quality) but one who was humble of heart, who lived to do good.

Her religious belief – however one might rate it intellectually – sustained her and enabled her to console and help simple people in the way no rationalist could. I remember her coming back dejected from an afternoon in Devonport, visiting homes where women had lost husband or son at sea. 'It's nothing but misery, isn't it?', looking into some poor woman's face and holding her hand – I suppose, praying with her. Consolation that we high and mighty intellectuals could never give, I reflected, as Nancy told me how her afternoon had gone. She could give people something of her spirit – she was always giving out. Looking out on Plymouth burning, 'There goes thirty years of our lives,' she said; and immediately added, 'But we'll build it up again.'

The Astors had done so much for Plymouth – I don't know the full tale of their good deeds. They created a social centre and built a children's *crêche*; at Exeter a hostel was given to the university. From the Hoe one looks down upon a rather nondescript tail-end of the town, in a prominent position fronting the bay, looking towards Drake's Island. Before the 1914–18 war, when Waldorf was rich indeed, they hoped to clear that area and make a fine public park of it. What might not have been achieved, if it had not been for the two wars the Germans let loose upon Europe!

There was always fun where Nancy was about; taking me under her wing, she let me in for a number of amusing occasions, meeting the local worthies, some of them bearers

of historic names – all grist to the mill for a budding historian. One year I had to make the speech at the annual Feast to
celebrate Sir Francis Drake's bringing water to the town – a
considerable feat, cutting a channel for miles to bring a leat
down from the highlands of Burrator. Up there we gathered,
civic dignitaries in fur and feather, plumed and robed alder-
men, Commander-in-chief from Devonport and other naval
and military grandees, clerics to sanctify the proceedings.
Assembled on the sacred spot, the silver loving-cup was
passed round. When it came to me I wondered whatever the
liquid tasted of – until I realized that it was Sir Francis Drake's
water, nothing more nor less. At that the heavens descended;
we were deluged. It was fun to see the dignitaries picking up
their skirts and skedaddling for the marquee, where, slightly
sodden, I had to make my speech.

Among the naval personnel I met with her was an heroic
submarine-man, Dunbar-Naesmith, then in command at
Devonport. When he was a young officer, his submarine
went to the bottom and failed to come up for some appalling
number of hours – while Dunbar-Naesmith coolly kept all
under control until their rescue. Admiral Lord Chatfield,
First Sea Lord, I remember – but wasn't he a Chamberlainite?
– I've no idea how good he was at his job. Rumbustious Cork
and Orrery turned up, a red-headed fire-eater; what a title,
however historic! One of Nancy's introductions led to a firm
friendship with the dear Mount Edgcumbes – only son killed
in the war, so that the title passed to a remote cousin in New
Zealand. Something romantic as well as historic about that:
back this representative of an ancient Cornish family came,
from more congenial farming, to take up the burden of
Mount Edgcumbe across the water from the Hoe. In the Blitz
the house was gutted, historic contents – pictures, books,
archives – all destroyed. West Country folklore liked to think
– when people still had that penumbra of interest to their
minds – that the Duke of Medina Sidonia in '88 fancied
Mount Edgcumbe for himself. 1588 – those were the days!

One thing Nancy could not make me do, that was to visit
her children's crêche. She found this incomprehensible: 'Just
like Bobby', the son of her first marriage. And indeed it was

just like Bobby – though whether he had the excuse of preferring to look into St Budeaux church of the Budocksides,
cousins of Sir Richard Grenville, with its Elizabethan tomb
of a Gorges, I doubt. Anyway, it provided an alibi from
philanthropy for me.

The house on the Hoe, 3 Elliot Terrace – the 'lodging-
house' the Astors called it – became very familiar, with its
first-floor drawing-room looking out to sea; over the chimney-piece a contemporary picture of Winstanley's baroque
Eddystone light-house. (He boasted that it was so staunch
that he would not mind being in it in the worst of storms –
and was. And that was it: it totally disappeared.) The house
was ultimately given to the city as an official residence for the
Lord Mayor.

I remember, at my first lunch there, wondering who the
glamorous young RAF officer was who gaily contradicted
me from the bottom of the table. This was Bobby, whom I
was not to meet until after the war at Cliveden. Talented, but
a problem for his mother. She had her own private griefs. It
was over this that she eventually became friends with T. E.
Lawrence, who, a misogynist, had refused to meet her,
though a friend of Curtis and a Fellow of All Souls. When
Nancy was in trouble, he came to her rescue: sailed her down
and up the coast of Cornwall in his speed-boat one night of
crisis, until day came and she had to go through the hoop of
meeting the Prince of Wales on an official visit to Plymouth.

She had indeed done her bit to try to help the Prince in the
duties that attended upon him – these he regarded as 'chores'
(his own word), and so in the fullness of time, aided by
another American woman of spirit, he demoted himself to
Duke of Windsor. One of Nancy's leading ideas – since she
was totally without snobbery herself – was to bring people of
different sorts together. She had helped to arrange for stiff
King George V and Queen Mary to meet the Labour leaders,
improbably clad in knee-breeches and silk stockings, at a
dinner-party at 4 St James's Square. It was a great success –
the formality of the occasion lightened by Nancy telling J.
H. Thomas to pull his stockings up. Jimmy became a favourite with George V – they talked much the same language,

though I doubt the exchange: 'I've got such a 'orrible 'eadache, your Majesty.' 'Take a couple of aspirates, Mr Thomas.'

An anthropologist well understands the aura that surrounds royal personages – or used to; so I will say no more than that Nancy, bless her heart, was anxious that I should write the official biography of George VI. I suspect that it was no advantage to be pushed in those quarters by her, and anyhow I rather fancied a career (in writing) for myself. I had already turned down the more enticing offer – pressed upon me by both sides of the Lloyd George family – of writing his official biography. And I had already rejected proposals to write the history of the RAF in the war, and that of the DCLI, our own Cornish regiment. I recall the colonel of the regiment, a general in fact, coming down to All Souls to persuade me to undertake it, and his inability to understand that I really couldn't do it – I knew some of my limitations. A conventional royal biography was certainly not my idea of bliss – I was bent on the more exciting Elizabethans. Jack Wheeler-Bennett was their choice, and an appropriate one: George VI had little historic importance to speak of, such as even his father had had. Wheeler-Bennett turned out a dull, over-long volume – to be rewarded suitably with a knighthood, along with such luminaries as Sir Stanley Rouse, Chairman of the Football Association in his day.

Far more important historically than this kind of thing was the whole issue of Appeasement; for, though I became a friend of the Astors and knew well their friends, leading Appeasers – Geoffrey Dawson, Halifax, Simon, Lothian, Tom Jones – I was militantly opposed to them and their policy. I agreed with Vansittart, who was 100 per cent right about Germany, and with the Foreign Office view on the matter. The Foreign Office was well informed about it all – it was its business. The Appeasers were prejudiced against the Foreign Office: they did not know what they were dealing with.

I will not go into the historic issue here – merely record that I had a controversy on it in *The Times* in 1937 with Nancy's mentor, Philip Lothian. Anyone who wants to read it can look it up in my book, *The End of an Epoch*, and see who was right – the noble Marquis (Vansittart used to call him a Mr Know-all, but it was worse) or the young historian who knew Germany and her record in the past century.

So, since I was a friend of the family and a familiar at Cliveden – though after Appeasement was over, and it had brought its consequences down upon us – when I wrote my little *aide-mémoire, All Souls and Appeasement* (C. P. Snow wrote, 'This is exactly as it was'), I sent the first copy of the book in honesty to Bill Astor, who had then succeeded his father. He wrote me a reasoned letter, which in itself made clear why they had been so wrong.

> As to the misapprehension of the German character, Halifax, Lothian, Dawson, my father and others were very sincere Christians, who could not believe that people could be basically evil. This was, of course, all the worse with those who were Christian Scientists (Lothian and Papa) who did not believe in the reality of evil at all.

[One sees how silly they were to believe any such thing. Lord Hugh Cecil knew better, and said that the trouble with Halifax was that 'Edward did not believe in Original Sin'. Naturally such types had no idea what they were dealing with in Hitler, Göring, Goebbels, Streicher, Heydrich etc.]

Bill went on to explain why they had been anti-French – though that had proved equally mistaken and disastrous – and hostile to the Foreign Office, which was better informed. 'The Foreign Office was not helped by their very bad public relations and by Vansittart's way of expressing himself, which seemed to be hysterical and exaggerated and offering no hope.' But it was precisely these people who gave the Foreign Office and Vansittart a bad press; and Vansittart was driven to distraction by the evil emanating from Nazi Germany, the increasing threat, and the refusal of the politicians to recognize it for what it was.

Lord Brand, who knew Germany from the City's dealings

with Schacht – who made Hitler's rearmament possible – knew better. He wrote me about my Appeasement book:

Philip [Lothian], Geoffrey Dawson, and Halifax were among my closest friends and I feel, if I reviewed your book, I would have to say how wrong I thought they had been in their judgment of Germany, and I do not want publicly to criticize them . . . You have been very fair to me and I make no criticism.

Brand wrote again:

The Baldwin and Neville Chamberlain period is a very curious one. We so happened to have two Prime Ministers who knew nothing whatever about the Continent of Europe. Baldwin was a more able man in my opinion than Chamberlain. Chamberlain was a courageous man in many ways, but extremely limited and extremely sure of himself.

I quote his opinion, since he knew both of them; I did not – and did not want to.

There were plenty of people who remained mum, and many more who had been Appeasers to the last and resented my little book. So it made no impression and had no success in Britain (though it had in America). Nevertheless, the book stands for what it was intended to be – an *aide-mémoire pour servir à l'histoire*.

Interestingly enough, young David Astor was right about all this, since he had the advantage of knowing the German situation intimately through his friendship with Adam von Trott, as I had. No attention was paid to him or me: we were too young and unimportant. Bill's brother, Michael, tells us that Geoffrey Dawson and Barrington Ward on *The Times* went further than Waldorf thought wise in pushing Appeasement; while John Walter, of the historic *Times* family, raised an official objection to the fatal policy *The Times* was pushing. Michael tells us, 'I thought at the time, and I still believe, that Geoffrey Dawson was blinded by a form of self-conceit'

– and that was true enough; a powerful man, he was totally ignorant of Europe. As for Barrington-Ward, Foreign Office people thought him a 'wet', and that was about right. As for Philip Lothian, he wrote to Lionel Curtis, 'I am increasingly convinced that Christian Science is the real key to all our problems, political and economic, no less than personal.' He should have told that to Hitler. Isn't it extraordinary what fools intelligent people can be? When H. A. L. Fisher's brilliant book came out, *Our New Religion*, Philip wrote a review in *The Observer*, which was always at his disposal, to answer Fisher and advocate this profound nostrum for our troubles.

As for Nancy, an American observed that, though the Astors owned two of the most influential papers in Britain, she had a wider circulation than both put together. Surrounded by such men – actually I never met Dawson at Cliveden, but regularly at All Souls, where he was impermeable to argument – how could Nancy be blamed for the nonsense she thought about Germany? It fitted in with her emotional prejudices: the French were immoral, and Catholic when they weren't atheists, the Germans were moral and largely Protestant. After all, this was the dominant point of view in nineteenth-century Britain, of such asses as Carlyle.

How did I get along with such nonsense? Really, quite easily: I never took seriously anything Nancy thought, about politics or religion. I was fond of the essential woman, the wonderful creature she was, and her intuition told her never to argue with me on any of these subjects. On Sunday mornings at Cliveden, when she and Waldorf went off to their Christian Science meeting, she would place a Bible on the arm of my chair stuffed with markers to places indicated, I suppose, by the sainted Mary Baker Eddy. I never took the slightest notice. And I was already sufficiently sceptical to know that human beings can often be helped by nonsense, when rational sense can do little for them.

I am sure that Nancy's faith helped to keep Waldorf going, who was not strong, as indeed it had recovered her from serious illness and breakdown earlier. It was no use to her daughter, Wissie, when she had a fall from her horse and injured her back, indeed it did positive harm; as, ironically, it did to Philip Lothian. Ironically again, Philip, who was such a fool about Germany, was very successful as ambassador to the United States. *You never can tell*, Shaw says; or as William Shakespeare puts it better: 'The web of our life is of a mingled yarn, good and ill together; our virtues would be proud if our faults whipped them not, and our crimes would despair if they were not cherished by our virtues.' I expect Nancy would have agreed with that, if she had ever come across it – it would have done her good to read more Shakespeare and less Bible. The nugget of sense in her faith was just that the state of one's mind is related to one's physical well-being, and affects it: that is all.

I was surprised when Nancy told me that Belloc had for a time been one of her literary lions. With her anti-Catholic nonsense, her 'doxy could not have got on for long with his 'doxy. Though he was an educated man, a man of genius, his 'doxy had no more to be said for it than hers – rationally. Historically, of course, and from the point of view of civilization and culture, it had almost everything to be said for it. She would not have appreciated that; but she had been kind to him and his family in a time of trouble, and put them all up for weeks – I don't know whether in one of the cottages on the place. There was a delightful one down beside the Thames, where usually some lame dog or other was being put up. Their generosity of spirit and kindness were boundless, and sometimes taken for granted. She told me that her Labour MPs hardly ever said 'thank you' after a meal.

Bernard Shaw worked in with her pattern of things very well, where a Belloc could not possibly. Shaw became a friend, and they all went off on a historic mission to Moscow in the thirties together. As usual stories were told against Nancy, about her innocently quaffing a glass of vodka thinking it was water, etc. Actually, there was an exchange with Stalin the significance of which escaped her. Winston Churchill was out of power and out of favour; he never was in much favour with her, and not more than a handful of Tories were with him in the House – that deplorable assembly that led the country bound and gagged (willingly, it must be admitted) into the war. Stalin pressed her for information about political leaders in Britain, and their prospects. 'Chamberlain is the coming man,' she said. 'What about Churchill?' said Stalin. 'Oh, he's finished,' said she – which was what most people thought at the time. But Stalin, who had a first-class political brain, replied, 'If ever your country is in trouble, he will come back.' The sense of power – which is what politics is about – recognized itself in another.

Nancy had no success with T. S. Eliot. One day she rang him up out of the blue to come and meet Shaw. What she got was that quiet, precise voice at the end of the telephone: 'Lady Astor, I am sorry to say that I do not have the pleasure of your acquaintance.' She did not resent it: too good a sport to resent snubs. Eliot would have been no more her cup of tea than Belloc was. I can't think how I was, for my whole outlook, Oxford and the rest of it, was much more in keeping with those two Oxford men.

She had a real feeling for Oxford, a kind of respect and deference that was rather endearing in one with little deference in her composition – it was partly, I think, a touching respect for learning. She came over to All Souls for Encaenia fairly often – I recall her once in a costume of rarest blue, which went with her eyes; upon which my friend, Arthur Bryant, always an appeaser, not only of the ladies, complimented her with enthusiasm. Sometimes she came to cheer fellow Americans receiving honorary degrees. The university should certainly have given her one, if only as the first woman Member of Parliament, who had thus made history. And, if Oxford could confer degrees on those entertainers, P. G. Wodehouse and Charlie Chaplin (rightly), it should have extended itself to include her, peerless (if that is the word) among women entertainers. The authorities simply hadn't the imagination.

One little success I had with her was once when she came to my rooms before making a speech. She was tired and out of sorts, and I actually got her to drink half a glass of sherry, against her principles. I achieved it by telling her that it was against my principles too, as a 95 per cent teetotaller; but for a good purpose we were to give ourselves a dispensation. She obeyed – I can see her now, sitting on a stool, a good little girl doing as she was told. She went off and made a rousing speech.

To understand her, one had to know something of, and allow for, her American background – she was far more American than Waldorf, an Etonian and Oxonian. As an historian I have always been surprised by the way Americans remain, indefeasibly and irreducibly, American after a lifetime in England. It is remarkable evidence of the strength of American characteristics; that there is such a thing as an American national character is again a remarkable achievement after only two or three hundred years of national history. Perhaps that is long enough – it is certainly an answer to Leftist illusionists who cannot see that national (or racial) characteristics even exist.

Nancy was born in 1879, a Virginia Langhorne. ('I was born a Virginian, so naturally I am a politician.') This meant that she had no inferiority complex about Astor wealth and grandeur; though the first Lord Astor regarded himself as a Renaissance prince and Nancy once remarked that at that time the Astors were treated in the US as semi-royal. (There had been a grand progress earlier in the United States with Waldorf and the Pierpont Morgans. Pierpont Morgan had a proboscis of a nose which grew and grew, for all the operations he had upon it to reduce the offending feature. Nancy said that when he kissed her, it stuck to her.) Even Waldorf, an unsnobbish man, once told me with innocent pleasure the number of 'royals' Cliveden had collected for the weekend, as against none at the Kemsleys, his rival newspaper proprietor across the way at Dropmore.

Naturally I didn't know Nancy in those early days of her first glory, when as the first woman MP she was world news, and when the world regarded what took place in Britain as important. The Americans were proud of her; no public woman competed with her at the time – those were the days before the rise of Eleanor Roosevelt. And I never knew until quite recently that the Langhornes originally came from Cornwall.

Not long ago on a visit to the Library of Reading University, to which the Astor papers were bequeathed, I was surprised to find that Nancy had kept my letters to her. I had naturally kept hers to me, for, a regular magpie, I keep everything. The Library very kindly gave me a Xerox, so now I have both sides of the correspondence. Mine begins by being properly deferential, goes on to become flirtatious and occasionally teasing, and ends up with genuine affection. The trouble with her letters is that they are largely illegible: after a lifetime of Elizabethan handwritings I can make out only half of what she is saying – her friends would say that this was to disguise her shaky spelling. It certainly succeeded.

My first letter was to try to persuade her to buy and save lovely Elizabethan Trerice (near Newquay), when it was empty and in danger. I suggested it might make a base for one of her sons setting up for a nearby constituency. I got a characteristic reply: 'It was funny you should write and ask me to have a corner in my heart for Cornwall, because I have fallen completely in love with it, having spent several weeks at Rock and played on the St Enodoc Golf Course quite alone . . .' Then, 'being Cornish there is a hitch in your mentality which I long to talk to you about! There are a lot of hitches in mine – or shall we call them stitches?'

She regarded Bertie Abdy's fabulous Newton Ferrers with disapproval, because he had given its Queen Anne interior the *décor* of a Louis Philippe house in Paris. It certainly was a bit exotic with its Winterhalters and Hubert Roberts, books with precious bindings from French royal libraries, its Houdon bust of Marie Antoinette, etc. – exquisite creation, I suspect Nancy thought it the least bit wicked because French.

An undated letter refers to the death of Adam von Trott, who had been David Astor's friend as well as mine, and an intimate at Cliveden. Adam had been in the generals' plot against Hitler and was hanged on a butcher's hook in Plötzensee Prison. Nancy:

> Oh dear. David feared this some time ago. Are you certain that it was Adam? I can't feel that death is anything save an open door. The real suffering is for those who are left and who believe it's the end . . . I've had

four weeks with my Bible and Books in a horrid house at Trebetherick. I wondered where you were as we truly want to see you. You are not a very sociable friend. Would you come to us at Cliveden any time? . . . Adam had a full life and great faith, but still how ghastly it is. A world that Hates and Kills and Envies. There are good Germans but no good Nazis, I agree. Do come soon and see us.

In October 1954 it was:

You know perfectly well that you have entirely forgotten me – I suppose for some dumb duchess! I have waited anxiously and never a line! You always win me back again with a book, and it looks very interesting. If I can tear myself away from the Book of Samuel I will read it.

Next, from Sandwich, where there was a quiet bay and golf at hand – a kind of millionaires' *enclave*:

I am bothered on all sides about my Life. I think you will have to write it – would you like to? If so you better go to Virginia and pick up what you can, *or* are you too busy for that? [As usual, I was.] I wrote you and had no reply before you left . . . General Slim wants me to come to Australia. I am torn. I'm no traveller . . . I know you will love my native land, tho' alas there are no Duchesses there. How you could fall for Duchess — — has rather shaken me. But then you are Cornish! *Not* Devon. God help and keep you in the strait and narrow way. Nancy, Her Grace of Sandwich, Kent.

In September 1955,

I wrote you before you left and never got an answer. I have now had your letter from the *Britannic*. I see you have fallen for Winston. I haven't yet. He is paying his usual visit to Lord Beaverbrook. The Bible says 'he is known by his friends.' I see you will be in the East [of

U.S.] from Dec. 1st. I hope to come over about January 1st. This is to know if you can wait so long.

I was so much enjoying myself in America that I wrote to her: 'Shall I stay over here for good? People are so good to me – so much more so than Cornwall has ever been, or Oxford, or the intellectuals.' To this she replied from Plymouth: 'Please don't go to Charlottesville or anywhere in Virginia until I get there. If possible change your programme, because I could ask you to stop with me near Charlottesville, and you would love it.' Of course, I couldn't change my programme of lectures, and didn't. 'I certainly don't advise you to leave your native land, though I admit you'll want to if you go to Virginia. Naturally a prophet is never with honour in his own country: have you forgotten your Bible? If you are returning for Duchesses it isn't worth while,' etc. More banter.

In October 1955,

> Your book has come [this was *The Expansion of Elizabethan England*] and I am looking forward to reading it – particularly the part about Virginia. I am off to Cumberland to unveil a tablet to the memory of G. Washington's Grandmother. I ask you, your Duchess has asked me to dine tonight!

There follows more banter about falling for duchesses . . . In February 1956, from Hill Street: 'I went to Cliveden, but no word of you. I sent you a wire. I sail for USA Sat 25 as ever is – I wish you could go with me. Ring me up here. I go aboard *Queen Elizabeth* Friday night.' [I don't suppose I did, I so much hate telephoning.]

Virginia regarded her as a favourite daughter, and had her portrait painted for the Capitol in Richmond. I have seen Mirador, where she was born, standing up on its bluff above the road from Richmond going up to the beautiful Blue Ridge country, which Nancy cantered all over as a girl on her horse, a fearless rider to hounds. It was as a hunting-woman that her father sent her and her sister to England –

for a change after the disillusioning experience of her first marriage. Propositions, as well as proposals, came from the Edwardian gallants of the hunting field to a beautiful, unattached young woman, full of spirit and daring. They got precious little change out of her, except some pretty smart repartees, and she took time before making up her mind even to Waldorf, as virtuous as she. She disapproved of the 'fast set' of the Edwardian age, and gave no encouragement to Edward VII himself: he was not welcome at Cliveden. Once he turned up, she told me, with his escort of dubious ladies, and commented that he had not had the pleasure of a visit from her. He had a mania for cards, among other things; she wouldn't play, and is said to have said to the old *roué* that she couldn't even tell the difference between a king and a knave. I don't know whether that was authentic, but certainly no Virginian ever felt inferior to anybody.

She made Cliveden a great centre of Anglo-American *camaraderie*, and what a contribution that was to good fellowship. One met any number of people in public life from both sides of the Atlantic, ambassadors and admirals, cabinet ministers, politicians, writers. I cannot remember them all: charming and cultivated Frances Perkins, close friend of Franklin Roosevelt, the one woman member of his Cabinet; Governor Darden, with all that Virginian charm, who on ceasing to be governor, became President of Jefferson's University of Virginia; Herbert Agar and Leonard Brockington, Canadian publicist; Vincent Massey, to become Governor General of Canada; Mrs Vincent Astor, rather distant and grand, in pearls; genial and friendly Field-Marshal Slim. And always a wide spectrum of the British aristocracy, along with a sampling from politics; hardly any writers, publicists rather, such as Alan Moorhead; and even one artist, Stanley Spencer, diminutive as a cock robin, up from neighbouring Cookham.

The young historian watched it all as so much history unfolding, for the benefit of his education, from the sidelines or, rather, from a front seat in the stalls. For, as Nancy once said in her wobbly French, I was '*bien placé*', usually next to her on her left-hand side. One certainly observed some funny scenes. She was a marvellous mimic, and could do Margot Oxford so convincingly, that one was reduced to helpless laughter – Lady Oxford with Nancy's boys at the theatre, wondering what they found so much to laugh at, unconscious that it was herself with a nose more like a limb than a feature and baring her teeth for the extraordinary things she would say, describing someone: 'She hasn't got a roof or a rafter to her mouth.'

If the table lagged for a moment, or things became too solemn, politics or whatnot, one looked round and there was Nancy, the anarchist, at the head of it with a false red nose, mimicking somebody else's way of talking. She could do the nasal accent, as if with a cold in the head, of the German 'royals' of the Edwardian royal family to perfection. No superfluous reverence, or conventional English flunkeyism, in that quarter.

Awkward moments occasionally occurred. She was giving a large tea-party for Paul Hoffman, the Administrator of European Relief, a key post after all the devastation of the war. It is a pity that, now that we know blacks are better than whites, only whites may be regarded as a subject of amusement, blacks not; while *Huckleberry Finn*, a work of genius, may be withdrawn from schools and libraries for its use of the term 'niggers' (not very nice) or even, affectionately, 'darkies'. Nancy adored the darkies she had been brought up with, loved them as they loved her, and she had a mass of good stories about them, could speak their lingo to perfection and sing their songs. Paul Hoffman was sitting beside her when she began on some of these imitations; Mrs Hoffman was sitting beside me, a do-gooder who, like many who have gone to the good, was without a sense of humour. I sensed her gorge rising, and felt her beginning to rise from her seat to do battle; I managed to restrain her with, 'Wait, you'll see he'll deal with her.' And, of course, he did. The golden rule was not to take too seriously whatever she said, at least place a large pair of inverted commas around it.

It was on that occasion that I took the opportunity to suggest to Paul Hoffman the desirability of an Anglo-American literary magazine to draw us together – out of which I rather think *Encounter* ultimately took shape. I may be wrong, but they wouldn't know about this *éminence grise*.

Sometimes things were more awkward – as with Nancy's broadside against Mrs Admiral Nimitz: 'Why did you allow your daughter to become a Roman Catholic nun?' That was not funny, and none of her business anyway. But Nancy was a past master at the quip direct, not sparing her own children, and that embarrassed them dreadfully. Once she attacked Bobby at table, in my presence, drawing the contrast with 'Look at what *he* has done,' meaning me. I wasn't going to have that. After lunch I took her aside – I can see her now standing above me on the stairs, holding her tiny wrists jangling with Astor jewelry – and said, 'Nancy, I won't hear a word against Bobby. All you can say is that he's a bit idle, and everybody ought to do a job of work. Bobby did his duty in the war, and you should be thankful they all survived,' etc. She took it like a lamb and, I think, was pleased at my standing up for him; for the trouble with Bobby was that he loved her and she him, perhaps too much.

She never once put her nose into my affairs, except to say innocently, 'What do you want to get married for? You don't want to get married – you are best off as you are.' Since I knew that already, and had no intention of getting married, it made me laugh; for it was just the line Elizabeth I used to take with *her* ladies-in-waiting.

Nancy had confidence in me, deserved or no – she certainly had in my taste. Once down in the Barbican at Plymouth we were looking into the window of an antique shop, in those days when they had antiques worth looking at – before they had been burgled or sold out of a run-down country, a dispiriting society. My eye was taken by a pair of pretty Victorian stools with seed-pearl decoration; while I hesitated Nancy was in like a shot, and beat me to the post. I thought that rather naughty of her; but it wasn't the only time that a gamesome lady has made up her mind by noticing what caught my eye. I shouldn't have hesitated.

I made it a principle with these grand ladies not to dine out at each other's expense. Plenty of them were malicious about Nancy – she wasn't malicious herself, though she could give

as good as she got. I always stood up for her with others, and
for the others too when their turn came. After all, I didn't
need to dine out at anybody's expense; it was more fun standing up for people, carrying the game into the opponent's
camp. Any fool can criticize – it is far more worth-while
analysing a person's good qualities, and exposing those. More
difficult too! – goodness, if I devoted my brains to criticizing,
what could I not do, with my view of human beings
(Swift's)?

I think this ultimately paid off: it won their confidence,
and the historian who was a complete outsider learned a lot
of things, without giving them his, or giving himself away.
He knew all about them; they knew little about him. Nor did
it matter: he was not one of them, for ever outside. The man
on the margins of life sees most, and this was the right thing
for a writer, at any rate for the kind of writer I was – never to
be involved. Henry James said of the human aquarium that
a writer should be half outside life, so as to be able to see
what was going on, and half inside, enough to know what it
was like. Most humans don't ever glimpse the aquarium, or
realize that they are inside it. I sometimes vary the image
and, as I watch their antics, think of them as my menagerie.

When poor George VI's reign was over and it came to
Elizabeth II's coronation (I was rather sorry that that sacred
name was to have a second innings), I had the job of reporting it for the *Western Morning News*. This paper had treated
me outrageously as a candidate during the appalling election
of 1931, which led to a disastrous decade under the 'National'
Government. (Pure humbug, of course: a frame-up against
Labour. They have paid for it since.) However, it was my one
way of seeing a coronation – I should not have been invited
otherwise, unlike the Sitwells and Willie Walton whom I was
enskied amongst, up in the north transept of Westminster
Abbey. London was full up – nowhere to stay so as to get up
at 5.30 a.m. and present myself in my best fettle, doctoral
scarlet and all. Nancy came to the rescue and got Bill to put
me up; with whom, resplendent in his peer's robes, I duly
sallied forth and all was well.

What ever could I do for her to show my appreciation of

her – no possibility of return for her constant kindness? Well, I could at least dedicate a book to her – not even Shaw had done that, though he wrote *The Apple Cart* mostly at Cliveden. I thought my Trevelyan Lectures on *The Elizabethans and America* a suitable offering, with its theme that English-speaking America went back beyond the dreary Pilgrim Fathers (G. K. Chesterton: 'The Pilgrim Fathers landed on Plymouth Rock: would that Plymouth Rock had landed on the Pilgrim Fathers!') to Virginia, beyond Jamestown to Ralegh's colonial enterprise, backed by Elizabeth I. In fact, English-speaking America, along with the Shakepearean drama, was the greatest creation of the Elizabethan Age. I don't know whether Nancy appreciated the dedication to her two chief loves, Virginia and Plymouth; I'm pretty sure she didn't read the book.

What was a weekend at Cliveden like? Of several accounts in my Journals I choose one of the most interesting for readers next century – in case no one else has taken the trouble to write them up.

Mid December 1952. 'I missed Nuffield lunching there, though Nancy insisted I should come over in time; for I had already promised dear Geoffrey Hudson and didn't want to let him down . . . Arrived late at Cliveden, I was flung into the middle of the large round tea-table – Nancy Mitford's image occurred to me, the flock of starlings all rising up to settle on the newcomer. Menzies, Prime Minister of Australia, and his pretty daughter were there, and Field-Marshal Slim just going out as Governor General; Bob Brand, Bill Astor and Nancy herself, looking like a girl, elegant in black, jangling the jewelry on tiny wrists. Another very noticeable woman whom I couldn't make out had been a close former friend of the Duke of Windsor, now disguised as an Italian Marchesa, flashing brilliant green ear-rings.

'Slim turned out a largish, square-shouldered, pleasant, very masculine type – and full of himself: in the manner of these strong silent soldiers, very loquacious. Not a public-school man, but from King Edward's Birmingham: he talked across the wide space of that table mostly at, or to, me.

Conversation pitched on me at once. Did I know A. J. P. Taylor, whom they had seen and heard on TV? (Indeed, only too well, from his undergraduate days.) From that to the Leftist intellectuals and their influence. I said that business magnates paid no attention to literature and writing; for example, their next door neighbour at Dropmore, Kemsley, had the literary pages of his *Sunday Times* written by *New Statesman* types, and was probably unaware of it. They thought these things didn't matter, and were surprised when the young people at the universities turned out Leftists. From that to the intellectuals in general and the BBC. Brand is on its advisory council, but couldn't find out who appointed people to give the talks – it was done much lower down, invisibly from the heights of high policy.

'Slim, pleased with himself but equally impressive and likeable, thought Western propaganda misconceived in always attacking Communism as such – particularly American propaganda, for reasons of internal American politics. This had the effect of aligning the Iron Curtain countries, and China, with Soviet Russia – stressing their one common bond. Our line should be directed against Russia as such, attacking Russia's interference with their internal affairs, running *their* countries.

'I said that this was not only right in itself but in line with the profoundest force we had with us – the desire of peoples to run their own affairs their own way. If this could be elicited and canalized, it would eventually win. But we mustn't neglect to frame Communism for the malign thing it is – witness the Prague Trials and the sickening effect they had on some English Communists, e.g. the composer Arthur Benjamin leaving them. The wonder was that anybody stuck.[1]

'Towards dinner the party filled out. Mary, Duchess of Devonshire came down looking infinitely distinguished in black dress, rather short, but with long Spanish-looking fringes. Everybody says that she is the most modest of people, simple and good and kind; but I find such sensibility

[1] It was not until Hungary and Krushchev's revelations of Stalin's crimes that many became unstuck.

and distinction rather paralysing, so I never attempt to talk to her. Besides, she has been through a great deal in late years – I remember *how* she looked last time at Cliveden after her husband's death. This time she said to me she was much better, with that impulsive Cecilian girlishness: I saw how irresistible she was, and observed her at night go up the staircase alone, a wonderful, rather sad, figure.

'Menzies made a friendly, cheerful impression, also well pleased with himself in the manner of the ordinary male animal. Much more at ease in Zion than fifteen years or so ago when he came to All Souls with Dick Latham. Ambition now satisfied, he was more relaxed, fatter, eupeptic, complexion positively blooming. "The trouble with me," he said to the observant young historian, "is that I'm a very bad butcher. Gladstone said that, to be any good as a Prime Minister, you have to be a good butcher. I just can't do it: I haven't the heart. The result is that I let a lot of chaps go on when they are past it." The historian registered the way of commending oneself by running oneself down, commented on by La Rochefoucauld, Swift, and other cynical observers of mankind.

'He realizes, rather pathetically, that it is his obvious ability that has always stood in the way of his being popular with Australians. Similarly, Smuts's trouble in South Africa – "Slim Janny" – a great man. So Menzies has to bring up his heart for the benefit of the dear people. Now I should say that, in spite of his ability, he probably has a good heart. He is touchingly proud of his daughter – like her father, very good-looking. The girl fell asleep and didn't come down in time for dinner. Nancy was in favour of letting her sleep. "No, let her get up," said her stern parent; and when she appeared in pretty frock and I remarked on her charm – "No," said father fondly, "I rather like looking at her myself."

'They had naturally been at the Buckingham Palace party, and the PM had to tell me the latest Winston story. The Prime Minister of Pakistan is a teetotaller, as a Muslim; when drinks came round after dinner and he rejected them all, Winston said, "What, Mr Prime Minister, you don't drink?"

On his affirming no, Winston said, "Christ! – I mean God!
– I mean Allah!" Tommy Lascelles thought the footman
would have dropped the tray.

'At dinner I was placed beside Joan Hammond – Nancy
never told me who she was. When I tumbled to it, we got on
like anything, and we spent most of the evening together:
luscious, glittering look of an Italian *prima donna*, black wave
of hair, collusive smile, pretty mole on cheek. After dinner
we chummed up in the library with Bill Astor and Leonard
Brockington – asthmatic, hunch-backed, ginger-grizzled
hair, close-fitting gold-rimmed spectacles, endlessly cigar-
smoking; clever, humorous, benevolent, full of stories – too
many. Canadian friend of Lionel Curtis and all the Round
Table group. Like all such lonely men who can't sleep, he
wanted me to stay up talking with him. But I had arrived
fagged out, almost faint with fatigue over proofs, several
nights up to 1 a.m. at them; never have I arrived at Cliveden
so flagging.

'We had a pleasant evening in our little group, jokes,
stories, giggles – the *prima donna* beaming down from behind
the glittering armour of her Brunhilde corsage. I didn't know
Bill was so interested in music or moves in these circles, and
goes to Aldeburgh (on B.B., "Oh, he's a happy little fairy").
He had had a chamber orchestra giving a concert in his house
to celebrate his baby's christening. I was happy to see him so
cheerful and gay – after the melancholy appearance he has
been making since his wife walked out on him . . . He is a
good host, with kind, affable manners. Joan Hammond is a
dévote of Beecham, to her no conductor like him. Bill told us
about "Rule, Britannia" having been first sung in the little
open-air theatre in the grounds here, at the end of the first act
of Thomson's *Masque of Liberty*. (I suppose that a piece of
Frederick, Prince of Wales's nonsense directed against his
father, George II.)

'At the end of the evening when Joan was leaving, Nancy
said to the assembled group, "This girl can fill the Albert
Hall any time: that's more than you can do!" Menzies was
taken aback, quite nettled by this *boutade*; and instead of taking it in good part stumbled rather clumsily with, "Oh, well

– we can do other things perhaps.'' Nobody seemed to notice the comedy; I was rather amused.

'One elderly dame appeared in what looked like a bath-robe plus a solitary rose at her waist. Little did I realize that she was to be my buddy through the weekend. But she was a Cornish Vivian from Glyn; beneath white hair, dark, coal-glowing eyes, full of intelligence and vivacity. She had married into the Yarborough family, grand Brocklesby, which I visited a year or two ago to see a portrait of the Elizabethan soldier, Sir William Pelham. The usual story – two lots of death-duties had reduced that vast estate to something quite small. Now the case of someone just managing to hang on by cheese-paring and prudent land-management, the house much reduced.

'So unlike the state of things at Glyn, where her nephew, the dance-band leader, made no effort. Result – that beautiful estate in the most romantic of valleys is in the hands of the estate-breaker. [This man lived on the opposite side of the road to me at home, in a hideous villa called Soulsbyville – I thought of calling my place All Soulsbyville. He recouped the price of the place simply by cutting trees – couldn't the dance-band peer have done as much? I would have done, if only it had come to me.]

'After breakfast we walked out, December mildness in the air, peacock-blue sky, sun up. Down the glen we went to the river, church bells ringing across the suburbanized Thames countryside. We got on easily like two Cornish folk in a foreign land. She had spent much of her childhood abroad, though refusing to learn languages out of exaggerated patriotism. I saw something masculine in this descendant of dashing Hussey Vivian, Wellington's cavalry leader, Waterloo and all, who made a fortune out of soldiering and bought Glyn from the Glyns, who had gambled their patrimony away. Now – the Vivians in turn make way – what will become of the lovely place?

'Her life-story simple, husband killed in the first German war, no children. We talked about the responsibilities of governments and parties before the second war. These people of the governing class are uneasy on the subject – as well they might be. One and all, they defend themselves; some of them, like Nancy, blame the Labour Party. (Of course, they were idiots to oppose rearmament, when the Germans were working all hours to rearm; but Labour was kept in a small minority, theirs a secondary responsibility.) These people realize that their record in the twenties and thirties – when they had everything their own way – needs defending. She had rushed to the defence of Edward Halifax, when someone called him a collaborator. (He was not that, but he was in favour of compromise with Hitler.)

'She made a sensible claim for her own line: "I had neither husband nor son, nobody to lose, but I should feel all the more blameworthy if I didn't do all I could to support peace." I recognized the Chamberlain line, and said – unfortunately we learn from history and experience that to make concessions to thugs and criminals is the very way to bring war down upon us. And I did not fail to make the point on behalf of my own people that Labour, when in power, had done better in standing up to Communist Russia than the Conservatives had to Nazi Germany. A sensible, honest woman, she had once admitted it, and spoke with real appreciation of Attlee and Bevin. A lady-in-waiting to the Queen Mother, she is above the humbug of party allegiances.

'Coming back along the river, we paused on that delicious eighteenth-century Italian bridge with steps down to the water's edge, a stream made for it to arch over. Michael Astor told me a lot about his grandfather, my picture of him as a buccaneer coming over from the jungle of American politics evidently quite wrong. A much stranger and more complex, unhappy, solitary man, thwarted in his ambition to become a US Senator, left New York for Europe, was Minister in Rome for a bit. Whence he picked up the terrace of the Borghese Villa and placed it admirably at Cliveden, with the Giovanni da Bologna fountain to terminate the vista. A connoisseur – hence too the French Renaissance chimney piece in the hall, the dining-room panelling from the Pompadour's Château d'Asnières, the Louis XV portraits of the French royal family in the small drawing-room. Michael told me a great deal about the strange personality of this remarkable man, walled up in himself after the early death of his wife.[2]

'Sunday afternoon a shorter walk around the grounds with Bill, Miss Menzies and the American Rear-Admiral (who spoke so long at the Berger Lunch that I had to cut my speech down to five minutes). We did a round of the temples – the Leoni temple has been made a family mausoleum, where Waldorf is buried. Another was built by Lord Orkney, Marlborough's cavalry-general; his clever screw-eyed wife was William III's mistress and Swift's friend. After them came Frederick Prince of Wales –

> Here lies poor Fred,
> Who was alive and is dead . . .
> Since it's only Fred,
> There's no more to be said.

Next came the Sutherlands, who called in Barry to build the present house, 1851; then the Westminsters from whom the first Lord Astor bought it. I suggested to Bill that he write up the history of Cliveden; it could make an interesting book, based on proper research, going into all the associations, and embellishments. Bill was unenthusiastic: "I am much too idle," he said; and unfortunately I believe him.

'Before dinner the household was keyed up and unusual preparations were evidently being made: the Queen Mother and Princess Margaret were coming to dinner. "I have given you a very good place," said Nancy to me – only two away, between the Marchesa and charming Pam Ruthven, whom I had met several times with the Gowries. Last time I read the poignant book about her husband, their only child, killed in the war, based on his letters from childhood up. How touching – simple and courageous and loving, heart-breaking for the old couple; gallant old war-horses, both of them.

'When we joined the ladies in the library after dinner, Princess Margaret was ensconced in the sofa by the fire. I made no effort to talk to her, considering myself much too old to

---

[2] Since he has written all this up in his admirable *Tribal Feeling*, I omit the account in my Journals.

interest a young girl: I left her to Bill, then to Michael, then to A. P. Jones's brother, a Korda young man. I devoted myself to the Marchesa, an interesting study. Twice she said, "If you had a wonderful time when you were young – what is called a mis-spent youth . . . when you get older you find life disappointing, things pall." I said, if you had had a great deal of illness all the years of your youth, you would be grateful for life when you got older: I have never been so happy as since I was forty: I enjoy being middle-aged.

'She was obviously *mécontente*, perhaps I should say *malcontenta* . . . She was still somebody to be looked at – not to talk to, but to study. I studied her. She carped at the party, at the royal family. She thought they should do without all this formality (her own contact had been on a less formal level) – why can't they be more matey? I said that the People would be disappointed: since they paid out all the money to keep the thing up, they expected something different for their money. Mrs Jones of the Surbiton Conservative Ladies adored going down on her creaking old knees and would feel cheated not to be able to do it. Besides life was so monochrome and boring for ordinary people, wasn't it a good thing to have something *different* in the plum pudding of society?

'The Marchesa, herself a Conservative, couldn't deal with this one, and fell back on – "But need it be so stiff and silly? Look at it!" I looked: the Queen Mother was seated at the other end of the library, across an acre of parquet flooring – which Bill means to cover with a savonnerie rug. I turned round: there she was sitting upright in her regal chair, talking one by one to the person presented to her. "But *they* insist on keeping it up: they shouldn't insist on it: they should give it up." (I suppose this was the Duke of Windsor's line, and he had certainly given up.) I conceded that it did make people shy and nervous. "Well, of course: look how ridiculously they are all behaving, just because *they* are here."

'I looked: a charade was going on – not very successfully – Nancy and most of the others were seated in a ring on the floor, she and her nephew, Reggie Wynne, making fantastic noises. "How ridiculous of them," said the Marchesa, "all sitting on the floor, because *they* are here. Nancy is a nervous hostess. What is the point of it? It's ridiculous." It was a bit absurd; but why take against it? I was amused – and I never thought Nancy a nervous hostess: quite the contrary.

'The charade broke up and I was next to be summoned to the Presence. I gave the Marchesa an incriminating glance – not too obvious a one: even so it was intercepted by the Princess Margaret, on whom nothing is lost, sharp little girl. Reggie Wynne was hanging over the QM's chair: I waited till he had gone, I wasn't going to have a conversation *à trois* with him. The QM, looking more beautiful than I have ever seen her, was resplendent in an enormous crinoline, black velvet, black silk (I thought of Queen Elizabeth I's dresses in her Account Book in the British Museum – black velvet, puffed sleeves slashed with ivory satin – in the 1570s); three rows of huge pearls, a diamond ornament in (Balzac's) *place la plus mignonne*, diamond ear-rings dangling. All like something out of the Victorian Age, Queen Victoria again.

'We took up the conversation where we had dropped it at the tea-table at Lambeth – as the QM said to Nancy we always did. Nancy disappeared. I asked about the Castle o' Mey she had recently acquired at the furthermost tip of Scotland, and said that if she moved any further away from her loving subjects she would find herself right off the island. She laughed, "Perhaps it was all a mistake." I said, "Yes, if they ran Sunday buses from neighbouring towns to have a look." "They won't see much," she said; it was the nearest thing to going abroad, now that it was so difficult to go abroad. Very like Norway. I said she ought to be able to go abroad more – she said that it meant about eleven persons going, all told. Couldn't she go incognita? She said that once when the King was Duke of York they had gone to Belgium as Earl and Countess of Inverness. But it wasn't any good: everybody behaved very well, but they looked . . . She made a pretty *mou*, from which it was clear that she rather enjoyed recognition.

'I talked about Spain, and that she would enjoy the Escorial: her security would be looked after now, or Alba would look after her and show her everything. (I forgot that that would be impossible for political reasons.) We talked a little

about the King. I said that history would record how much
he owed to her and all she had done for him. "Oh, no. I did
nothing – except that I was his loving wife. It was he that had
the character. He made the decisions – I think he made the
right decisions." I said I hoped that he knew the great feeling
his people had for him – though people can't express it very
well to a man: they can more easily to a woman. She said that
there wasn't time for that (as there had been for George V;
so the son died without realizing how much people felt for
him). First, there was the Abdication, and all the trouble that
gave rise to. (The historian reflected to himself on the ironies
of history, with the Marchesa in the offing – but she had not
been responsible for it.) Then came the war, and after that
there was never any time . . .

'We talked of the social revolution that had taken place –
she said that it had been led from the top. Certainly those
two had worked hard enough . . . "I am rather a revolutionary," she said, eyes smiling, those most expressive eyes,
sometimes the suggestion of tears in them. "Ah, *la belle révo-
lutionnaire*," I thought, but did not dare to say. What I said
was, "I thought you were a Jacobite, not a Jacobin." "Oh,
yes, a Jacobite and a Jacobin too," she said gaily; "it doesn't
prevent me from being a revolutionary." I said that the English social revolution meant that a Prime Minister who was
an Old Harrovian (Winston) was succeeded by a Prime
Minister who was an Old Haileyburian (Clem Attlee).

'We were certainly having fun, Nancy now hovering to
give someone else a chance, quite rightly. The Queen said,
with more than *politesse*, "Oh, but we were *just* beginning to
have a real talk." "I'll go away," said Nancy, "don't let me
interrupt." But I had had more than my fair share, and was
going to make way. Nancy whispered, "I'll get him to come
to a party in London." Will it, I wonder, eventuate? Bob
Brand took my place; I saw the elderly peer, with the frosty,
rimless-spectacled banker's appearance, settle shyly into my
chair.

'Was the Marchesa right after all? For, not long after, the
Queen Mother gave the signal: the formal circle gathered
once more, as on her entry, and we all bowed and scraped, or

curtsied. Arrived at the other end of the circle, she stopped specially to have a few words with the Marchesa, David's former friend, not forgotten. That was nice of her, considerate and thoughtful as always. Did the Marchesa appreciate it? The irony of the encounter was not lost upon the observant historian nor how prettily the *convenances* were kept. What memories, it flashed across my mind, those two women could exchange!'

Nancy was as good as her word: I take from my Journals the account of the party she gave in London for various literary people to be presented to the Queen Mother.

'Nancy had asked me to recommend some, and I sent her a list with John Betjeman, Arthur Bryant, Carola Oman and Veronica Wedgwood, among others. Very few writers had she asked, it was more like a journalists' party, with editors of *The Times*, *Observer*, *Sunday Times*, *Literary Supplement*, etc. I arrived early in case she wanted help with writers like Veronica and Carola whom she didn't know; but she had not asked them.

'All the Astors were there in force, though they must have plenty of opportunity of meeting the QM – Bill (without wife), David (with new wife), Jakey, Michael (no doubt *with* wife), Bob Brand, Nancy Lancaster without either husband but wonderfully dressed: her vibrant sexy figure appearing out of a sea–foam of white-pearl-grey tulle, another Venus with resplendent pearls and rubies. Nancy A. herself equally impressive in black velvet with long train and a superb jewel looking like a three-tiered Boadicea's buckler. (What it is to be an Astor!)

'The house was looking lovely – never such flowers in the depth of December, cyclamen, African violets, orchids; pictures rich against the background of a savonnerie carpet, honey colour, dark browns, rose-red flower-festoons. Nancy however, complained that this [Hill Street] wasn't the same thing as at St James's Square, where all you had to do was to give orders and the whole thing was done.

'We were not a large party for dinner. The QM was rather late as usual, I suppose *pour faire impression*, so we were caught in some disarray. We had been standing up waiting; then we sat down; *then* she appeared, with Nancy at the door saying, in her serjeant-major's voice, "Get up, all of you." Curious that with all her looks and experience, she doesn't bother about dignity – perhaps the American allergy to dignity, as in their public life. [I have seen Nancy at a garden-party on the lawn at Cliveden doing her Barbican fish-wife's turn to the crowd, the QM only a few paces away trying to appear oblivious of the indignity.]

'The QM looked girlish as ever, fresh as a flower. The presentations began the other end of the half-circle and finished with me; she seemed pleased, but stopped, not thinking of anything to say. So I stepped in with some gallant nonsense about how fine it was, driving through gloomy December London, to see her flag flying over Clarence House – she was "keeping the flag flying", the only one to be seen. This closed the gap – it must be so boring for the royal family that people are so petrified on meeting them that there is nothing to say. She responded at once with the girlish enthusiasm that is so effective, "Oh, everybody ought to have a flag: there should be flags all over London."

'Arthur Bryant's wife, Anne, in a terrible state of nerves, was agog to know what I had found to talk about. Nothing much.

'The dinner, as always with Nancy, was first-rate, though the QM declined soup, with an eye to her figure, I registered. None but the Astors can have such a chef – I don't suppose the royal family has, though I don't know, for I haven't eaten their food. After dinner in came the party, among the first Harry Hodson (my first election when examining for the Fellowship at All Souls) – evidently embarrassed and excusing himself for the nasty photograph of me and malicious comment the *Sunday Times* had published – the usual literary animus. I took the opportunity to make the point that what Arthur Bryant and I have to say was far more in keeping with the readers of the *Sunday Times* than anything their recruits from the *New Statesman*, Mortimer and Connolly, have to say. "I dare say," he stammered, "but that is – that is a matter of policy" – which gave the game away.

'Next tripped in David Cecil and bright-eyed Rachel, followed by Harold Nicolson. I don't speak to him, after his shocking review of *The English Past* in *The Observer*. This is what humans are like – I have always been nothing but kind to his son and his nephew at Oxford. I know as well as the next man that one is supposed to take no notice, but I wrote in to protest; I always do react. After all, I don't want to know people – I am here only as an observer, watching the fish in the aquarium gawping and gaping. Just like Henry James, a *voyeur*, uncommitted, an outsider, inassimilable.

'Then came the dear Betjemans, much more congenial, whom I had suggested to Nancy: Penelope bringing her air of a country farmyard into this metropolitan atmosphere, John in the usual disarray, looking like a clergyman who had lost his way. I propelled him forward to the little formal circle in the inner drawing room where the QM was holding her levee – it was more like the doctor's waiting-room where we awaited our turn in the outer room.

'Nancy called me up along with A. P. Jones of the *Lit. Sup*. There couldn't have been a worse choice: he so sophisticated, so "cultivated", as John said, it made me shy and awkward. He was very much at his ease; I would have done better by myself. It was frightfully hot, with Nancy's American standards of central heating; the QM was occasionally reduced to lifting one of the enormous emeralds sticking to her. We talked away about Disraeli, and Harold Macmillan's having something of his forward-looking quality. (I did not mention other things.) I uttered some nonsense about too many houses being put up everywhere, spoiling the countryside; the QM protested, with an understanding smile, "O, *not enough* houses!" She had evidently learnt her lesson well: no mistakes in that quarter.

'Mrs A. P. Jones chipped in dexterously about her daughter's tour in the South Seas. Had I read Herman Melville? No, I had not. This gave the QM an opportunity to score, and she promised to send me *Omoo* and *Typee*. Fancy her remembering! Shortly after Christmas there arrived a little parcel, addressed in her own clear hand, along with a grand coloured photograph of herself and Margaret in their coronation robes. Autographed too – all very well conceived: she had done her bit for the monarchy.'

And what of Waldorf?

Quiet and reserved, shy and content to sit back while Nancy performed, his rôle was far more important than people suspected. He was the real ruler, not Nancy. At times she behaved like a naughty girl, and pestered and bounced him into things. He was doubtful about some philanthropic project of hers – I forget what – and dragging his feet, when she said, 'If he doesn't do it, I'll sell all my pearls.' I don't know how often she used that threat, but it is not impossible that she might have carried it out.

It happens that she has occasionally asked me to stay on when the large weekend party had gone, and then one could see the terms of mutual understanding between them, the long dining-room table contracted for the three of us, a simple teetotal meal that suited this perpetual member of the Duodenal Club. Waldorf adored her good qualities, realized all that he owed to her for releasing him from the shadow of his father's presence, the endemic family shyness that held up communication with the outside world. Her dynamism was indispensable to him, a precious element in his own life; they had created a wonderful life together, and accomplished what neither of them could have done without the other. A selfless man, a good deal of a saint, Waldorf put up with a lot; but, in the last resort, he had the last word, the withdrawn presence ruled. It wasn't only that he held the reins of this very flighty mare, but he provided the steady element in her life that prevented her from going too far – to mix the metaphor, and frankly, from going off the rails. An educated man, of an achieved spirit, he set the standards, and she knew it.

Nancy was a democrat – I was not; Waldorf had a pathetic belief in the principles of democracy – I had not. No aesthete can be a democrat; I was about as much of a democrat as Proust was – or, for that matter, Karl Marx or Lenin (perhaps a bit more than the latter). If anyone wonders then why I was a Labour man – it was that I was desperately anti-Baldwin and Chamberlain; I may add that they had the great heart of the democracy with them. (And how I hated the fatuous people for that, allowing themselves to be so bamboozled. I suppose now I was in revolt simply against *la condition humaine.*)

Waldorf and Nancy were too independent and liberal-minded to be hardened partisans: reliable enough members of the Conservative Party, they were certainly not Tories. I think that, during the second war, Waldorf was glad to escape party controversy and operate as a genuine Independent, as Lord Mayor of Plymouth. He held that office all through the war, something like a German burgomaster – such as Adenauer was in Cologne; he worked night and day for the city, trying to find housing for the people whose homes were shattered, and planning to build up again, as Nancy had promised with the city in flames before her eyes. This exceptional span of office enabled Waldorf to plan well for Plymouth: it was owing to him that Plymouth was first in the field with Abercrombie's scheme for replanning and rebuilding the city as we see it today. For all Waldorf's good work, the Conservative caucus hoofed him out before the job was finished, and installed an old war-horse of the caucus as Lord Mayor in his place.

I never heard a word of resentment from Waldorf – but judge if he was just a party-man.

The election of 1945 was to visit upon the Conservatives retribution for their record over the past twenty years. As Lord Boothby admits in his memoirs, they were governed throughout by their own economic and class interest. So, when the election of 1945 initiated a social revolution, they had only themselves to blame. Waldorf plainly had no such narrow views, though he had more to lose than almost any-one. He saw, however, that it was time to withdraw Nancy from Parliament; her day, her contribution, was really over.

Waldorf was right, but Nancy was both furious and miserable. She fought hard against the decision; she argued that, if she had been allowed to fight her seat again, it would not have been lost to Labour. That may have been so; but Waldorf

did not want to expose her to defeat, or indeed allow her to
expose herself any more. She had fought seven elections, and
never once been defeated. (I found it intolerable that the Conservatives were in power virtually in permanence between
the wars: they alone bear the responsibility for what happened to the country.)

Nancy's fighting spirit took the form of a line against the
Astors – this was unreasonable of her, but reason was never
her strong point. If only she could have taken to reading,
developing the inner resources of the mind – with that, one
is no longer dependent on outer circumstances or other
people. She was like other women of natural ability but uned-
ucated – she had not the resources to fall back upon. 'Oh
dear, I should never have believed that I should miss the
House of Commons so much.' The limelight had become a
drug she could not do without.

Waldorf was happy to retire and withdraw from the conflicts and bitternesses of politics. He had had a heart-attack,
and lived quietly to himself in a ground-floor suite giving on
to the terrace, whence he could propel himself about the
grounds in his electric chair. They took all the care he could
give them. One post-war weekend when the house was full
of guests, the place was visited by expert lead-thieves who
rolled all the lead off the roof of a garden-temple: portent of
the Brave New World, the society we enjoy with the people,
on every hand, out of hand. The last time I saw the dear good
man, frail in his chair, we were alone with Frances Perkins;
he turned to each of us, with tears in his eyes, 'What am I to
do with Nancy?' There was nothing either of us could suggest.

She went on grieving for the House of Commons. Almost
the last time I saw her she told me that, sitting beside Winston at dinner the night before, he had said, 'Nancy, we very
much miss you in the House.' The old couple who had
sparred there so often – Winston could not bear being interrupted – had at length made it up, in view of the end, having
experienced so much, been in so many fights.

Sometimes Nancy regretted Bill having taken her place at
Cliveden. 'The Astors have no taste.' This was not true of the

younger generation: Bill much improved Cliveden with
exquisite French eighteenth-century furniture, savonnerie
carpets laid upon the creaking parquet floor of the library, his
own collection of water-colours upstairs, and resurrecting the
rare books his grandfather had collected from a closet where
they had been put away out of view. Sometimes she wished
she had taken over beautiful Bletchingdon when he left it,
within easy distance from Oxford, whence she could have
drawn a salon. In the end she spent a good deal of time not
far away, with her niece, Nancy Lancaster, in the exquisite
house with topiary garden she brought to perfection, out at
Great Haseley.

'It was here that I saw her the last time. There was smart
company, and I much wanted to see what her niece had done
to make the house so ravishing, since I first saw it with her
when derelict from the war. Actually I spent the greater part
of the time with dear Nancy – worth all of them. It was nice
to talk to her in a quiet mood, no public turn at all – come
back to the country girl she had once been. She was sad,
worried about the country and what is going to happen to us
(as we all are), and about Bill's matrimonial troubles. [We
need not go into those, as she did, the intolerable joys of
family life.] Nancy wanted to talk to me so much that I
hadn't much opportunity to see the house. It tantalized my
imagination the more. *Such* taste, such flair as Nancy Lancaster has got . . . I have never seen such candelabra and giran-
doles, Italian coloured glass, the whole place winking in pale
misty winter sun across level fields, glittering in the coloured
glass like raindrops.

'Nancy A. took me into the high saloon occupying two
storeys of the east front looking out on the topiary chess-
men. Her niece had decorated it herself, pale blues and pearl
greys, ovals and garlanded Adam wreaths in the high coved
ceiling, long slim Chippendale mirrors and Chinese silk
curtains from Ditchley. The house has possessed my mind.'
Nancy came to occupy the most splendid room upstairs, the
Chapel room, with fine canopied bed in the middle.

She was very much lost, withdrawn from her world of
politics, Westminster and Plymouth. 'Why don't you marry

her?' said Nancy L. 'It could be a *marriage blanche*.' 'I don't see
why it should be a *marriage blanche*,' I said, to her amusement.
She knew very well that, like Arthur Balfour when someone
thought he might marry Margot (who ruined Asquith, or at
any rate weakened his fibre), I rather fancied a career for
myself.

And now they have both gone, Waldorf and Nancy, from
Cliveden, the great days over. I have never been there since,
the place too full of ghosts: Nancy coming out from her
boudoir to galvanize a party of inert menfolk in their capa-
cious red seats in the hall; or appearing on the terrace, a
bunch of grapes in hand for breakfast; or suddenly boasting,
'I haven't a hair on my body.' (She didn't invite me to inspect
– if I were to lay a hand on her, 'I'd kick you in the belly.'
I'll bet she was as beautiful and chaste a figure as a marble
Diana.) She could still turn cartwheels at seventy. Or Nancy
in London, going to the theatre with her and her friends,
the King and Queen of Sweden; or meeting at Cliveden,
Queen Margarethe of Denmark with the beautiful eyes.

Or I see her on the rounds we did at Plymouth, over to
Mount Edgcumbe, to Admiralty House at Devonport, or out
to Buckland Abbey, which Drake bought with the money he
made from the Voyage round the World – which was then
being refitted as a museum after the fire – with Nancy wondering why her car wouldn't start up the hill, having forgotten about the gears.

Frequently as I go to Plymouth, I never go there without
thinking of her. The centre of the new city – Armada Way
and the rest of it – we owe to Waldorf. Still, without her,
somehow the spirit is missing from the place; the vivacity,
the magic of her presence gone.

One Sunday after the war, I went into St Andrew's, roof-
less and gutted, the church-bells ringing, a garden growing
in the empty interior. I was reduced to tears by the scene, the
destruction, to think of all we had been through, church-
bells ringing to empty space. Since then St Andrew's has
been restored, more beautiful than before, a splendid west

window in the tower, to Waldorf's memory: designed by John Piper, a work of art.

Today I still sometimes take shelter from the noise of traffic in the new Plymouth, in St Andrew's, and there in the quiet of the church remember Nancy and Waldorf and all the good they did, there by myself, alone.

3

Agatha Christie

So much has been written about Agatha Christie, besides what she wrote herself – getting on for a hundred books when one includes her plays and half-a-dozen straight novels under the name of 'Mary Westmacott' – that I must concentrate on my friendship with her and Max Mallowan, her husband. In any case I am not a detective story addict: I knew Agatha as a person before I ever read one of her detective stories. She knew that I was not a reader of hers – which put our friendship on a different footing from the beginning. Most people thought of her only in relation to her detective stories – 'Queen of Crime', 'First Lady of Crime', etc.; quite a number of her friends were professionals, publishers or theatre people. It was only slowly and gradually that I came to read any of her books.

So I am not going to write about them, but about her and Max. All the same – Agatha wrote me a warm and encouraging letter about my Shakespeare discoveries. 'From the mistress of low-brow detection to the master of high-brow detection' – so the discoverer of Shakespeare's Dark Lady could, if called upon, sleuth the trail of Agatha and her own story in her work. Max is quite right in saying that, for all her personal reserve, an impenetrable armour, she reveals herself fully in her books. All writers do, after all; but it is rather fun following up the clues to herself strewn across her work.

But I had another clue to the crux in her life, the near-tragedy of the breakdown of her first marriage, which was so important, abnormally so – to so sensitive and vulnerable a nature, with old-fashioned religious standards. It may be said to have shaped her subsequent life; it was always there in the background. Nothing was ever said about it, it had wounded her so deeply, and well nigh cost her her life. I never knew if she knew that I knew; in their last years Max realized that I was aware of it, though of how much he did not know. I had learned the story from an old friend of Agatha's – married to a Cornishman – who had known them before ever Max came on the scene.

In the end it worked out happily, though it might so easily not have done – and very narrowly did not.

All that the world knew was that Agatha Christie disappeared, and was lost for a matter of ten or twelve days. This was in the twenties, when it was possible to disappear – not so easy today. I remember the papers being full of the hue and cry – 'Disappearance of Agatha Christie', her abandoned car found, a shoe and scarf found on the Downs; an organized search for her, photographs of how she might have disguised herself, how she was to be recognized, age thirty-five, etc. Hundreds and thousands of people joined in the search. She was eventually recognized staying in a quiet hotel in Harrogate, suffering from complete loss of memory. When brought back to London by her husband, crowds gathered at King's Cross to greet the train.

After that, as a detective story writer, she never looked back. She jumped to first place, and held it for the rest of her life.

Most people thought that it had been a stunt, and she was acting out one of her own mysteries. But it was far more serious than that. As an historian, and the discoverer of Shakespeare's secret, I know that the truth about people, if only one can find it, is far more interesting than third-rate conjectures about it; and an experience such as she had undergone is far more powerful for being authentic and true, than any put-up job.

It was Max who reconciled her to life, their marriage and mutual love that readjusted her and gave her happiness. But the mark remained; such a wound never heals.

I never knew them until Max was elected a Research Fellow, in archaeology, at All Souls and for some time took little note of them. They were away a good deal in Mesopotamia, Max making his wonderful finds of ivories at Nimrud, about which he produced a superb book a few years later. Each winter I was away in California researching and writing, with a couple of months in Cornwall.

Coming back to All Souls for summer term I used to have a large lunch-party, occasionally filling the long table in the Hall, to mingle Anglo-American friends. To one of these I invited Max and Agatha, along with her West Country publisher, Allen Lane, creator of Penguins. I remember the extraordinary hat she had bought for the occasion, a large, floppy black shiny affair that looked like an eighteenth-century parson's shovel hat. I had no chance of talking to her, with so many guests on my hands, devotees of hers like Christobel Aberconway, Geoffrey Harmsworth, Jack Simmons, all anxious to meet her.

But I remember Max later on telling me something of her publishing experience. A Devon girl herself, she had gone to a Devonian publisher, canny John Lane, who gave her £25 for her first book! (One remembers his extraordinary meanness with poor Corvo, and Corvo's curses.) The nephew Allen Lane became a friend as well as publisher, with a castle in Spain, having made a million. All the same . . . said Max.

From Agatha I received my first letter in her own hand, large and clear – she had old-fashioned courtesy and good manners, very much a lady; for all her being the world's best-seller, nothing vulgar about her – retiring and modest. What a contrast to best-sellers today! She actually avoided publicity all she could, never gave an interview or made a speech, let alone appeared on TV. She was an old-world lady – and, for the rest, her fearful experience in the twenties, hounded by the press, made her keep it at arm's length ever after. 'We did enjoy your luncheon party so much,' she wrote. 'Too bad Max had to forgo the very pleasant coffee drinking and sitting about in chairs, which really was delightful, and how glorious to be able to sit.' We used to sit out on the terrace between the twin towers, the most splendid scene in Oxford, like a stage-set before us, the majesty of Gibbs's dome of the Radcliffe Camera, St Mary's spire, with the eighteenth-century spire of All Saints behind – all framed by our own chapel, cloisters and Codrington Library.

Max and Agatha had an eighteenth-century house right on the road at the end of the town at Wallingford, Winterbrook House, very convenient for Oxford. I used to wonder at first how they could put up with traffic right on the road. But the house had a heavy cushion of shrubbery in front, and for the most part went back in depth to a garden and meadow going down to the river. The rooms they occupied were mostly in the back, a spacious drawing-room giving on to the garden, a long wing projecting where, upstairs, each had a study for their so different work.

In Devon they had a finer Georgian house, Greenway, in a splendid situation on a bend of the river Dart with a view right down it, steamers passing, and a magnificent garden, full of the rare shrubs the West Country can grow. This had been created by the Cornish family of Bolitho, from whom Agatha's growing earnings – after parting from Christie – had enabled her to buy it. Here I was invited to stay for a wedding anniversary – I remember that Max had had his classic work on Nimrud, with its astonishing illustrations, specially bound in two large morocco-and-gold volumes for Agatha. At that time I had not realized how closely associated with the work there she had been: it was there that she had met Max on the job, who insisted on her marrying him, and she had gone out year after year with him. How well it had turned out – the experience of the Near East, the expertise and personnel of archaeology, new fields and subjects for her prolific pen!

Greenway was of interest to the West Country historian because it had been the home of the Gilberts, half-brothers of the Raleghs. Hardly anything of their time remained, but not far away – nearer Agatha's home-town of Torquay – was the medieval home of the Gilberts, rose-red Compton Castle, rehabilitated by Commander Walter Raleigh Gilbert, who came over with his wife. His saving Compton was a romantic story. As a young Dartmouth cadet he used occasionally to have a farm-tea with the farmer who owned the Castle, then more than half a ruin. Gilbert determined that one day he would restore the home of his ancestors – and lived to do it.

He began by reroofing and restoring the ruined wing. There remained the gap between the two, where the great hall had been – you could see the line of gable upon the walls. The Castle was complete once more; we went over to see it – the Commander chaffing me that it was I who had pointed out the gable-ends aching for a roof years before and he had carried out my command! He always intended to do it; Agatha said – let him have his way about Greenway and he'd rebuild it too: suspiciously he sniffed around the old foundations at the back. I don't recall much more, except looking into the church at Churston Ferrers and over the wall at the old manor-house – and the good fare Agatha provided wherever she was (she was a good trencherman): a fine Devon turkey and Devonshire cream.

That same summer I was able to take them over to Hawksmoor's grandiose *palazzo*, Easton Neston, under the aegis of my friend, Kisty Hesketh, who much appreciated the architecture of Hawksmoor's All Souls, similar idiom and idiosyncrasies. Later on, I took them over the hills and up the valley to medieval and Elizabethan Stonor, fascinating house with its Catholic associations, where they made friends with the Stonors and became regular visitors.

From the first Agatha was interested in my work on Shakespeare, herself a life-long devotee, very familiar with the plays on the stage and very well read in and about them. When I eventually found the Dark Lady, contrary to my expectations – right there across the way from All Souls, in the Bodleian – she gave me public support with a letter to *The Times*, and came to my lecture about the Simon Forman finds at the Royal Society of Literature.

It was consoling to have her support, for though she was not a so-called 'expert' in the field, she had a first-class brain, an extraordinary combination of perception and common sense such as few of the experts possessed. And, after all, she had the kindness, as well as the sense, to see that the findings of the leading authority on the Elizabethan Age, Shakespeare's lifetime, were probably right. They have proved unanswerable, for they are the answer. The problems have been solved.

She herself was extraordinarily good at setting and solving problems, as all the world knows. What the world does not know is, what Max knew, that this came from her exceptional combination of 'inner sensitivity with an intuitive understanding of situations hidden from mere normal mortals'. To a degree that made her rather formidable, until one found out how kind and good she was. But it made her a personality that I was rather wary of, to begin with – those silences in which one was aware that she took in everything about one and saw right through one. (I was rather intuitive myself.) No taking any liberties with her; one had to be rather careful what one said – nothing off-beat, even one's jokes had to be proper, for she was very much a Victorian lady. She once said to me, 'There is nothing immoral in my books – only murder.'

Max thought of her books as moralities as much as thrillers, and that she was much concerned with the struggle between good and evil. Naturally I didn't appreciate that side, but he was emphatic that she was a good *novelist*, not merely a detective story writer. That I did come to appreciate: her gifts for creating character, her wide understanding of human beings, especially of children (sympathy too), her natural and convincing dialogue, her firm construction and setting of the scene.

In one of her straight novels written as Mary Westmacott, *The Burden*, there is wonderful dialogue between a crusty old don, Mr Baldock, and a little girl, Laura.

> Mr Baldock, grinding his teeth and snorting with venom, was penning a really vitriolic review for a learned journal of a fellow historian's life work.
>
> He turned a ferocious face to the door, as Mrs Rouse, giving a perfunctory knock and pushing it open, announced:
>
> 'Here's little Miss Laura for you.'

There follows a virtuoso performance in dialogue, if it were not so utterly natural and funny. Agatha knew all about children and the way they talk. (In one of her detective stories she actually says that children's evidence is best and most to be trusted.)

In the earlier days of our friendship I used to think of her as a geometrician, and she did say to me that in writing a detective story you begin at the end. As a girl she had been good at mathematics – I don't wonder at that. Max corroborates that she had a mathematical brain, and that this appears in 'the neat solution of the most complex tangles, an ability in analysis as well as synthesis'.

Though she was not communicative, one way and another she came to tell me a good bit about her writing. People were for ever sending her plots of stories which they fancied for her to write up. Courteous and patient, she always replied that thinking up her plots was the one great pleasure she took in writing: all the rest was hard work. That this was so one sees from the revealing preface she wrote – a rare thing – to *The Crooked House*, a favourite of hers. 'I saved it up for years, thinking about it, working it out, saying to myself: "One day, when I've plenty of time, and want to really enjoy myself – I'll begin it!" I should say that of one's output, five books are work to one that is pure pleasure.' There is a rare glimpse into the workings of that mind, naturally secretive. Max speaks of her horror of the invasion of her privacy (redoubled by its exposure to the world in the twenties, a veil drawn over it ever afterwards) and her refusal to talk about 'the esoteric world of her invention'. This was the fantasy world in which she lived her imaginative life, to outward appearance the most conventional of middle-class old ladies.

Considering that, I am touched by how much she did tell me about her work – never about her life. She would give people her autograph generously – she was naturally generous; never a photograph. She was very careful and cagey about her public relations. One can see that in a significant respect in regard to the handling of her straight novels, by 'Mary Westmacott'. Her publisher would never allow her to deviate from what her enormous public expected of her as

Agatha Christie – she had to be as cautious as a pope or prime minister. Whatever the reason, her straight novels had no success whatever – ludicrous, from the most widely read woman in the world: it shows how stupid people are, for, in my opinion, they are excellent – and more to my taste than detective stories.

In the course of my campaign for common sense about Shakespeare I sent her my biography of Marlowe, which was a strategic move though people hadn't the sense to spot it. As the result of the hopeless confusion perpetuated by the Shakespeare establishment, the gates have been needlessly left open for all the crackpots to canter through. Many innocent folk can't feel sure whether Shakespeare ever existed, or whether his plays weren't written by Bacon or Marlowe – both 100 per cent homosexual, by the way; while Shakespeare, the author of his own work, was 100 per cent heterosexual, all for women in love. Some of these crackpots actually make a living out of confusing the poor public – for ordinary people cannot tell a good egg from a bad egg intellectually. So my *Marlowe* was intended to close one gate to the crackpots – though the third-rate academics never saw the point, for they perceive nothing.

I sent the book to Agatha down in Devon, who replied courteously as always, for all her burden of work. (Lesser people, even in the peerage, are apt not to acknowledge the gift of a book: Agatha was very old-fashioned, better brought up.) She had been away from Greenway much of that summer: 'I've been judging at a rose show in Holland. What do I know of the finer technical points of roses? *Nothing!* It's a great world!' Evidently she had enjoyed it. But just like her modesty – I'll bet she knew a good deal. There were always roses in the garden at Wallingford, and I have been struck by the extraordinary number of things she did know, the sheer range of her experience – apart from archaeology, the Middle East, the law and police, medicines, poisons and all that. She was knowledgeable about china, and at Wallingford had a special collection of slagware. I have noticed in just one of her books the mention of things I have never heard of. What is a 'tantalus'? I don't know. What's a 'shebunkin'? I don't know – quite apart from innias from Baghdad. It may be a truism, though it will be news to some people: Agatha was a *writer*.

What was she like at home?

Here I have my Journals to fall back upon: 'Sunday, 23 November 1969, a crisp golden day, out to Wallingford to lunch with Max and Agatha: a cosy, warm, hospitable, upper middle-class interior, with all the comforts and amenities, the pretty china and good furniture that Agatha's prosperity has brought. Better still the warm, generous, kindly atmosphere both radiate. Max has (Austrian) charm and kindness; Agatha large-chested, full-bosomed English comfortableness, plus the American strain of generosity. Wine-coloured autumn sun came flooding into the blowsy, cosy room – the too-large billowing chairs (like Agatha), the lavender colour of the slagware on the chimneypiece. She brought out piece after piece of old china for me – nothing spectacular, like Jack Plumb's Sèvres, just pleasant Victorian pieces (again like Agatha herself).

'I have always been curious to know the truth of *her* detective story – that of her first marriage, her background, whether the episode of her losing her memory and being identified (at Harrogate) was true. Last week, lunching in London with a Cornish fan of mine, I learned the truth from his wife, an old friend of Agatha's . . .

'It must be remembered that at this time nothing was known except the external facts of the famous disappearance. Before they died Agatha and Max each wrote an autobiography, in which they told as much of the story as they felt they could. They corroborate what I was told – and kept to myself (and my Journals) as long as they lived. Agatha said that during that appalling experience she had lived in a dream; but there was more to it than that . . .

'I knew that Agatha's father was an American expatriate, who lived at Torquay and married a Devon girl. Agatha is very patriotic about Devon and, when the thousands began to roll in, bought Mary Bolitho's Greenway on the Dart. She married Christie, had one girl, and lived in London, not well off. She went back to Torquay for some time to look after her sick mother, leaving her best friend [according to Mrs X] to look after her husband while away.'

What happened was just like the Windsor story, when Lady Furness left David (then Prince of Wales) to her friend, Wallis, to look after him and 'keep him out of mischief' while away in America. When she got back, she found that the friend had *got* him, and for keeps. The same thing happened to Agatha. Plenty of people have broken marriages nowadays; what made the experience shattering to her was that she had never dreamed of it. She had had a peculiarly happy and sheltered childhood, loving and beloved by her parents; she was more than conventionally religious, but had old-fashioned conventional standards, believing in the sanctity of marriage and horrified by the idea of divorce. She knew that the dashing army officer, who had had a brave record in the first German war, had a ruthless streak, but had no idea that he would behave brutally to her throughout this ghastly period of strain. Psychotic elements entered into it on both sides: he was brutal and abrupt *because* he had loved her; she continued to love him throughout it all, but it shattered the world of fantasy in which her spirit – her genius – lived. This is what led to her breakdown.

I have never felt at liberty to say what Agatha's former friend told me, until Max gave a hint in his *Memoirs*. He told me that he had only once set eyes on Christie, in later life, greying hair, but still an upstanding 'good-looking fellow'. Agatha, when young, had been beautiful: he had swept her off her feet. With her abnormally sensitive nature – the delicate balance of genius – and her exceptional fabric of security, the shock was terrible, and pushed her over the edge. Mrs X told me that Agatha had been prevented from throwing herself over the balcony; this is now corroborated by Max's 'acts which came near to *felo de se*'.[1] This is why the wound was

---

[1] In Max's *Memoirs* by a slip of the pen he said *auto da fe* for *felo de se*. The fool who saw his book through the press passed this obvious mistake, as well as getting my well-known initials wrong. It is a duty to describe a fool as such; I deliberately do all through my work – how else are they to learn?

so deep and, though she made a marvellous recovery – largely through Max – it had left its traces all through her work. It also made her the great woman she became.

I continue from my Journals.

'I just remember the furore in the newspapers, the nation-wide hunt; and her being identified in the hotel: "You are Agatha Christie," someone said, and received the monetary reward. "Am I?" she said, and it all came back. Everybody thought it a publicity stunt; but it was genuine – so much better than the best of jobs. After that every book was a best-seller, everything fell into her hands.

'Agatha's woman friend thought that the original Mr Christie had reason to regret his conduct since. She was very much in love with him, a perfectly contented wife, geared to domestic happiness. Max has achieved this with and for her – and has had the reward of his goodness and niceness. Everything genuine about the old couple. Actually Max is my age, but he has had a slight stroke, left hand and arm dragging – which brings him up more to her age in appearance.'

Mrs X had told me about Agatha's innate modesty. She hadn't thought highly of her play *The Mousetrap* – it surprised her that it had gone on year after year, now for nearly twenty years, bringing in £4,000 a year to her grandson. No wonder he can afford to collect pictures. Max had placed this (to me unknown) youth beside me when dining in Hall. We talked about painting. He said he had bought a Sidney Nolan. 'That must have cost a lot,' I said. 'It did,' he replied. 'How did you manage that?' I said in wonderment. 'I have a rich grand-mother.'

'Max told me, "Money means nothing to her." It pours in, in hundreds of thousands – and nearly all is lost in taxes. She is trustified, trusts in every direction for her family, very much a family woman. Poor Mr Christie – what a story he would make, looking at it from his point of view! What a mistake he made! Latterly she has had to join some corporation to deal with tax getting beyond her – and has to turn out a detective story a year, like some bank-manager turning in his annual account.'

Actually, what a waste this was – going into the maw of

the trivial consumption of a consumptive society, the shopping bags of the people bulging with rubbish. Think what it could have done in preserving historic houses in Devon falling to ruin; or saving historic treasures from dispersal abroad, or simply burgled, like Lord Clifford's at neighbouring Ugbrooke. A contemptible society. Max said to me that, if they were younger, they wouldn't stay here five minutes. I agree. With his long acquaintance with the Middle East, he said that, much as we used to laugh at the Arabs for their unreliability and slatternliness, the general squalor of their society, ours was now just like it. (Look at the filth and dirt of railway platforms – and the men striking for the heavy responsibility they carry in checking tickets.)

I agree with him, but I do not subscribe to the word 'ours'. I have no part nor lot in it, nor obligations to it. I am Cornish, not English – if I were, I should be ashamed, after the record they achieved in history, under the direction of their governing class. But only *under direction*, for of course ordinary people are incapable of operating without direction. As on one of Max's archaeological sites in the Near East, so in any industry in Britain.

I had an independent link with Max, besides All Souls, for we were of the same seniority at Oxford. He was at New College, and was criticized for saying in his *Memoirs* that Warden H. A. L. Fisher, though a great man, was pompous. Fisher *was* pompous; and it was more than generous to call him a 'great man' – he was just a distinguished, an eminent, man. At Lancing Max had been one of a group with Evelyn Waugh and Hugh Molson, an undergraduate acquaintance of mine. Hugh was known to them as 'Preters', from his addiction to the word 'preternaturally'. Waugh has a description of his extraordinary affection of pomposity, which Evelyn says he adopted out of mockery. It used to mesmerize me as an undergraduate, it became second nature to him: he carried it through life and indeed into the House of Lords.

Max used to tell me how unpopular Evelyn was, a distinct streak of mischief, getting other people into trouble and himself out of it, a vein of cruelty. What an extraordinary character his was! With him too there was a strong element of affectation which entered into his character and formed his personality. Why ever? Why not be oneself? But his was not a very nice self. Max's was. I think life was straightforward for him. He was always simply heterosexual; the homo side to public school life seems to have meant nothing to him. I used to chaff him about this – not in front of Agatha, of course. Like Christie before him, Max made the running and carried off Agatha captive, several years his senior. Only once did I gather a hint. After my stimulating lecture to the Royal Society of Literature about Simon Forman and the Sex Life of the Elizabethans, Agatha did say, 'I hope it won't start up Max again.' Though love normally appears in her books, there is nothing about sex as such. I wonder if that wasn't an element in the failure with the dashing, perhaps demanding, army officer?

Agatha's friend may have been wrong about his missing the millions. Max rather contradicts this; he says that Christie did quite well for himself in the City, but was not much interested in money. I suspect that sex, raising its ugly head, was responsible for more.

Agatha showed what a dear, good, Christian soul she was, after all she had suffered, the irreparable wound he had inflicted upon her spirit. When, some fifteen years after, the woman for whom Christie had left her and whom he had married, died of cancer, Agatha wrote him a kind, consoling letter. I regard his reply as rather unfeeling: perhaps it is difficult for a proud man to accept forgiveness. Agatha knew all about the defects of men henceforth, how inconsiderate they are compared with women: in one place she has a tell-tale phrase about someone who was 'rather considerate for a man'; in another, that where men are concerned there is no end to the flattery that may be applied; for a third, that 'women can put up with a lot – when they have got what they want'.

I did not realize the religious side to Agatha until I read her *Poems*, and her beautiful little book of Christmas fables, *Star over Bethlehem*, both of which she gave me. I did not know that she always kept Thomas à Kempis' *Imitation of Christ* by her bedside. I should have noticed from her books how familiar she was with the Bible, the phrases continually coming up, especially those about loving kindness which truly guided her life. This comes out more openly in the 'Mary Westmacott' novels, along with other clues. 'How often he had heard and said those words: *Thy loving kindness to us and to all men.* Man himself could have that feeling, although he could not hold it long.' And then: 'Those are the magical moments – the moments of belonging – of everlasting sweetness – not sex. And yet if sex goes wrong, a marriage is completely ruined.' And again, 'We all have fantasies that help us to bear the lives we live.'

And here is a penetrating historical reflection – life with Max gave her a good historical sense, such as life with Christie could never have done:

> People were burned at the stake, not by sadists or brutes but by earnest and high-minded men, who believed that what they did was right. Read some of the law cases in ancient Greece [that came from Max, a classical scholar], of a man who refused to let his slaves be tortured so as to get at the truth, as was the prevalent custom. He was looked upon as a man who deliberately obscured justice. There was an earnest God-fearing clergyman in the States who beat his three-year-old son, whom he loved, to death, because the child refused to say his prayers.

I see that my gloss on that passage is: 'They *were* brutes. Right and wrong are absolutes – not relative.' And then the Swiftian condemnation, appropriate for an historian: 'They were idiots.'

There were other clues. In *The Crooked House* – 'Never explain': a maxim I adhere to myself. In *Five Little Pigs* a woman thinks of taking poison – Agatha knew about poisons from her nursing days as a VAD in the first German war: 'I had received a bad shock. My husband was proposing to leave me for another woman. If that was so, I didn't want to live.' The husband had said, 'Do try and be reasonable about this, Caroline. I'm fond of you and will always wish you well – you and the children. But I'm going to marry Elsa.' That was exactly it. I don't suppose that anyone has noticed that the husband's initials, Amyas Crale – A.C. – were the same as those of Archie Christie. Then comes in Agatha herself:

> She had that enormous mental and moral advantage of a strict Victorian upbringing denied to us in these days – she had done her duty in that station of life to which it had pleased God to call her, and that assurance encased her in an armour impregnable to the slings and darts [Shakespeare's image] of envy, discontent and regret.

As for the absurd suggestion of her disappearance being a publicity stunt (Henry James: 'Nobody ever understands *any-*thing'), Agatha herself gives a pointer, in the voice of Hercule Poirot, no less:

> But consider two points. First, that the lady had by that time not the slightest need for publicity. She had a full measure of it already. Secondly, a more important point . . . the known character of the suspect. Can you really visualize a lady of genuine modesty, with a retiring disposition and an extreme dislike of public intervention in her affairs deliberately making herself the centre of a *cause célèbre* and bringing down on herself the country-wide attention of the sensational press?

Murder in Mesopotamia has several corroborative clues. A woman says: 'Lots of people wanted to marry me, but I always refused. I'd had too bad a shock. I didn't feel I could ever *trust* anyone again . . . Of course, I thought at first I was mad or dreaming.' Later on after various sensational happenings, 'another idea flashed across my mind. Perhaps soon, in the natural course of things . . . a new and happy state of things might come about.' We recall that it was Mesopotamia that brought Agatha and Max together, where he proposed marriage, to be held off for quite a time, for like the woman in *The Curtain* who had suffered too deeply, she was mistrustful of life – and, anyway, 'a good brain, yes, but women seldom fall for brains alone'.

I was getting to know both of them better: a real feeling of affection grew up, barriers lowered. From 'Dear Mr Rowse', or 'Dear Dr Rowse', Agatha's letters began 'Dear Leslie' – my name in family and College – though she never dated them by the year. One November day in the late sixties she is writing:

> What fun your party was! I enjoyed it immensely – and liked talking to both of my neighbouring guests at lunch. I also enjoyed eating what was certainly one of All Souls' best lunches. Delicious trout. Thank you very much for the book you have bestowed on Max and myself. There is lots of Devon I don't really know – and this will, I see, fill in interesting gaps. Time to begin to be industrious again – How hard one has to drive oneself to begin a new book. Only disgusting weather outside really drives one on.

So much for those who think writing is easy for even natural and gifted writers. As she said, planning and thinking about the book beforehand is all the fun – the rest is hard work.

When the Dark Lady was discovered, Agatha was fascinated and wrote in her own contribution to the discussion in *The Times*. She was, as I have said, well versed in Shakespeare and had thought a lot about him. So she said that she had always thought that in the character of Cleopatra Shakespeare was remembering his own experience – and someone he had experienced and suffered from: a dark, bewitching, foreign beauty, gypsy-like in her moods and tantrums, temperamental, mercurial and not to be trusted; yet whose spell was so irresistible her man could not break free from it. This was certainly Shakespeare's situation in the Sonnets, and I dare say Agatha was right, with her abnormal intuition about human beings. It is a brilliant conjecture – and Agatha's sheer cleverness has often been commented on. One never saw that in life, she was so modest; her essential self so subdued and withdrawn in society; her persona as a writer was something quite different, almost as if there were two personalities. Her intuition was really rather alarming – one felt one had to pass the test to be admitted to confidence. But though she may well have been right that in Cleopatra Shakespeare was remembering Emilia Lanier (born a Bassano), the historian could not use even the most penetrating of conjectures.

On the other hand, we *know* that Rosaline, Berowne's lady in *Love's Labour's Lost*, was the Dark Lady of the Sonnets, for both are described in practically the same words. I always realized that, if ever the Dark Lady were discovered, she would be found to be someone known to the circle of Southampton, Shakespeare's patron. And this turned out to be so: she had been the mistress of the Lord Chamberlain, patron of Shakespeare's Company – one could hardly get closer – while Southampton's stepfather, Sir Thomas Heneage, was Vice-Chamberlain.

Agatha, with her first-rate detective brain, could see the bearing of all that; the third-rate, of course, couldn't. No point in discussing it with them: they had nothing to discuss with: a first-rate authority was telling them.

Here's for another of those happy visits out to Wallingford.

'Sunday, 17 January 1971, I drove out to lunch alone with Max and Agatha – always a pleasant homey atmosphere, largely due to his Austrian charm – in that sunny house where the living rooms at the back look over their flat water-meadows to the river. They have been there since 1930, perhaps immediately after her marrying Max. She has been celebrating her eightieth birthday, with lots of public notice and hundreds of letters to answer – one of the most famous women in the world, and just been made a Dame by the Queen, one of her constant readers. Max knighted. But, thirteen years younger, he is less well preserved than Agatha, a powerful big woman with prominent features.

'It is impossible to penetrate her reserve – that mixture of shyness and formidable resources of power, of outer diffidence with a massive inner confidence, as Max puts it – and no wonder, with that story in the background. We talked about money, as all best-sellers will, Agatha complaining at the amount of tax lifted off her – on top of all the trusts she must have made for the family. She told me one couldn't even donate a story to a cause now; years ago she gave to the Westminster Abbey Appeal, a short story which fetched £1500. I told her what I was doing for Charlestown Church bells, no tax relief. And was rather surprised to learn that they had bought a plot to be buried in neighbouring Cholsey churchyard. I should have expected Torquay, where she was born. She said that it was so spoiled, one of those ghastly great town cemeteries.

'She is not one to encourage questions, said that she had always hated being questioned from a girl on, and never gives interviews. But a little boy from the local school had come to interview her for his school paper; she took a fancy to him and asked him in. On her birthday came a sheaf of flowers from his parents. All Wallingford must know the world celebrity living in their midst, in the Georgian house right on the road, if invisible behind thick shrubbery growing up to the top windows.

'She has a secretary to deal with her correspondence; says firmly when asked for large donations for this or that, "It's no use asking authors for £30,000 or whatever – they're far too heavily taxed: you must ask a tycoon." She has had jacket trouble with her American paperbacks, when the publishers, without consulting her, would come out with a naked girl recumbent in a park – nothing about sex in the book. Or in any of her respectable books, "which deal only in murder" (this a little apologetically). Two years ago she had had a showdown with the Americans and insisted on seeing the jacket designs. I told her that I had suffered similarly with two American paperbacks: one, by some ill-attuned Slav, had given Shakespeare the hairless head of a surprised egg; the other made him a doddering old man with straggling beard, in imminent decay. Idiots!

'About five years ago she had accepted an interesting and very lucrative assignment from Hollywood to do a TV script of *Bleak House*. She became very much interested, had never done one before – only plays of her own (this with modesty). Hollywood interfered so much and it involved so much discussion, so many changes, etc. that she gave it up. She had done two parts, and received the money, but was not going to do the third part. She said that she had never got headaches from worry over her work before, as with this. She was never going to finish it. A pity, for she had found it fascinating. [The fools – fancy frustrating a famous writer with their constant interference. I know what 'editors' in American publishing houses are like from experience – most of their authors can't write, so their books have to be rewritten in the office. Not good enough for Agatha, or for me.]

'At the moment she has stopped after writing two chapters of a new story – the energy, at eighty! What characteristic has all genius in common? C. E. M. Joad was asked, and replied unhesitatingly – Energy. I should qualify that only by – energy *of mind*. Since all the letters came pouring in and the book wasn't going very well, she has stopped work on it for the time to attend to the letters. "You know how it is – you have to give yourself to a book, you can't do anything else." So that is how she works – in spells, with concentration. I told her that I don't waste time answering most of my letters: Napoleon's secretary Bourrienne said that, if you leave them a fortnight, most of them will have answered themselves. And of course I never answer dotty letters about Shakespeare's plays having been written by Queen Elizabeth, or Richard III having been as innocent as a new-born babe.

'She talked a good deal, without vanity – she has no vanity, remarkable in an author, especially a world-famous author (contrast —, or —,) and about the nuisance people will make of themselves. Never at Wallingford, but sometimes in Devon. Once a woman invaded her summerhouse, where she was sunbathing – just to show her to her young hopeful of a youth, who was covered with embarrassment at his mother. Then a party of Finnish journalists got through the barriers and pursued her into the house, where her brother-in-law backed her up in refusing an interview. She was thereupon described in the Finnish press most unfavourably and as protected by an armed guard – her harmless elderly brother-in-law.

'Worst of all was Spain, where they couldn't get any peace for themselves on holiday at all. It ended with a woman getting into her bathroom when she was changing for dinner:

"I thought you wouldn't mind – anyway you've got to see
me now", etc. Agatha put on her dress, and went straight
down to the management.

'The house is always warm and cosy, with a nice wood
fire, sun coming cheerfully into the back drawing-room from
the side. There's always good food, they both like their food
and have second helpings – today a favourite of Agatha's,
boiled silverside with dumplings. Max likes his wine, face a
bit flushed. She's an apple-juice drinker, like me. The dining-
room, on the road side of the house, is small, with rather low
Victorian French tapestry chairs, good silver not scarce, and
a *very* good cook-housekeeper. She tells me that Wallingford
is far better than Greenway for milk, cream, butter, poultry,
provisions – in Devon the best is skimmed off to London.

'Max and she must have had good times together in his
diggings in Iraq, when the going was good – and several of
her books came out of it. He's had an interesting life and
friendships, with Mortimer Wheeler (what a character!),
Leonard Woolley, archaeologists all. We talked a bit about
Preters, a nice man under the extraordinary mannerism, and
Evelyn's Anglo-Catholic religiosity at school – Rome let him
down in the end, dropping the Latin Mass and going
demotic, all that he hated. Unlike Tom Eliot, he didn't die in
time; he saw his world crumble.'

I find that on a golden day that autumn, 3 October 1971,
Max and Agatha came over the hill to lunch at Stonor, 'Agatha having recovered marvellously from breaking her hip that
summer . . . Agatha was warm in praise of my 'Chalky
Jenkins' story [about the half-grown cat that used to come up
from down in the valley at Trenarren, liked visiting at the
big house, and then was lost]. She said it made her cry – as it
did me to write it . . .

'After this friendly lunch, a wine-coloured light came out
over the pastures.' Max, who as an archaeologist was virtually professional as a photographer, took pictures of us all
standing in front of that historic house. 'Max and Agatha
took off across country to Wallingford, I up and up the Wat-
lington road into the hanging beechwoods of the Chilterns,
where the Britons survived into Saxon England.'

A prominent and troublesome character in those last years was Bingo. Agatha had always had a dog, and this was a present of a very idiosyncratic kind. He was a Manchester terrier, black and tan, so overbred as to be positively neurotic. Noisy, he would snap and bite for tuppence, or less – he bit the cook: he didn't know which side his bread was buttered. She couldn't bear him, neither could I – though I became intrigued by him, he was so odd; as he was by me. At tea-time he would come sniffing around me, curiosity aroused, one dared not move, he might bite. If the telephone rang Max had to shut him out or he would snap at his heels. Agatha had a fantasy that Bingo believed there was a devil who lived in the telephone, and he meant to warn Max and pull him back by biting his heels.

Both Agatha and Max loved him; I couldn't understand it, and would say, 'You know, Agatha, your dog's dotty.' She rather agreed, loved him all the same, and would recount his endearing ways. The source of his trouble was nerves: overbred, he was frightened of everything, terrified of get-ting up the stairs; but once having overcome it, new every morning was the love with which he snuggled under Aga-tha's eiderdown while she had her morning tea. I think that Max gave me the answer why they put up with him, always having to put him on a lead if anybody came into the house, etc. – it was that they would have found an easy conventional dog uninteresting. He had his uses: he gave the alarm when a burglar set a ladder up against Agatha's bedroom window, and made off with only a couple of old fur coats, interrupted in his intentions. It was a drawn battle between Bingo and me: no love, but mutual curiosity: I never met so odd a dog. As for Max, Bingo provided him with a tease for me: he pretended that Bingo had a special devotion to me, held me in high regard, etc. and regaled me with the latest news of him and his dear little ways, how he had bitten the postman, etc.

When I wrote a little book about my beloved cat, *Peter the White Cat of Trenarren* – of an angelic disposition, never once bit or scratched anyone, no horrid Bingo – Agatha wrote to me: 'I enjoyed your book about the White Cat so much that

I really must ponder seriously about your suggestion of a little book about my cats and dogs, possibly in the Christmas Season, though I rather doubt whether my publisher would care for the idea!' There you are, the old lady was the prisoner of her world *réclame*. Max wrote me a characteristically charming and intuitive letter – that the book showed my need to give, as well as receive, affection. I knew that well enough, but it was very sweet of him to say it. There must be other letters from both of them, that have not yet come to the surface in my enormous *Archiv*.

Agatha said that she was not ambitious, and everyone who knew her accepts that that was true. You could see her innate modesty in her bearing. She never put herself forward, but held back. I have seen her at a lecture of Max's in a crowded room at Cal. Tec. (the California Institute of Technology) in Pasadena, the whole audience keyed up that the most famous woman in the world was present. For her part she might not have been, sitting away close to the wall in the third or fourth row, in an anonymous position. She was given an ovation, to which she responded with a brief curtsey politely, never turning round – and that was that.

But we must not underrate her literary ambition and accomplishment, as her publishers did, simply because she was the first of detective story writers – any more than we should write off Churchill's paintings because he was Churchill. I have said that Agatha was a *real* writer – I mean by that that she was a compulsive writer: writing was her life. Or one of her two lives – for outwardly she had a full and normal social life, family, two marriages, friends, hospitality, entertainment, housekeeping (which she was very good at), shopping (which she much enjoyed); she had even, through Max, something of an academic circle, more in London than at Oxford, to which they came late. All ministered to Agatha's inner life of the imagination.

I remember an odd story of the old witch Margaret Murray, an authority on witchcraft, who dabbled in it, and lived to be a hundred. One of Max's London colleagues crossed the beldame in some departmental matter. She proceeded to boil up some witch's brew, with appropriate curses – and, sure enough, the offending man's face came out covered in pustules. I couldn't make out whether both Agatha and Max believed this – certainly Max did: one of Koestler's unexplained 'coincidences' perhaps.

I had never read a detective story until Agatha gave me her *4.50 From Paddington* and, no professional thriller reader, tended to take the story *au sérieux*, if not *au grand sérieux*. So I was able to tell Agatha that I was now rather alarmed at taking the regular 4.45 from Paddington to Oxford, which we relied on to get back in time for dinner. Similarly with *Passenger to Frankfurt*: now I was frightened to take a plane to Germany. I find from my Journals that I did not much care for *Hallowe'en Party*. which she also gave me – nor is it one of her best. I must say, however, that her gift extended to titles: she was a dab hand at them. Nor did her American publishers improve on them, though they had, of course, to change *Ten Little Niggers*.

I am not competent to estimate her form in this (to me) esoteric field; though another Fellow of All Souls, Geoffrey Faber, who was a good judge, always put her first. Oddly enough, another Fellow, G. D. H. Cole – socialist writer on dreary politics – made a regular income for some years from his detective stories. I read only one, which he gave me, because the scene was placed in Cornwall. Nor had I read Agatha's real Oxford rival, Dorothy Sayers – quite unlike Douglas Cole's undistinguished prose, and a contrast with Agatha. Dorothy Sayers was a first-class academic scholar, witness her work on Dante; but when I read her *Nine Tailors* I was bowled over by her sheer virtuosity, her knowledge of campanology.

I remain convinced, with Max, that Agatha was a better novelist than people realize – her creation of Miss Marples, for example, is a lasting one, a character added to literature. Poirot is, of course, a caricature, of whom Agatha tired: she never tired of Miss Marples, into whom she put something of herself. Other characters, too, are authentic personalities, some of them recognizably drawn from life. So, she was a novelist, and that will keep her best books alive, not mere thrillers.

A real writer, she had been writing all her life, from girl-hood, stories, fables, verse. She wrote, I believe, something like a score of plays, some of them eminently successful, like *Witness for the Prosecution*. Max thought *Akhnaton* the finest. I am not qualified to judge: I must be the only person in Britain who has never seen *The Mousetrap* (suggested to Aga-tha by Queen Mary, of all people!).

Agatha was a devoted reader of poetry, and a fairly con-stant writer of verse at times throughout her life. Here was a field where we could meet – and, of course, her poetry gives clues. I am surprised that there are not more Devon poems, or perhaps I have not found them; there is one on Dartmoor but, as Agatha said to me, large parts of Devon she did not know – only South Devon around Torquay and the Dart. Here is a clue, however, to that earlier suffering:

> Love passes! On the hearth dead embers lie
> Where once there burned a living fire of flame . . .
> Love passes out into the silent night,
> We may not hold him who has served our will
> And, for a while, made magic common
>   things . . .

And a witness to the later happiness she found with Max, written in his absence:

> Now is the winter past, but for my part
> Still winter stays until we meet again.
> Dear love, I have your promise and your heart
> But lacking touch and sight, spring birds bring pain.
> *Friendship* is ours, and still in absence grows.
> No dearer friend I own, so close, so kind.

I wonder whether there wasn't a further bond they may have been unconscious of, but which means something to the historian. Everybody thought of them as a very English couple. But Max was Austrian by blood, and Agatha's mother was a Clara Boehmer. Agatha had been when young a beautiful Teutonic blonde, with a fine singing voice. In old age she looked like a large cushiony German *frau*. Both were, however, witness to the English genius for *Verschmelzung*, for the peculiar power of environment and tradition – and no one could have made more distinguished contributions to it.

Latterly, we exchanged poems and, as Agatha grew old, Max took over letter-writing.

> 1 June 1979. What a charming appreciative letter you wrote to Agatha [I don't know whether they kept letters, they must have received thousands] on receiving her Poems, and what pleasure it gave us both to have these words from one so sensitive and artistic. Yes, we have been lucky in our companionship and in the enjoyment of things shared together. May you not feel lonely too often, for you must know that you have many good friends who are sensitive to your affection – among them the two of us, however much guarded by a black dragon who holds you in high esteem. I have no doubt that we should very much enjoy *Strange Encounter* if you can find a copy . . . I shall hope to see you at Gaudy [compare Dorothy Sayers' *Gaudy Night*], if not before.

So I sent them *Strange Encounter*. Max wrote,

> We have enjoyed your poems very much indeed, and I particularly love 'Strange Encounter' [the title piece], dramatic and the reflection of you. It is strange that you, a poet, would believe and cannot and that I, who am not a poet, can believe and would not. We admire your variety and range: the 'Portrait of a German Woman', and 'Before Cortés', a frightening glimpse of what art means. Agatha liked 'Dover Pier' and I enclose the list of her favourites. Perhaps one day you will write a poem about Bingo, an inscrutable character who has his own particular and private regard for you. Love from us both.

The acquaintance that began so casually ended then with affection on both sides. Agatha appended and autographed a list in her own hand of her favourites in this volume, no less than nine, beginning with 'Dover Pier' and 'Strange Encounter', both elegiac poems (Dover Pier a Civil War bastion in Magdalen walks overlooking the Cherwell). The old couple had evidently taken trouble: they took literature seriously – unlike the third-rate 'critics' of literary journalism.

I saw them together only once more, when they crossed the Tamar and came over the border into Cornwall to lunch at Ince, a paradise almost wholly surrounded by water. Agatha was visibly failing, memory going, this time for good. I went out to say a word to Bingo, on guard inside the big black car: fatter and more quiescent now, he didn't even growl – did he recognize me after all, since I addressed him by his name, extraordinary little character?

Max I saw yet once more, in the Athenaeum, pressing me to look him up at Wallingford. But we had both retired from Oxford, and shortly he too was dead.

Away in America, or marooned on my headland in Cornwall, I did not attend either of the crowded memorial services for them in London. But when, very infrequently now, I pass Cholsey Church on the railway line from Oxford to Paddington, the fine tower standing planted on its dead, I do not fail to send a thought of those dear good souls, among all the souls of the faithful departed, in that direction.

4

G. M. Trevelyan

A whole book could be written about Trevelyan as an historian. He was the leading English historian of his time, admired and read more widely than any other, in Britain as also in America; and we looked up to him as the head of our profession, its *doyen*. He should have had the Nobel Prize, rather than his contemporary, Bertrand Russell; as his *compère* in America, Samuel Eliot Morison, should have had instead of a second-rate writer like John Steinbeck. But Steinbeck appealed to popular Leftist sentimentality, and the half-educated of today do not realize that history is a department of literature. Think of English literature without Clarendon, Gibbon and Hume, or without Macaulay, Carlyle or Froude! Or Latin literature without Tacitus and Livy; Greek without Thucydides and Herodotus!

Trevelyan stood staunchly throughout his life, and exemplified it by his practice, for history as an art, and the writing of it as a literary art. As a young man at Cambridge he had been admonished by Seeley, with his Germanic standards, 'Remember always that history is a science, no more and no less.' As he went away, Trevelyan told me, he said to himself, 'Nevertheless, history *is* an art.' That was his *eppur se muove*, from which he did not depart for the rest of his long and fruitful life.

I am not going here to estimate his qualities as an historian, except to say that they were very much part of the man. In his case the man and the writer were singularly homogeneous – as they are not with many men of genius, with whom there

is often a split in the personality, some conflict within producing tension. Trevelyan was all of a piece, monolithic,
presenting to the spectator who did not know him a rather
bleak surface. He had indeed no small talk, and no time for
it, or for little human foibles – unlike that endearing side to
Gibbon, which mitigates the pomposity of the manner.

Trevelyan was, in some ways, not easy to know. I knew
him better than most, and over a considerable number of
years in his later life, when he had by all accounts mellowed.
Indeed, I saw only a warm and generous side, as his letters
will show; true, he was a formidable, no-nonsense man,
direct and crashing, liable to knock down any piece of silliness. I think that people found that alarming. Trevelyan was
never one who stood fools gladly, or wasted any time on
them. He was an uncompromising man, rudely direct, who
could be crushing. I never found him anything but kind, and
encouraging as only the first-rate themselves are. I could take
knocks – and answer them back; Trevelyan enjoyed sparring
and a good argument with someone who knew what he was
talking about.

He was consistently encouraging to young people and their
work – though he had singularly little influence on the generation after him at Cambridge. That may need explanation;
but the explanation is clear. Genius is inimitable; literary art
cannot well be imitated. Academic methods and preferences,
'lines' of investigation and fashions in subjects taken up can
easily be imitated, like the populist school among the
younger historians today, complete with graphs and statistics. Anybody can compile statistics, and computerized history is on the way. A work of art stands by itself, in its own
right, and cannot be repeated. Nobody else could write my
books, any more than they could Trevelyan's.

One further point, the bigness of the man and his achievement. Quite good academics are content to have accomplished one or two good books; Trevelyan did it a dozen or
more times over, a shelf of substantial works which go on
being read today, while his critics are forgotten. (One
Montague, for example, who wrote a nasty review of *England under the Stuarts* in the *English Historical Review*, and is

now forgotten, wrote nothing himself. That is the way it is with them. Why don't they have the sense of humour to see it?)

I don't think Trevelyan bothered his head much with critics, or perhaps even noticed them. For he had the advantage of being born on Olympus – all those generations of Trevelyans, his father, Sir George Otto Trevelyan, an eminent historian in his own right; his great-uncle Macaulay, of whom the family had a cult and for whom he was named, to whom he might be said to have been dedicated at the font. Indeed, observing the family over a long period of time I sometimes suspect that they think there are Trevelyans, and then the rest of the human race. They are certainly rather a race apart. I once heard G.M.T. refer to the Regius Professor at Oxford, H. W. C. Davis (who first introduced me as a young Fellow of All Souls to the great man) as 'the excellent Davis': I saw at once what that particular professor's place was in the scheme of things. Regius professors recur; there was only one G. M. Trevelyan.

The scale and quality of the achievement went with the greatness of the man. Those few men I have encountered who could be called 'great' all had something in common: an indefeasible integrity, something rock-like in their character. Churchill obviously had it, and so had Ernest Bevin. One saw it in Vaughan Williams, as in Robert Bridges, for all that it is the fashion of lesser people to depreciate him now. Nimitz had it, for all his charm; Eliot, for all his diffidence. Samuel Eliot Morison had it, that rock-like quality. It may be that Lloyd George had something of it, in spite of his obvious defects of character. Genius does not necessarily go along with character – Dylan Thomas had no character to speak of, any more than Edgar Allan Poe or Baudelaire.

I saw little of Trevelyan during the years when he was at work as Regius Professor at Cambridge (how he disliked the chore of lecturing – and how bad he was at it, just reading from a typescript!). Then Churchill appointed him Master of Trinity. He did not want to take on this chore either, but Winston said, 'If you don't take it, I will appoint somebody you don't like.' Apparently a scientist – and it did stand out that the grandest of English colleges, so far as science was concerned, came to be presided over by someone with no feeling for science at all. (No more had Winston: he depended on 'The Prof', Lindemann.)

Early in our acquaintance, in June 1942, I had a long letter from him à propos of A Cornish Childhood, which he found

> an extraordinarily fascinating story, made up of the two threads of Cornwall and yourself. I have, as you rightly suppose, a very strong Cornish feeling. As you know the Trevelyan papers in the Camden Society you realize the origin of that feeling on my part. I have walked round the whole coast of Cornwall twice and many parts very often, in my younger days, and I should be quite a good guide to all the old Trevelyan places near Fowey. In the eighteenth century the Trevelyans were settled in the beautiful old country house of Nettlecombe in Somerset, where they had been for two hundred years, but they still kept their smaller Cornish estates and connexions. Then in 1777 my branch of the family inherited the Wallington estate in Northumberland by marriage with the Blacketts, and moved up there at one step . . .
> I think in some ways the part of your book that interested me most is the part about the Church and its effect upon you. I was, by the way, delighted to find how much you admire Frere [Bishop of Truro]. I always thought from his history books that he must have been a delightful person.

He was more than that: not only scholar and musician, but a gentleman, a saint. Joe Hunkin who followed him was a poor come-down.[1]

Trevelyan went on to a slashing attack on the Labour Party's record, and charged me with letting them off lightly, which I had done.

> I do not at all disagree with your attack on the Conserv-

[1] See my A Man of the Thirties.

ative statesmen, but . . . the Left Wing parties were violently opposed to rearmament . . . and this was utterly
incompatible with the other part of their policy, which
was to oppose and check the Nazis and Fascists in
Europe.

Trevelyan was right – it was.

I am in a great many matters a Socialist, and I am certain
that after the war we shall become Socialist even more
than we have already done. *But Socialism means duties as
well as rights for the working classes.* One of those duties is
military preparedness and readiness not only to fight in
time of war, but in peace time to *prepare* to fight. This
the working class and its leaders have hitherto steadfastly
refused to believe, and it seems to be a matter which you
also have not taken into account.

Alas, I was only too well aware of it, and what we had to put
up with from the illusory pacifism of the lunatic fringe.
Even Attlee admitted afterwards that he had been wrong – in
the endeavour to keep party unity – for he must have *known*.
    Trevelyan himself had come a long way from the extreme
radicalism of his youth – while his brother, Sir Charles, had
taken the pacifist line in 1914. G.M. was writing from the
Master's Lodge at Trinity: 'If ever you get to Cambridge, be
sure you let me know beforehand, so that we can see you
here. We can have good talk.' Busy as he was, he was ever
hospitable, though I have always been chary of imposing
myself upon people with such burdens, and only once called
on him while he was installed in that historic Lodge, about
which he wrote so well in his little book on Trinity.
    When Trevelyan appeared in London to give some
National Book League lecture, at a private dinner party afterwards I was suddenly called upon to make a speech in his
honour. Somewhat at a loss, I could not think of anything to
lighten the occasion except to twit him on so Cornish a name
– the Trevelyans go back to the early Middle Ages at Trevelyan in St Veep parish – getting annexed to Northumberland.

What were they doing there? And how ironical that so radical a family, almost republican, should have got its first leg-up through a royal favourite, John Trevelyan, favourite of Henry VI. It did not appear that G.M. was amused.

We were to have many better opportunities of getting closer together – especially, as it happened, in Northumberland, where I stayed with him several summers running, though at Cambridge also. I could not get him back to Cornwall. In Northumberland an attractive small estate fell to him from a remote cousin, just as the money coming in from his *History of England* enabled him to live there. It was only a dozen miles or so from the family home at Wallington, the splendid William and Mary house where his brother, the radical baronet, lived.

G.M. loved Hallington. Northumberland was in his blood; from the garden one could see Housesteads on the Roman Wall. The house was a small Georgian country house, improved and made more roomy by the Victorians, with a high-walled kitchen garden to shelter from those northern blasts. In front was a remarkable deep 'dene', a ravine with a pond at the bottom, and luxuriant vegetation, rhododendrons and such as one might find in Cornwall. It was a striking contrast with the bare uplands of the home-farm which he loved to stride across, the squire on his own place.

For all his attachment to Northumberland he had never seen the most dramatic of the fine houses within it – Vanbrugh's Seaton Delaval – until I persuaded him to. He did not appreciate it: his taste was Victorian, he was one of those people who could not appreciate the imaginative nobility of Blenheim. He was a moralist, not an aesthete.

This leads to the philosophic difference of opinion between us. I do not think he understood any form of scepticism, any more than Macaulay could: he was too downright. He would take me to task for my dislike of the Puritans: if it had not been for them, he would say, the Elizabethans would not have fought the Spaniards. If it had not been for the Counter-Reformation and the Jesuits, I would reply, perhaps we should not have had to. He did not seem to appreciate that it was the extremes on *both* sides, who make life intolerable for

sensible people in the middle, that I detested. He did not like
Laodiceanism.

Trevelyan never grasped how sceptical I was – but an
aggressive sceptic, detesting extremists on *both* sides. I think
he assumed that I was just on the other side – a simple point
of view. There was a grand simplicity about him: there was
right, and there was wrong.

He was also liberal-minded. When we talked about the
French Revolution and Pitt's repressive measures against the
Corresponding Societies and fellow-travellers, nuisances like
Horne Tooke, G.M. talked like a Foxite Whig. 'Billy Pitt –
damn his eyes,' he said with indignation; it was all contemporary to him. All my sympathies were the other way: I
should have had no compunction in shutting up the trouble-
makers, only bringing suffering down on people's heads. The
paradox was that I was a man of the people, standing for
order, authority – as it might be Bevin or, for that matter,
Stalin who well knew what to do with trouble-makers. Trevelyan was an aristocrat; he could afford to be liberal-minded.

This is not to say that I was not prepared to learn from
him. I was out to learn all I could. About John Bright, for
example. So, on one of my visits to Hallington, I read his
biography of Bright, the only one of his books I had not read
and – allergic to the subject – I remember nothing of it.
Disraeli was much more my cup of tea (not Trevelyan's):
genius, romantic imagination, humour, a cynical turn about
humans, no humbug, no illusions, fun. I remembered his
summing up of Quaker John Bright: 'He was a self-made
man, and adored his creator.'

Then, too, G.M. had been a Baldwinian, not a Churchillian. He knew that I was strongly anti-Baldwin and Chamberlain; nor did I regard with much sympathy his own
progress from the radicalism of his early days to the inert
complacency of Baldwin, the reign of humbug which led us
to 1939 and war. Trevelyan had the honesty – the most trans-
parently honest of men – to admit that he may have been
wrong in supporting Baldwin. He then made the best
defence of him he could. He said that it was very rare for a
man to be good at both home affairs and foreign affairs. Take

the case of Sir Robert Walpole, first-class at home, a failure in his foreign policy. Baldwin had been good about home affairs, a failure on the foreign front. (Myself, I do not think that Baldwin's home record is much good either: the settlement of the war debt to the USA on extremely harsh terms; the return to the gold standard when he was Prime Minister and First Lord of the Treasury; his behaviour over the coal-industry, taking the line of least resistance. He always took the line of least resistance, instead of giving leadership; for all his humbug about helping Labour to take responsibility, the artful party-politician kept them in a perpetual minority position, fatally so in the elections of 1931 and 1935.)

However, we did not talk politics much – G.M. was as much disillusioned by the contemporary scene as I was, though he did not take so badly the loss of the Empire: he had always been anti-Imperialist, a little Englander. *Ich nicht!* I agreed with Canning: 'England is either great, or she is nothing at all.' It was curious that he was not more interested in the British Empire, for he several times repeated that 'the best of us' was Sir Charles Trevelyan, the Indian administrator, who shaped that historic institution, the Indian Civil Service, by the introduction of entry by examination. Trevelyan's disenchantment reached further back: I was amused one day to discover that he disliked practically everything since the Industrial Revolution. Even I thought that that was going a bit far – eliminating the Age of Steam, of the Railway, the Victorian Age, the apogee of our history!

It was consistent with his country gentleman's view of landscape and history. Then the country was at its most beautiful, all was still on the human scale and yet at its most creative – the age of Walter Scott, Wordsworth and Byron; of Gainsborough, Reynolds, Lawrence, Constable; of Robert Adam, the Wyatts and Soane, of Georgian architecture in town and country; the country-house life which presented the best and most balanced way of life the world has ever seen.

His conversation was not very personal – rather a defect, I think – no gossip, nothing mean or malicious. But he did express disapproval of Bertrand Russell, and in reasonable terms. 'He may be a genius at mathematics – as to that I am no judge; but he is a perfect goose about politics.' Russell was incapable of seeing that: he had little human perception. We now know about the struggle within the Cambridge Apostles between the conventional heteros led by Trevelyan, and the homos led by Lytton Strachey. The latter won – to G.M.'s disgust; for he was not only conventional but positively prudish. Though he kept the formal *convenances* with Strachey over their books, he deeply disapproved of Bloomsbury: 'A dreadful lot!'

He was a late Victorian, his chief admiration Meredith: G.M. had met his wife, Janet Penrose Ward – Matthew Arnold's great-niece – over and through Meredith. All very high-minded. And, since both were rationalists, they had a Unitarian marriage service put together for them and celebrated at Oxford. G.M.: 'If anybody had told me when young that I should be sitting in the Master's seat in Trinity Chapel, I should have been *scandalized*!' Well, he matured and mellowed, and sat there all right. His daughter Mary married an Anglo-Catholic bishop; his Cornish nurse-attendant was also High Church. G.M. would say, 'You and I seem the only rationalists left'; and once: 'I am a flying buttress of the Church; I support it, but from the outside.'

We did not talk literature much, though poetry was a great love in his life. Here we might not have been *en rapport*: his taste was late Victorian, couldn't see anything in Eliot, and was geared to Browning and Meredith, to neither of whom do I respond. In any case he has told us all about his love of literature in his delightful *A Layman's Love of Letters*, which he sent me with a p.c. 'It is a real issue how literature should be approached – for love or by some rule. P.S. So glad the great Eliza is getting on full steam ahead.'

It is a personal book, its message clear.

> It is the love of great poetry and good prose that we want to instil into the young. It is our greatest national inheritance, and how little use we make of it . . . It has been to me a great part of the value of life . . . Poetry in particular but good prose only to a less degree appeals

through the ear to the heart; by sound and melody and the happy use of words it touches the inmost soul in each of us. That is how great poetry works if it works at all. It is not a set of intellectual conundrums, to be solved by certain rules. It is joy, joy in our inmost heart. It is a passion like love or it is nothing. One's passion for a poem often lasts all one's life.

That this was true he knew from his own experience. Poetry often moved him to tears, 'tears of pleasure in the sound of words, tears of gratitude for the beauty of the world in which we live' – and he quoted, for example, Dante's *Dolce color d'oriental zaffiro.* He speaks of 'the unbearable pathos' of Keats' sonnet on the presentiment of his early death, 'in view of what actually happened to Keats'. The truth was that, under the granite of G.M.'s exterior, the formidability of manner, there was intense pressure of feeling liable to burst out, as I found. In his last years, with eyesight failing, so that he could not read, and he would not listen to wireless or music, almost his only solace was to repeat reams of poetry he knew by heart. It is rather paradoxical that he criticizes Housman's pessimism about 'nature, heartless, witless nature': 'I have not this feeling. The Wordsworthian joy in nature is not dimmed for me by the knowledge that I shall not possess it for ever. We come and pass and are not, but nature remains, the friend of each of us in turn.' He was desperately sad towards the end himself – he had not Housman's stoicism: he was a romantic at heart.

He shared Housman's judgment, characteristically stated in prosaic terms, that there were passages in Blake and Shakespeare that give us 'poetry neat or unadulterated with so little meaning that nothing except poetic emotion is perceived and matters'. In other words, the touchstone was *'la poésie pure'* – so much for the cult of Meaning and the Word in the Cambridge school of Richards and Leavis. Though he did not mention their names the whole gravamen of the Lectures was, salutarily, against their dogmatism, or dogmatic criticism in general. 'Above all I object to excommunication ("debunking") of great writers of the past on some modern theory, or to suit some phase of thought or feeling, which like all phases of thought and feeling will itself pass away.'

No one knows that better than an historian. He scored two bull's-eyes in his demonstration of the silliness of E. M. Forster's depreciation of Scott, and of Raymond Mortimer's denunciation of Kipling. From his own long experience he had observed two deplorable examples of the temporary effect of critical prejudice upon great writers. Victorian moralists so objected to the theme of Meredith's *Modern Love* that they excluded him for a whole generation: the second was the absurd decline in Trollope's stock upon the publication of his *Autobiography*. Trevelyan proposed a positive formula: 'Any author who was for a number of years together, considered to be a great writer by a large number of the elect spirits of any former age must have some great merit.' Note the significance of the definitive word 'elect', left unemphasized.

Trevelyan was able to sum up:

> So you see these wholesale condemnations of writers who have for many years been admired by competent literary opinion are not always right, or even final. The fashion of the hour, even of the latest hour, will change some day, and is moreover quite as likely to be wrong as the fashion of earlier times.

This is not merely true, but a commonplace with historians. Trevelyan was always looking for the positive, even in criticism: 'the positive side of criticism is more important than the negative'.

He did detect in 'the English language as we have developed it in our own time' a deficiency in poetic quality. He was at one with Housman in diagnosing the highest levels in literature as poetic – 'that grip of the vitals, that disturbance of the whole being, which the *sound* of very great poetry alone can give'. There are literary people to whom that means nothing. Trevelyan was happy in his generation – and his position in that elect society: for him they did not exist. We are not so lucky.

Trevelyan understood quite well the way things were going.

> It is possible that the country may become even poorer than it is now, and it is probable that what wealth it has will be yet more evenly distributed. In that case the more expensive newspapers, weekly and daily, who still do serious reviewing are likely to disappear, and we shall be left with nothing but the cheap Press.

Not a good prospect for literature, as writers today find; but in a social revolution Quality is the first thing that goes.

> Now that economic and political circumstances are rapidly finishing off what is left of the independence of the English middle and professional classes, posterity will perhaps soon be able to judge for itself how much literature has gained by the disappearance of the hated bourgeois.

Meredith had written that, if England fell, 'mankind would breathe a harsher air'. Trevelyan commented on that: 'Well, she has not fallen, but she has relatively declined, and the air is already more harsh.' When one thinks of what the England of the past stood for, and what it achieved! Trevelyan had not much opinion of the present or hope of the future.

He said to me once, 'When you were young, we thought you were never going to start. But, my goodness, once you started . . .' I told him of the years when illness held me up: I was working all right, researching hard enough, but hadn't the strength to write my books. When I had recovered and was getting forward with published work, G. N. Clark appeared in my rooms one morning with *empressement* and instructed me that I must be sure to be in – for the Master of Trinity was over in Oxford and wanted to see me specially. The Master's visit was characteristically brief and to the point. 'I want you to give everything to accomplishing your big work on the Elizabethan Age. I don't know anybody else who is writing a book on that scale: nothing must come in the way of it.' That made me sit up. I thought, if that is what he thinks and has taken the trouble to come and tell me so, I really must stick to my last and grapple with it. While still at work as Master, he took the trouble to send me a useful reference for the state of the Borders in mid-Tudor times, and followed this up with a letter, having sent me a book as 'a reminder and a stimulus for the great work you have got on hand, throwing aside lesser things. I have "great expectations".'

I didn't know then that the two volumes would grow into three, and the third volume bifurcate, so that my 'trilogy' on the Elizabethan Age is really a quartet. He later gave me some practical advice: nowadays one can't publish a book in two volumes. Take a continuous title to cover the whole, as he did with *England in the Age of Queen Anne*, and publish each volume under a separate title but with that connecting thread.

Of the technique of historical writing he was a master. He told me that one reason why Macaulay was irresistibly readable was because of his mastery of the paragraph: each firm as a shaped block in the building, so that you have to go on to the next. Macaulay, like his great-nephew, was suffused with the sense of the poetry of the past (and was a good poet – a rare thing for an historian). He thought Acton over-estimated, but was grateful to him for one thing; he remembered the exact spot in the Madingley Road where Acton said, 'Never believe these people who run down Macaulay: with all his faults he is the greatest of our historians.' Trevelyan had a very high opinion of Lecky, while I prefer Froude.

Paradoxically, though I was so much closer personally to Trevelyan, intellectually I was more in sympathy with Namier's tragic vision of history, his disillusioned view of human idiocy, violence, brutality, his clear understanding of what modern Europe owed specially to the Germans; and his scepticism and penetrating insight into political humbug – he was a Churchillian, with little respect for Baldwin, and a Tory with not much respect for democracy. Namier had a cutting, ruthless, sardonic mind, like an Old Testament prophet. I am not with him in his analytical technique of writing; in the writing of history I am with Trevelyan, the constructive builder, who was also an artist and saw the poetry and pathos of history.

He very much wanted me to be Regius professor at Oxford. When I said that I could not even consider it – the only person to whom I gave my confidence in the matter – he said, with his usual brusque directness: 'Why not?' I said that the only thing I cared for was writing my books. He replied: 'I wrote my books while I was Regius professor.' I replied, 'There are two things to remember: you were much stronger than I – I have always had to be careful of my health. Secondly, the whole conditions of the job have changed: there are now so many research people to be directed, so many more committees to waste one's time.' At once: 'Then you mustn't have it. What about —— ——?' I said, after some thought, 'That would be all right.' Actually, the whole succession at Oxford went agley: the two most eminent Oxford historians were Namier and G. N. Clark, whom Richard Pares might then have followed, if not stricken with fatal illness.

At Cambridge Trevelyan was curiously followed by Dom David Knowles, a Roman Catholic monk. But that was much to Trevelyan's broadminded satisfaction: 'He is so polite, you can say anything to that man.' Strangely enough, Knowles wrote one of the most perceptive pieces ever written about Macaulay. He saw that under Macaulay's front was an extra-ordinarily emotional temperament, passionate feelings pent up – and, as I have said, there was something of this in G.M. Few knew it.

There was the extraordinary intensity of his and his wife's cult of their dead child, Theo, a boy of brilliant promise, who died at five, I think. Never spoken of, but always there in the background – yearly pilgrimages to his grave in the Lake District, uncontrolled grief and lamentations one must not go into, it was so strange. And his wife's death actually broke G.M. – no less strange: 'I am finished,' he said to me. His elder brother, Sir Charles, tougher and more resilient, less sensitive, spoke to me with disapproval of G.M.'s giving up. But here was the difference: the brother had genius, and something about that is inexplicable.

G.M. had his reservations, on the other hand, about his elder brother, head of the family, which we will also not go into. Suffice it to say that, where G.M. was a complete Victorian, his handsome brother was more of an eighteenth-century type, proper companion for Charles James Fox whom he adored − tutelary deity of the family. Once, when Sir Charles was showing me a box of counters which had belonged to Fox, the compulsive gambler, I said, knowing that Sir Charles was careful about money: 'Do you remember when Charles Fox as a lad at Eton, with another fellow, gambled away £32,000 one weekend? Really, he should have been horsewhipped!' The baronet was taken aback, then recovered with, 'Well, if he hadn't afterwards horsewhipped George III, then he *should* have been horsewhipped.'

I laughed to see the religion of Charles Fox still going on in the family − my own sympathies, of course, being entirely with poor George III. Fancy having a compulsive gambler, however gifted, at the head of the Treasury! Still, Sir Charles went on to make a good point against the great man, his younger brother. The baronet was way out on the Left, a sympathizer with the Russian Revolution. He said to me, wasn't it strange that G.M. who had made name and fame with his sympathy for the Italian Risorgimento should have no understanding whatever of the Russian Revolution? It was a debating point, possibly no more. For perhaps G.M. had had second thoughts about his early enthusiasm for the Risorgimento when he saw what it had led to in Mussolini.

When eventually, rather deferentially, I called at the Lodge of the grandest of English colleges, Trevelyan took me upstairs to see the portraits assembled in the drawing-room overlooking the Great Court. I remember his leading me up to pay my respects to Newton, and the Master telling me that such was the intensity of Newton's mental concentration that his friends were afraid of his going off his head, and conspired to get him made Master of the Mint, to remove him to London and society. He certainly looked mad enough in that portrait.

By my next visit Trevelyan had retired, to the house in West Road which became familiar. The visit is described in my Journal. 'Sexagesima Sunday, 13 February 1955. The taxi slushed across snowy Cambridge to a road behind the Library and an Edwardian neo-Georgian house. G.M.T. came to the door, looking an old man at last, after so many years of healthy walking and tramping. (One of the original Tramps, under the lead of Leslie Stephen.) He was quite white and hadn't shaved well for days – a Victorian outcrop of white hair on jaw and neck adding to the distinction of his appearance. He was warm and welcoming, lithe and energetic as ever.'

I had never met his wife, Janet (descended from the Cornish Penroses), now stricken with paralysis, but gay and lively, ready to giggle and chaff G.M.T. We had plenty to talk about, Cornwall and the Penroses, Oxford and the Arnolds. Over the chimneypiece was Will Arnold-Forster's engaging portrait of her – 'the woman you married, George' – sunlight filtering through the sunshade under which she was seated. One saw the cultivated circle, Cambridge of the early 1900s, superior and secure, refined, given to high thoughts and good causes: Trevelyans, Darwins, Sidgwicks, Keyneses, Butlers.

'Lunch was very gay, Janet T. prepared to be amused and ready to be flirted with. I don't suppose she gets much of that; I liked her enormously, and apparently excited her too much, for after lunch G.M. took me sharply away, for fear of exhausting her. "As brilliant as ever," said G.M. – and I remembered that, with the older Cambridge, "brilliant" has a questionable note. No one could accuse G.M.T. of being "brilliant", nor would he welcome it; absolutely solid, big-minded common sense, plumb right judgement, plus imagination and poetry, rather than brilliance or subtlety.'

His attitude to his wife's illness was strange – it made him ill. His Cornish nurse told me that no Trevelyan was allowed to be ill. He could not accept the fact of illness. Two nurses were in attendance, Janet practically helpless. She didn't look it at the table, rather flushed with excitement; I had amused her, given her a change. What pathos in the phrase, 'the woman you married, George', all now coming to an end.

'He took me away into his study. It was some time after Winston's H-bomb speech. Trevelyan hates the modern world, more completely and consistently than any of us – and no wonder, after the hopes of that late Victorian circle with their radical belief in progress. He hates modern science and the world it has made – rather piquant for one who was Master of the most distinguished scientific college in the world. I said that all these horrors sprang out of the Cavendish Laboratory, where they had split the atom. "Yes," said G.M., "there are Rutherford and J.J. [Thomson] buried in Westminster Abbey; when the atomic ash rains down on London, they will be well and truly buried under it."

'I said a word for science as the most important development of rational thought in the past three centuries. "But I don't like the world it has made – the Industrial Revolution, with industrial development all over the country and all that has come with it." I suddenly saw that G.M.T. is really an eighteenth-century figure; I had always thought of him as nineteenth and early twentieth century. He would like to go back beyond the whole development of modern industry to a world of coaches and carriages, farms, villages and estates, of squires, farmers, labourers. He saw himself as a squire in a stable country society. (Even I don't go back as far as that – I see 1914 as the terminus of the civilization I care for, smaller, on a mere human scale.)

'Thence to history. What he has to say about Elizabethan Ireland was old-fashioned to me, coloured by the sentimental pro-Irishry of the Gladstonian Liberals (right enough as they were about Home Rule). *There* his views hadn't kept pace with the rest. His attitude to history springs from the proximity of the old governing class to government, rather than the specialist outlook of the historian. Therein lies its advantage. When I asked if he was writing anything, he said sadly, "No, I'm too old to write any more." He had what will be, I suppose, his last book lying out before him, *A Layman's Love of Letters*.

'Something touching about the scene – as I walked away over the Cambridge snow I registered: "Work while it is yet day, for the night cometh in which no man can work".' However, they were pleased by my visit, for he wrote to say, 'let us see you whenever you come to Cambridge'.

In the autumn of 1955 I was able to send him my second volume, *The Expansion of Elizabethan England*, which he considered 'extremely well planned'. Next autumn,

> Your jolly letter about the ultra-Whig pleased me well, for I saw clearly you had not heard of Janet's death. She has suffered so much mentally and physically, for so long a time, that it is a mercy which she hoped for. It leaves me indeed the shadow of a shade. I am glad to stay here alone [at Hallington] till Christmas. I am sure I shall love your *Early Churchills* when I see it.

A week later he was pleased to think 'I had had a share in pushing off the happy voyage of so remarkable an historian as you'.

In October, 'I have now read all your *Early Churchills* very carefully and with great pleasure and great admiration. Though only a parergon, it will certainly add to your rapidly rising historical reputation.' In January 1957 he wrote:

> I cannot imagine a nicer letter than the one you have written me and I thank you most sincerely. It touches me closely. I am also greatly touched by your kind suggestion about a possible visit to you in Cornwall for April. It is an extraordinarily attractive suggestion, but I am afraid I am too old to carry it out. The journey back from Northumberland was really too much for me and as I shall need to go to Northumberland again in May, for the greater part of the year, I do not think I could manage another long expedition like that which you suggest, however pleasant it should be. My gratitude for the suggestion is none the less.

That March he had learned that I was to give the first Trevelyan Lectures: 'I want to tell you at once that you are the person I should most of all wish to be so chosen to open that show.'

In June of that year, I was bidden up to stay with him at Hallington, and duly scooted up via Nottingham in my large Humber along A1 to Scotch Corner, Corbridge, and thence on. Next morning we drove out to see over Housesteads, the camp on the Roman Wall – which he bought out of his royalties and gave the farm there as an endowment to the National Trust, to which he had also given many years of work as Chairman. How public-spirited of him, with all the other work on his hands – no wonder he had always been a man of no small talk and no waste of time. He told me a curious story of Kipling, who had the Highland 'second sight' and certainly was psychic. In one of his Roman Wall stories he had placed a certain legionary detachment somewhere along the Wall, purely out of his head; later, a coin came up from the soil, which showed that it had in fact been stationed just there. (One of Koestler's 'coincidences'?) G.M. wrote to Kipling, who was thrilled, and immensely pleased at Trevelyan's appreciation of his historic sense.

Trevelyan's books had made him a comparatively rich man, though earlier old Sir George Otto had kept him rather short. At the end of the war his English Social History had made in its first year £42,000 – of which, with double British and American income tax plus supertax – he paid out £39,500. I said, why ever didn't you hand the book over to the National Trust? He said he would have done, if he had thought of it. Instead of that money going on some historic or cultural object, of significance to the heritage if not to the people, it was swallowed up in the maw of the trivial consumption of a mass society (one should see the rubbish they buy in their bulging shopping-bags); the earnings of those who work confiscated for the benefit of those who do not, eternally striking over nothing, like a lot of stupid kids. (What could I not have done for Cornwall, if I had not had my hard-earned savings confiscated so wastefully, purposelessly! I suppose society today was always intended for the benefit of the third-rate, so naturally the third-rate like it. The elect despise it.)

Next morning we took another turn out around upper Tyne country, passing by Errington, I suppose the Catholic house whence the redoubtable Anne Lucy, Lady Arundell of Wardour, came (whom I had put into a short story, 'All Souls Night'). We saw also Brunton, best preserved of the Roman towers along the Wall, and stopped to look at splendid fourteenth-century and Jacobean Chipchase Castle, tawny in the sun. Doubt was expressed as to its future. I remember thinking dejectedly how uncertain was the future of these splendid houses from the historic past – hundreds of them destroyed every year. What historian of any taste could care tuppence about the rubbish proliferating in their place?

Next morning we walked in the plantations G.M. had himself been able to make, from his own earnings, before taxation got such a stranglehold on the cultured classes and the cultural life of the country. He was a fundamentally constructive man, a positive not a negative type – the antithesis of the destroyer, the estate-breaker, on top in the squalid society of today. Though we came from opposite ends of society – he from the top, I from the bottom – G.M. and I were at one in our fundamental values.

One thing surprised me: he had no such disapprobation as I had of the Jacobite Rising of 1715, which led to the ruin of Derwentwater and his family. He thought that anyone was justified in taking a sporting chance. I was surprised at the old sporting instinct coming out, myself not being ever in favour of taking such chances. There never was a chance of the '15 succeeding.

On my return he wrote: 'Yes, what a lovely and memorable time we had.' I had sent a volume of my poems for his daughter, Mary Moorman, who wrote the finest biography of Wordsworth – of which he was very proud. 'I have been reading the poems with great pleasure myself' – I had not intended them for him, doubtful as I was of his liking modern verse.

Of my next summer's visit to Hallington, in June 1958, I

have a full record in my Journal, a close-up of the great man, which tells one what his conversation was like.

'This year he looks better, in better colour, was even a little pink and obviously delighted to see me. Talked animatedly with vigorous gestures, argued with conviction and even passion – the old G.M.T. one used to see before his wife's long illness got him down and killed his writing. Why this should have done so, I don't understand. (Like Elgar.) On our first walk down in the dene: "I am finished."

'I had urged him several times to devote himself to a history of the Trevelyan family – such a remarkable story. But he wouldn't – said that it broke into two distinct parts, the West Country – Cornwall and Somerset – and the Northumberland branch. We must hope that a junior member of the family will undertake it. He had written charmingly of its origins in his memoir of his father, and he certainly knew the Cornish background: he had twice walked the whole coast. He was a terrific walker in his prime, could do sixty miles a day; and had once walked from Cambridge to Oxford, a matter of eighty-three miles, within twenty-four hours.

'Apparently G.M.T. and Janet were not all that close together: in earlier years they were a good deal apart, leading their separate lives – Janet doing public work, children's playgrounds and other good causes (the Foundling Hospital, as I remember from my Bloomsbury days); he in Italy, or absorbed in writing. Only in later years were they so much thrown together, not wholly good for them. Amusing their upper-class domestic unhandiness: neither of them could make a cup of tea. G.M.'s only contribution is, when tea has gone on long enough (he is naturally impatient) to carry the tea-pot and hot-water jug out into the kitchen. Similarly with coffee after lunch. Not, apparently, a saving measure, just an odd habit, like so many things about him. (cf. Barrès' brilliantly observant *Huit Jours chez M. Renan*.)

'Conversation with him was much more rewarding this year, more vivacity and fire. Just as T. E. Lawrence noticed how Hardy talked of Scott naturally as an equal and of *Marmion* as if it were contemporary, so G.M. talks of Johnny Russell and Melbourne, Bright and Pam [Palmerston], judging the good and the bad about them as if he had known them. It is partly due to the immense span of life lengthened by his father's, so much of whose knowledge he absorbed: a double advantage – in addition to that of having been born into the old governing class, a fairly small circle of people who knew the circumstances and facts, the political lives and personal situations of those Victorians. What immense advantages! He has made the most of them by his inherited qualities of mind – absolute integrity, a devastating candour, no nonsense, genuine high-mindedness amounting to nobility, rare justice of mind. He knew Edward Grey, about whom he wrote, as a personal friend. (I observed him only as a guest at All Souls, dear, sad, good man – what utter rubbish the Germans and those pro-Germans, the Cambridge pacifists, wrote about that transparent character!)

'In consequence, he comes out with surprising things, no waffle, no havering or hovering. That is why we get on so well. He obviously enjoys our talk, always about history, sometimes literature – and was glum when the family threatened to descend. This evening we talked about Marlborough, Sarah and Sunderland. He admired Sarah: "For one thing, she was never up for sale. Now Marlborough was." I defended him as far as I could. G.M. allowed that he would not have sold the pass where the Protestant establishment was concerned or constitutional monarchy; however, "there were large parts of him, large parts of the time, that were for sale". With my sceptical view of human beings, I expect that.

'I told him about a new biography of Sunderland, where I had been able to help with a few bits from the archives at Blenheim. I said that Sunderland was now more intelligible to me. G.M. kept pressing me to condemn him. I wouldn't go any further than to say that I didn't approve. He then teased me about not being a moral man; which I improved on with an account of my scepticism, which people didn't understand. [Nor did he – too direct and simple, black or white.] He gave a vivacious sketch of Sunderland's reptilian career, and what it amounted to – to which I had to assent – and ended triumphantly: "There's a rogue." There was no denying that G.M. had won.

'We greatly enjoyed this banter. I stuck to my point of disliking James II much more for his (sincere) stupidity than Sunderland for his insincerity. I hate fools like James more than rogues like Sunderland: they do more harm.

'I have learned something I value: a better appreciation of John Bright. I have been reading G.M.'s biography, the only one of his books I had not read. He insisted how important the cause of the North was for us and for the world. The victory of the South would have meant an extension of slavery in the Tropics – witness the Congo – and a revival of the slave trade. The division of North America might have meant that, in the twentieth century, she would not be strong enough to see us through to safety against Germany. That was an argument to appeal to me.

'Only on one point do I differ, and G.M. himself has learnt since his early days, with its semi-pacifist radicalism. (His brother, the baronet, even opposed resisting the Kaiser's Germany, along with Bertrand Russell and other such asses.) Bright was too ignorant – and conceited – to learn the real meaning of the Balance of Power: that maintaining the liberties of Europe against the great aggressors – Philip II, Louis XIV and Napoleon, Germany in the twentieth century – has depended on it, really a Grand Alliance against the aggressor. Departing from this sheet-anchor of our security in the thirties had brought down the second war upon us in the worst possible circumstances. G.M. was forced to agree.

'I had not realized the significance of the Manchester Phillips element in the family – no doubt it accounted partly for his feeling for Bright. (By Sir George Otto's marriage came in a lot of money – G.M. was born in a second large country-house, Welcombe near Stratford-upon-Avon. Did there come in a foreign streak with this, the dark glittering look they all have, the marked intellectualism?) He told me of some Manchester meeting to protest against the Crimean War, at which grandfather Mark Phillips was presiding and took too long before opening. His brother shouted from the back of the hall, "Damn it, Mark! Ask a blessing."

'Saturday afternoon: a fire lit in the Library, a shelf or two of Macaulay's books marked M. on the wall, a late photograph of him with close-set puffy eyes and high stiff collar, while I sit in his slippery Victorian armchair on castors. (At Wallington the naughty baronet, whom G.M. never mentions, had made me place both hands flat on the table upon which Macaulay wrote his *History*, that some influence might accrue to me – more power to my elbow!) What a presence he still is in the family, what a cult! And yet there is the authentic story of Sir George Otto on his death-bed, having difficulty in communicating something on his mind: "Uncle Tom – Uncle Tom [what was it so important he had to leave as his last message?] – Uncle Tom was not a gentleman."

'When G.M. was writing his *Lord Grey of the Reform Bill*, Halifax's ancient father was helpful with information, but G.M. guessed it would not be without its price. Nor was it. When old Halifax read the book before publication, he was scandalized to find that G.M. had mentioned Grey's illegitimate daughter, born before marriage, brought up along with the other fifteen children. He added that, after marrying, Grey was completely faithful; nothing sexual in his relations with the Princess de Lieven. In deference to old Lord Halifax, he had cut this bit out of the book. "I knew what would happen: several reviewers got on to it and said that I was too favourable to Grey."

'Old prig, Lord Halifax. What *does* it matter? Lord Brand at All Souls told me that he was similarly descended from the great Lord Grey of the Reform Bill. His great-grandfather was supposed to be a younger son of the Duke of Devonshire, but in Regency days almost everybody who was anybody was somebody else's child. At Eydon Hall Bob Brand took me to look at a portrait of Lord Frederick Cavendish and then at one of the famous Lord Grey: Bob was the image of Grey, with that splendid high forehead and noble cranium. Who wouldn't prefer to be descended from a great man, rather than from some 'tenth transmitter of a foolish face'?

'Of Gladstone, a number of the Liberal Unionists, men of exceptional ability – like the men G.M. used to meet when he came to All Souls, Anson, Dicey, W. P. Ker – used to think that there was a good deal of an ass in Mr G.: witness his views on Homer, and on the Church.

'G.M. owed the original suggestion of his Garibaldi book to Bernard Pares. About 1905–6 some Italian Memoirs about Garibaldi had come out – Pares had given them to him as a wedding present. By then he could read Italian and saw that here was a subject. Never did he work so hard or so fast as in the year in which he wrote his first Garibaldi book. [The first three became best-sellers. I remember the appearance of the fourth, on Daniele Manin and Venice, after the 1914–18 war. At All Souls Keith Hancock wrote his *Ricasoli* largely in reaction to Trevelyan's Garibaldi books. No hero of mine anyway: I prefer the political type of Cavour.]

'Passing by a battered funerary figure in the loggia, of a lady from the Roman Wall: "She doesn't look much now, but I expect she was called the Rose of Procolitia in her day."

'He used to see a good deal of John Simon (of All Souls) in their radical days. Once, when the young Simon had been staying at Welcombe, Sir George Otto said afterwards that he wasn't really any good for politics. Then, with his usual fairness, G.M. added, "Of course, one must remember the blow that the death of his wife was to him. It shut him up like a flower in the evening. It was defect of character to allow that to happen – but that was the reason." [There were others.]

'He didn't ask me to like John Knox (I detest him); all he asked was to do him this justice: before Knox the Scotch peasantry were under the foot of the nobles, mere feudal vassals. Knox taught them to look the nobles in the face. Scotland didn't have a monarchy strong enough to carry through the Reformation: Knox was the best they could do. As for Henry VIII, he settled the Welsh problem, he extruded the Pope, was the real founder of the Navy and resuscitated Parliament: a big achievement for one man. A bad man, but a good King.

'One sees how personal his view of history is, and how moral: last of the Victorians.

'About his grandfather, Sir Charles Trevelyan – "the best of us all" – Trollope, who was much opposed to his introduction of the examination system into the Civil Service, put him into his novel, *The Three Clerks*, as Sir Gregory Hardlines. Afterwards the two became friends, without ever giving up their opposed convictions.

'How paradoxical it was that all three men – Palmerston, Lord John Russell, Gladstone – who were so sympathetic to Italian freedom and did so much to advance it, were all pro-South in the American Civil War. The aristocrats were more ignorant and out of touch with America; but they were always going to Italy and knew what was going on there. They hadn't yet begun to make American marriages; the working people were more in touch; through emigration and correspondence they knew the North, as the aristocrats did not.

'He was much interested by what I had to tell him about the historian Sir Charles Firth's background, and repeated to me his remark *à propos* of the Queen Anne material out of his splendid collection of tracts and pamphlets (Firth was always generous in lending him stuff): "You like writing about these old fellows?" "Yes, don't you?" "No, I only like reading about them."

'One day, walking in the Parks at Oxford with A. L. Smith, G.M. was astonished by his violent outburst against Firth. I explained that this came from the history tutors' inveterate feud against Firth: they never forgave him for his Inaugural Lecture, with its aggressive claims for research as against their teaching. Firth was a Yorkshireman, direct and forthright; the result was that they excommunicated him, and kept the most eminent Oxford historian of his day insulated and never sent their pupils to his lectures. His *protégé*, Godfrey Davis, good scholar, could never get a job in Oxford, and ultimately found a refuge in the Huntington Library in California. How small-minded academics are! G.M. thought the outburst all the more extraordinary coming from so fine a man as A. L. Smith. (He wrote nothing, gave all to Balliol.)

'Sir George Otto, after his First at Cambridge, missed a Fellowship at Trinity, so he decided to go out to India as private secretary to his father, the great Sir Charles, then Finance Member of Council, a terrific Reformer. As a result, Sir George wrote the book in my bedroom, *Cawnpore*, and *The Competition Wallah*, which Kipling admired.

'G.M. has just been into the Library, making up the fire and showing me books along the shelves: of Kennaway's *On Sherman's Track* – "he was in the House of Commons with my father in the sixties". An early edition of Purchas' *Pilgrims* had belonged to Holland House and was given to Macaulay by the Hollands. [That wonderful house with its splendid library was destroyed by the Germans in the Blitz. A friend of mine saw Lord Ilchester next morning, picking his way among the smoking ruins and saving here and there a rare book from his burned treasures.]

'G.M. wished that Macaulay had finished the reign of William III. He was imperceptive as to character; his great strength lay in his understanding of political situations, of mass-forces at work, and the movement of opinion. So that he wondered what he would have made of the reign of Queen Anne, where so much depended on the personalities of Marlborough, the Queen, and Sarah. He specified the three persons over whom Macaulay went badly wrong: Claverhouse, William Penn and Marlborough. He appreciated my point as to the defect of Macaulay's rhetorical method and the application of antithesis to character. Macaulay had blackened the portrait of the early Marlborough in order to make him appear the more shining as the hero of Queen Anne's reign – then Macaulay died before he got there. Unfair on Marlborough, unsubtle of Macaulay. He agreed as to this.

'This put in perspective a letter I had had from him about my own work, which had greatly elated me. I took it as the greatest compliment I had ever received: "You have a far subtler sense of character than Macaulay, but you do not have his tall measure of events." It took the compliment down a peg or two, when I reflected that Macaulay's sense of character was not very subtle after all.

'He was most interesting about Carlyle – most of whom I had read when young, and today cannot stand. One cannot understand anything of Carlyle, he said, unless one recognizes that there were *two* Carlyles. The Carlyle of *The French Revolution* had pity for men – this he said with great feeling and quoted a passage that moved him deeply, though not me; and then the Carlyle of *Frederick* – better not to read that.

How it could have happened, why the change, he could not conceive. At that I took over – he thought there was a good deal in what I said. Disillusionment above all – with people's folly, with democratic and Parliamentary cant, with the rationalist assumption, the idiotic liberal assumption that people are rational. Disillusionment too with his private life, the emptiness of it with no sex. He felt strongly against the later Carlyle, and evidently regarded what he wrote as immoral. I remembered how shocked the middle-class Quaker, W. E. Forster, was on tour with Carlyle in Ireland at Carlyle's views on the Irish peasantry: Forster thought him a moral scoundrel, and never held him in regard after. But, of course, one peasant would know better as to other peasants than a high-minded middle-class type like Forster, hopelessly gone to the good. He clearly thought Carlyle had gone to the bad. So too thought the high-minded G.M.

'Naturally, I feel this less strongly, and held forth on what made for Carlyle's originality: a peasant of genius who knew instinctively, as well as from experience, what nonsense the superficial rationalism of the *Edinburgh Review*, and of John Stuart Mill, was. Again, a lower-class man, an outsider, in their upper-class world, who was yet better educated and far more widely read than they were – not only in their classics, not only in French and Italian, like some of them, but also in Spanish, above all in German, which none of them knew. No wonder he was a phenomenon, who burst upon them from the north like a smouldering meteor. Actually, I preferred his earlier writings in conventional English, the *Scottish Essays* for instance, before he developed his appalling personal style.

'G.M. listened to all this, much impressed.

'Next morning occurred a *contretemps*. An ugly morning, would I walk with him? I had only my oldest shoes, most comfortable for driving, with a crack in the right sole. He led me up the road and straight across a hideously wet field, my shoes squelching, feet, socks, trouser-bottoms drenched (himself equipped with hobnailed boots, thick woollen stockings, breeches). All the while talking about the Reform Bills of 1832 and 1867, and why the Whigs chose Melbourne for Prime Minister; the paradoxes of the nineteenth century, that

the Liberals should have been so good at Army Reform with
Cardwell and Haldane, while the Conservatives should have
brought in Free Trade and the Reform Bill of 1867. To this I
added the Education Act of 1902, the most significant measure of social progress in this century.

'All the while I was in misery, squelch, squelch, squelch –
inwardly amused at my predicament. I might have known it
would happen, so I lost no equanimity. When I got back, I
had a complete change, the nice woman who looks after me
washed my socks and dried everything out. In earlier days
G.M.'s capacity for walking was terrific, and when he came
to a stream he walked right through it.

'This evening he was very lively – more conversation about
the contrast between the conduct of our policy before 1914 –
when we entered the war with Russia and France as allies,
and shortly Italy – and that before 1939, which left us alone
without an ally in 1940. The last time G.M. had seen Grey
was at Fallodon in 1933, after Hitler had come in. Grey said
that this was the end for Europe. All that G.M. could say was
that it wasn't his fault. (Of course it was the end of their
Europe – the old civilized Europe.)

'After supper G.M. was quite cheerful on the sofa, putting
little bits into the conversation. Once to the effect that there
couldn't be a better composer than Vaughan Williams, he was
by far the nicest man! (G.M. has no ear for music.) On going
to bed he scored joyfully off me. All the rest are going to
early service and breakfast at Wallington; so he said, 'Since
you and I are breakfasting alone tomorrow, *you*'ll be able to
get a word in edgeways.' Everybody roared at this sally, for
I have been talking nineteen to the dozen.

How much he appreciated it I overheard next morning, for
he dresses in the room next to mine and I heard him talking
to himself, 'Good friend. Good jaw.'

Writing the family history of the Churchills broke into the
sequence of volumes on the Elizabethan Age; but Trevelyan
evidently ceased to think of the book with which I hoped to
set a new model of readable family history as a mere parergon. For he wrote in August 1958 that he thought *The Later
Churchills* very good.

Indeed I think it is your best written and most readable book of all. Old Sarah and young Lord Randolph and, above all, Winston are A1, and all the figures are good. You have, what Macaulay had not, the power of drawing individual people rightly. His other qualities you have not, in his tall measure, nor has anyone had since his death.

> But thou Cornwall's and fortune's son
> March indefatigably on
> And for the best effect
> Still keep the pen erect.

When he had finished the book he wrote again: 'A very great book indeed – the Winston part of course the best of it all. How deeply moving. So grateful to you for doing it.'

In September he was very pleased by my telling him that I had learned from Macaulay my habit of noting down places and things just as and when I had them under my eye, to get them right and vivid when transcribing them into my books.

He was looking forward to attending the first of my Trevelyan Lectures on *The Elizabethans and America*. I much enjoyed those autumn jaunts along the roads between Oxford and Cambridge, picnicking in country lanes and looking in on the churches – as also the chance to explore Cambridge further, always a pleasure. Those two university towns, with their colleges and churches, so similar in character to a foreign eye, are two wholly different worlds with different luminaries, different tutelary deities to an inhabitant of one or the other.

'3 October 1959: afternoon at Hallington. I have brought my chair out to a favourite spot on the lawn, at the edge of the deep dene, the still water of the dammed burn spattered with fallen leaves, the noise of the water going through the weir coming up with the breeze that just stirs the beeches not yet turning. Some colour about: lemon yellow of chestnut, crimson blush of dogwood, striped scarlet of sumach.'

It was his remote cousin, the Taormina widow, who had re-created the place, Victorianizing the house rather well, 'considering it was done in the 1860s – nothing Gothic about it'. The essential thing was that she had bought the bank on the other side of the burn, pretty well impassable jungle and planted the dene as a whole; blocked the stream to fill the bottom with water, laid out paths on either side. The dene makes the whole charm of the place, purple and gold in summer, lemon, russet, scarlet in autumn. I have never seen it in spring.

'The Master's talk was as incisive as ever. I read to him from a new book about the Anglo-Florentines; he proceeded to quote forty or fifty lines from Browning's "Old Pictures in Florence". His memory for verse is astonishing. He said merely a good natural memory, nothing out of the ordinary; Macaulay could recite the whole of *Paradise Lost*. All the more remarkable with blank verse; G.M. remembered verse by the aid of the rhymes. I said that Edgeworth of All Souls, overcome by sea-sickness crossing the Atlantic, had lain in his bunk reconstructing the *Odyssey*, and found that he could do two-thirds of it. The older generation at All Souls, Malcolm and Oman, had hundreds of lines by heart.

'G.M. said that a great mistake had been made when they ceased to learn poetry by heart: it meant that the younger generation didn't care for poetry. Except Shakespeare – for they liked plays. "Shakespeare and Eliot," I said to tease him. "Oomph," he said with contempt. (However, he had been pleased when Eliot wrote him a nice letter about *A Layman's Love of Letters*, saying politely that he had no reason to regard him as a layman.)

'In truth he knows masses of poetry by heart, which he recites over and over, Milton, Wordsworth, Browning, Meredith. Walking in the dene he recited several stanzas of "Love in the Valley" – "the most beautiful poem of them all" – with more feeling than he usually puts into it. (Was he thinking of Janet? But only once had he fallen in love, at nineteen, for a girl who refused him. A second time he met a girl whom he thought he would like to marry. He studied her mother, and saw the kind of woman she would become – as I do the front photographs in *Country Life* – and decided against. The third time he met Janet – over Meredith. Was it a love-match? Janet was a personality, not content just to be the wife of a great man: she made a career for herself.) He was loud in praise of Browning for the courage with which he took Elizabeth Barrett away from her possessive father to the climate of Italy, which cured her illness. (Was it only the climate? Perhaps it was greensickness which Browning cured in her.)

'Henry Jackson was one day out at Madingley, about 1860, with some friends, well-read and educated. They were talking of Mrs Browning. One of them said, "Hasn't she got a husband who writes poetry too?" Mrs Browning was much the better known then. All Browning's best poems were written in the forties and fifties; his *reputation* was the work of the sixties.

'The lady who had created this place was the widow of Edward Spencer Trevelyan, younger brother of Sir Walter. Neither of them had a son, or Wallington would not have come to his grandfather, Sir Charles. This lady's daughter "had not much of what you and I call resources and was utterly bored at Hallington. She asked Sir Charles's advice, who suggested a six-month tour in Italy. She never came back, but lived in a large *palazzo* in the centre of Taormina. When I was there I called on her, and had tea with her; touched by this attention, she left me the estate. For the last twenty years it had been let: that came to an end in 1927, I came here in 1928."

'All very luckily for him – for, the most eminent member of the family, he was the youngest son: Wallington went to the eldest, Welcombe to the second son, Robert, poet and translator (whom I never met). Nothing for G.M., until out of the blue came this, and he made it his very own. "I had enough money then to look after it properly." Hence the loving care lavished on it: planting those belts of woodland, the coppices and spinneys he delighted to walk in, putting in the engine that brings water from the never-failing spring – "Hallington water is very good"; thinning and planting up the dene with flowering shrubs – like a patch of Cornwall in its luxuriance amid the bare uplands. He had filled the house with furniture from the antique shops at Hexham, books from Steedman's at Newcastle (with whom I had long dealt). He had some Edward Lear water-colours, Georgian prints of Cambridge colleges on the walls, good old wardrobes, chests, and clocks.

'In the dressing-room next my bedroom are family photographs: Sir George Otto and wife, remote and withdrawn, with family grouped on the steps at Welcombe. The eldest son, Charles, handsome, sexy, looking rather slyly out of key with all that high-mindedness; R.C., the poet; and the youthful G.M. looking abstracted, *mécontent*. (Thomas Hodgkin's daughter, who knew them all, said that G.M. was decidedly a prig then. Big brother Charles used to complain that out shooting he would break the line and wander away on his own. They would shout at him, and he would come back sulky. It is only in the second half of his life that he has broadened out, in his last years positively mellowed and developed a charm of his own.)

'I see that in his copy of "Bishop Blougram" he has marked the lines:

> Myself – by no immoderate exercise
> Of intellect and learning, but the tact
> To let external forces work for me.

(They worked for him all right: Baldwin, a Trinity man, gave him an O.M. in his fifties. And this was how he thought of himself.) This morning we walked along the terrace, he admiring the colour of the dahlias against the stone, for there is little that he can see – though this morning in the walled garden he could see a brilliant Red Admiral feeding on a chrysanthemum. He was modest about himself: in his will he had enjoined that there was to be no biography of him. He had written his *Autobiographical Essay* to forestall anyone else writing it.

'Why ever? He would not be able to prevent people writing about him. Consider the case of Thackeray, who insisted that no biography be written – and behold Gordon Ray's two, immensely detailed volumes. He rejoined that Thackeray was in a totally different class – a man of genius, where he himself was only a man of talents who had done his best with them. I said he was underestimating the value of the historian's work compared with the novelist's. And overestimating Thackeray – not in the same class with Dickens. He agreed with that. Historians like Gibbon, Macaulay, Carlyle were quite as important as novelists. He agreed about them, but did not compare himself with them.

'At one point in the discussion he paid me a grand compliment. I said that I did not count. "Oh, yes," with conviction, "you *count* – very much so."

'Today, I know that that is wrong. In a society where all contours have gone, all landmarks removed, nobody *can* count. So nobody counts, where all are alike: and what matter?

'I said that we historians had different things to contribute. Though Gibbon had a generalized interest in geography, he had not G.M.'s sense of the bone-structure of England and her landscape, which I loved in his work, and which he owed to his life-long habit of walking. For another, Gibbon had been essentially unjust to Christianity.

'I can admire his liberalism, though I do not share it. His income had come down now to £6000 a year: to pay tax on that, keep the place going with all its dependents, and the Cambridge house, with nurse-housekeeper – he must live on capital. He said, "I agree with death-duties and supertax. I think it is right. I pay my taxes gladly." I do not. What? – those who work hard pay for those who don't? We are sick to death with too much of all that – and many of the country's best writers and artists have left it on account of it. I think they are right to leave it to those who like it.

'G.M. has very strict and upright Victorian principles, irrelevant in a shiftless society like this. At tea he was approving of Dismal – the saturnine Earl of Nottingham – for holding no correspondence with Saint-Germain. (I forgot to score the point that this Right-wing Tory made an unprincipled deal with the Left-wing Whigs, over Occasional Conformity, to do in the men of the centre, Marlborough and Godolphin, who were carrying the burden of the war. Politicians are much of a muchness at all times.) To tease G.M. I praised Marlborough's subtlety. "Subtlety is another word for treachery," he said.

'I was admiring the subtlest intellect of them all, Halifax, the Trimmer. "But he would not sign the invitation to William," G.M. said. I replied that that was very understandable, with his point of view. "You mean to say that you wouldn't have signed the invitation?" (i.e. to come over and save the country from James II). I said, "No." "I think the less of you for that," he said. "You mean, you wouldn't?" I said that, with my scepticism, I should not have approved of signing it; I hope that I should not have been carried away emotionally.

'He was very disapproving. He said that Halifax was not disinterested. I replied that the Whigs who signed were even less so: they had every interest in bringing William in. Halifax's position was a consistent one: he had saved the principle of monarchy and James II's accession by defeating the Exclusion Bill. He may have thought that the best thing would be to retain James as titular King, with William, his son-in-law, exercising power as Regent. G.M. said that though Halifax knew James was a fool, he had not realized how great a fool, nor that he would bunk from the country. Precisely, I said, if James hadn't fled, Halifax's view would have been perfectly applicable. G.M. replied that William would not have accepted this subordinate position; and at the critical moment, as with a lot of distinguished men, Halifax was NO USE.

'That was that – just like G.M. to cut through all the cackle, all the complexities, to the core of the matter. But I do not share his view. When I was young, and a fanatic, I would have signed the party manifesto all right, and gone to the stake for my convictions. Not so today. I have seen too much of human foolery.

' "Why not?" said G.M., visibly moved.

' "Because I despair of the futility of so much of human action." (I did not quote an old-time Liberal friend of his: 'The longer I live the more I see that things really are as silly as they seem.' But that's what I meant.)

' "Go away with you," said he. "Take the tea things away, and come back again."

'I came back for another set-to, significantly on the issue of the Civil War. He was vehement that it was not avoidable. "For two reasons. One was that you could not trust Charles I. The other was that neither side had the idea of religious toleration. Bad as the Whigs were at the end of the seventeenth century, in many ways, they had the idea of religious toleration. I'm a great believer in liberty. I'm glad I live in a country where everybody can express his own opinion."

'He is a man of absolutely firm and simple principles, which he applies consistently to history, and this gives him a grasp of the essentials of a situation. I am left as a Laodicean to deplore the obstinacy of both sides that led to war, the destruction of beautiful buildings, irreplaceable works of art, which I value more than I do people's "principles" or their silly convictions. As against the inestimable losses – some irreplaceable lives of men of genius too – what gain?

'I did not tell him that I would have left the country with the philosopher Hobbes – to return when it had gained its sanity. That would have shocked him. No point in arguing that point: his mind was made up. So was mine.

'Sunday morning we went for a walk up through one of the plantations he made thirty years ago, giving protection to the fields from north-east and south-west winds. "I hope I die before I go stone-blind," he said, in one of those explosions of melancholy that afflict him. This made him think of Leslie Stephen, who made such an impression speaking for blind Henry Fawcett that the constituency asked him to stand for the second seat. "Damn you, don't you know that I'm a clergyman?" said he. The militant rationalist was in deacon's orders, and clergymen couldn't stand for Parliament. J. A. Froude was in the same case.

'He had no liking for Stephen's daughter, Virginia Woolf – a "horrid woman"; but, then, she had no liking for her father and gave a very unflattering portrait of him in *To the Lighthouse*. He detested Bloomsbury and all its works, making an exception for Keynes, who didn't really belong. "For one thing, he was infinitely public-spirited, and one of the things they discouraged was public spirit. Then, they were all very angry with him for getting married. One of the things they had no use for was marriage. He married one of the nicest women possible" [Lydia Lopokova].

'When I said of Bloomsbury that they wrote well, he replied that that made their influence all the more deplorable. A whole generation was ruined by them – gave them a debunking attitude towards great writers. He once listened to a paper of Lytton Strachey's and registered, "This is the end of all I care for. And it was."

'That night I had an acute attack of sciatica, excruciating pain all down my leg and had to stay in bed, under a drug administered by G.M.'s nurse. Now we were both invalid-ish, and G.M.'s real kindness came out, shuffling along the corridor to see how I was. When I got down he kept me by the warm fireside in the drawing room, charming with the colours of dahlias and Michaelmas daisies along the terrace, the room filled with October sunshine. He was lying on the sofa, silvery and frail in full sun, half dozing, almost blind, nothing to do but wait for death.

'Resuming our talk, he said: "The nineteenth century was better than the twentieth in a great many ways, and one of them was that it wasn't possessed with a passion for debunk-ing. Roger Fry, for instance, thought that Greek art wasn't any good! Pshaw!" When I reflected how Roger Fry pontifi-cated about art in those years, and was held up to us for mentor, his own painting lifeless and uninspired – King's is filled with his pictures, academic and dead – it is obvious enough that G.M. with his historical sense was right. *One* of Fry's portraits has life and was indeed inspired; an American friend owns his portrait of Bertrand Russell, which uncovers a real strain of evil in his face. Eliot, on Russell's playing round with his wife, upsetting her mental balance, already rocky: "Bertie has wrought Evil." He made up for it by unburdening himself of his armaments shares on Eliot, to ease his conscience as a pacifist. Michael Foot on Russell: "He is my man of the century." I share Trevelyan's view what asses these people were.

'What a contrast to them Henry James was – more genius

and a great gentleman. G.M. knew him well, and I have never heard him speak of anyone with more warmth and enthusiasm: a "lovable man", and then in a low voice, as if to himself, "adorable". It is the only time I have heard from him such a strong expression of that kind, though he spoke affectionately – who wouldn't? – of Gilbert Murray, "dear Gilbert". Of Henry James, "underneath the complicated and subtle machine there were simple and direct feelings. No action was more characteristic of him than his taking British nationality, out of anger that the Americans were keeping out of the war. He knew that the world wouldn't be a better place if the German militarists won. President Wilson couldn't see it".

'Well, by 1917 he did see it. Russell never did – until Hitler and the second German war, when his *volte face* showed up his attitude to the first for the nonsense it was.

'G.M. doesn't discuss people much: he sums them up incisively in a brief mention. Of Rupert Brooke: "he was a charming fellow". Of Belloc: "he was a liar" (he was; also a man of genius). Namier: "He's a good historical researcher, but I don't think he's a good historian. He has no sense of the past". Or, grandly, "You and I know that Veronica is a historian of the second rank".

'Next day I was well enough to risk driving. He came out on the terrace to see me off, and I took a photograph of him, looking sad and disconsolate, with that well known grumpy expression. There was the place he had re-created around him, hall-door open to the beds of snapdragons and dahlias, the curve of the drive with beeches as good as at Wallington; up on the horizon the Romans watching us from their Wall.'

In December he was thanking me for my

most interesting article on that extraordinary person, Hawker of Morwenstow. His love of the poor and understanding of their case, his selflessness and his poetry appeal to me very much. But his superstition repels me. Therefore on the whole I prefer a man who in general work and character was very like him – "wonderful Walker" of Duddon, whose memory interested

Wordsworth so much. He did on the Duddon very much the works that Hawker did in Morwenstow. I remember the wonderful region of Morwenstow, and its terrible coast, from walking there some sixty years ago. It is all very vivid to me still.

Next year my birthday message gave him 'special pleasure because it hailed me as a Cornishman'.

In July 1962 his faithful Cornish nurse wrote to me a touching account of the Master's death, and that she would be accompanying the body from Cambridge up to Langdale. There, I suppose he was buried with Janet, beside their little Theo, of so many years before.

It was sad that none of the family loved Hallington as he did. Janet, with her South Country background, never liked it, and in her last illness would not admit that she was there – she would be at Welcombe, or Stocks (her mother's place, Mrs Humphrey Ward, Matthew Arnold's redoubtable niece). Taken into the walled garden, where G.M. had set up her initials with his, along with Edward Spencer Trevelyan and his wife's, Janet would say, 'This *is* Stocks.'

This wounded G.M., to whom Hallington meant so much, and which he hoped would go on in the family, of which he had such an historic sense. When he died, his son at once took the opportunity to sell Hallington, and shortly died himself.

As with so much in our time of decline, decay and destruction, it made an end.

5

Samuel Eliot Morison

Samuel Eliot Morison was the opposite number to George Macaulay Trevelyan in England: each stood at the head of the historical profession, one in England, the other in the United States; each born in the purple, with a distinguished line and family tradition behind him; each the most widely read in his respective country. Morison was, like Trevelyan, not only a great historian but a great man. He had that quality of crashing integrity which I have singled out as possessed by all such men: his integrity, like Churchill's or Trevelyan's, crashed through all barriers, every kind of nonsense or humbug. I used, privately to myself, to call him a piece of Plymouth Rock – though he doubted whether the Pilgrim Fathers ever landed on that exposed piece of New England folklore.

On mature reflection I am inclined to think that Morison was the greatest of all American historians, when one considers the sheer range that he encompassed, the variety of his historical work, the amount of original research that he accomplished, and the quality of his writing, the honesty, justice of mind, his gift for words, the touches of poetry. Putting all this together, one must place him ahead of Parkman and Prescott, and even that more original and brilliant intellect, Henry Adams. Invidious as it is for a Cornishman to say so, in the end he beats Trevelyan – larger in scope, and he had the tremendous advantage of his knowledge of the sea, as well as the inspiration of it.

Curiously enough, Morison and Trevelyan had very little contact, for all that one was Cambridge *pur sang* (US) and the

other Cambridge (Eng.). All Morison's English contacts were
with Oxford, and he was a loyal Oxford man. His period as
the first professor of American History at Oxford, where he
was a student of Christ Church, exactly coincided with my
undergraduate years at the same college, 1922–5, though I
never set eyes on him. My history tutors, Feiling and Master-
man, did not encourage an interest in American history, and
Feiling thought the young Morison 'brash' – he would,
reserved and not very forthcoming as he was. I dare say Morison was brash; but he was quite right, as the first holder of
the chair, to be aggressive about American history, which
was disconsidered at Oxford.

As if the story of the greatest of the English-speaking
peoples were not immeasurably more important – with all
the lessons it had to convey, and just after Britain had survived Germany's onslaught only by the intervention of the
United States – than the intimacies of the Wardrobe or Privy
Seal under Edward II! I came to sympathize with Raymond
Asquith's unpublished Epitaph on a Tired Statesman (his
father?):

> He loathed affairs and hated the state:
> He wrapped his lunch in Livy;
> He threw the Great Seal into the grate,
> And the Privy Seal into the privy.

Medieval administrative history was the fashion then, in the
dreary volumes of Tout (to know Tout was *not*, as somebody
said, *tout pardonner*); just as today populist history is fashionable with Leftist historians, though it cannot be denied that
interesting people are more interesting than uninteresting
ones.

In his Inaugural Lecture at Oxford Morison made a
reasoned and unanswerable statement for the study of American history, very wise and mature for so young a man. He
always thought that 'the story of mankind, with all his nobility and baseness, wisdom and folly, is the most interesting and
fascinating of stories; that history is to the community what

memory is to the individual'. Where should we be without memory? And he was not afraid to say that the vast majority of people read or studied history for pleasure – very unacademic of him. He did not fail to make a salutary point against pedants: 'the study of roots is doubtless profitable, and pleasant for those who do not like the colour of leaves or the taste of fruit; but to learn something about a plant, you must give your main attention to what is above ground'.

Still more to the point is what he had to say about the upshot of the American Revolution, and the contentiousness that followed. 'This was not entirely the fault of one side, but it was unnecessary. Although the feeling of the American people was not friendly to Britain in 1783, the antipathy was recent and could easily have been allayed – it was allayed in New England, where the anti-British feeling had been strongest . . . But the British governments of the late eighteenth century refused to carry out the treaty of peace in good faith, refused to conclude a commercial treaty with the United States . . . No British minister was sent to the United States for almost ten years after the war, and the first one appointed almost brought on another war. But for Washington's resolute insistence on keeping the peace, war would have come in 1793 . . . Not that the British government during these years was hostile to the United States; its attitude may rather be characterized as one of contemptuous indifference; which is the very worst attitude to adopt toward a new or weak nation which, like the America of 1790, is suffering from what the current jargon calls an "inferiority complex".' Wise words.

Sam Morison was indeed a patriot. He tells us in his admirable recollections of boyhood, *One Boy's Boston*, that so far from Boston being snobbishly pro-British, 'the traditions of the American Revolution were central to my upbringing; memorials and landmarks of it were all about us . . . It was only after growing up that I began to entertain feelings of kindness and admiration toward our mother country.' This balanced judgment – justice of mind, rarest of qualities – is evident in the three big American histories he wrote: the *Oxford History of the United States*, which he wrote as a text-

book for students while at Oxford, the first book of his I
read; *The Growth of the American Republic*, in which he co-
operated with Henry Steele Commager; and his final *Oxford
History of the American People*, the book of which he was
proudest. It might be said that that Inaugural, more than any
that I can think of, provided a blue-print for what the young
professor would eventually accomplish.

I am not going to deal with his historical work as such,
but, as with Trevelyan, to present the man as I knew him: I
count myself honoured to have had his friendship for some
thirty years.

There is a clue to Sam Morison in *One Boy's Boston* which he
does not make much of and which most people miss. They
think of him as the essential Bostonian, descended from
Otises (of revolutionary fame) and Eliots, kinsman of the
celebrated Charles Eliot Norton and almost everybody who
was anybody in Boston, formed and shaped by Harvard, to
the service of which he gave his life, and ended up as its chief
landmark. He said in his Inaugural that 'the average American today is living in a different spot from his birthplace. A
house that has sheltered the same family for a century is a
curiosity'. His was one of the curiosities: he lived all his life
in the house that had been built by his Eliot grandfather, 44
Brimmer Street, Boston, an address that became very familiar to me.

But all that, the Boston purple, was on his mother's side;
his father came of Irish stock from Baltimore. One would
never think of Sam as a Southerner, and yet this element was
important in his make-up. Temperament is something deeper
than one's intellectual formation; and Sam had an ebullience,
an outspokenness, an enjoyable concern with himself and his
own doings, which made him unpopular with the faceless
tribe of his own profession. Trevelyan, a strong personality,
was yet rather withdrawn and impersonal in his contacts; he
thus avoided hostilities with lesser people who envied him.
Sam was very personal, apt to be contentious, rather liked a
fight and, I suspect, was out to provoke a fool and shoot him
down. He was a gentleman, all done in good sport without

rancour; all the same, he couldn't stand nonsense, and this made enemies. In fact, there was some Irish blood on both sides of his family.

Sam had a normal, extrovert boyhood, with all a boy's interest in horses – in those days of horse-drawn traffic, stables all round Brimmer Street – skating, camping, an igloo in the woods in those ferocious winters; above all, the summers on Mount Desert Island, swimming, sailing, everything to do with the sea, which generated his passion for the ocean and equipped him to be the greatest naval historian in our language. He admits at one point that his passion is almost indescribable: 'My feeling for the sea is such that writing about it is almost as embarrassing as making a confession of religious faith.' He then goes on to make a good shot at it. 'To ply, unhurried, the blue deeps, or skirt the shining margents of the land, communing with the element whence life sprang, hearing no other sound but the splash of the oar, the flap of sail, the whistling of wind in the rigging, and the swish and gurgle of cloven waves, revives one's strength and refreshes one's spirit.'

He then betrays himself: 'Once in a while some incident, view, or scrap of poetry strikes a bell that reverberates through the deeps . . . when that happens I feel impelled to write something immediately.' All his life, from early on, he was like that, keeping diary, journal or notes; and what it reveals is that he was *a born writer*.

For all that the Eliots knew that they were 'top drawer', there was a democratic quality in their life, which Sam carried still further in his, all the more for rubbing shoulders with everybody, especially the sea-folk along the coast. Boston itself was an open society. 'Once you were "in", more or less wealth made no difference.' How different from old Philadelphia, the most closed society in the States: unless you belonged to one of the old families there, you were nobody at all. No despising trade in Boston; nobody was too proud to earn his living; while the public spirit, which led to all those philanthropic foundations, was beyond praise – the best legacy of Puritanism. Hence it was that Bostonians bought Washington's original library, such an index to the man; it reposes in the Boston Athenaeum, to which Sam directed me. He was the heir to all this and improved on it.

All this is evident in his beautiful little book *The Story of Mount Desert Island*, which originated in a lecture he gave for the benefit of the public libraries there. Anyone who has written local history knows that in some ways it is more difficult than history on a larger scale, the evidence is often so minute and hard to get. Sam extracted the evidence from a vast quantity of sources for so small a space, and added to it his lifelong acquaintance with its local lore, people, folkways and language, its seacraft. All written in the idiomatic style of a master; Sam had such a command of language that he could afford to take risks which lesser people couldn't. He used the whole spectrum of the language from good, vivid, direct slang to the poetic and moving; his usage was as concrete as sea-objects themselves, instead of the nerveless abstractions of academics. He had a nose for rare words, his books are full of them, as for eloquence and poetry. And, of course, he was so much better educated than they, properly grounded in the classics – so that he could cite, along with St Jean Perse and Hérédia – Virgil's hexameters giving the very rumble of the sea:

et gemitum ingentem pelagi pulsataque saxa . . .[1]

Or

Di, maris et terrae tempestatumque potentes
ferte viam vento facilem et spirate secundi . . .[2]

Or the trumpet call of

dat clarum e puppi signum; nos castra movemus.[3]

From such a hand we accept 'Asticou's savvy salesmanship

[1] And the huge roar of the sea and battered rocks.
[2] Ye gods of sea and land, with power over storms, give us easy passage with following wind and breezes.
[3] He gives clear signal from the poop; we break camp.

succeeded'; 'Captain Argall ordered "Boarders Away", and in a jiffy his merry men were swarming over the French bulwarks . . . Argall gave Saussaye the longboat and told him to shove off'. So much more vivid, and in keeping with the genius of the language, than dreary Germanic academese. Since Sam kindly corrected a book of mine on a few nautical points, perhaps I may correct him, if only as a joke: this Captain Argall was not an Englishman but a Cornishman (the name means 'the shelter'), though I didn't know about his doings on Mount Desert.[4] Look at all those rare words – quahang, the 'long since departed porgy or menhaden' and the 'fry-houses' for extracting oil; beside the sea-terms, 'the fore gaff doubled as derrick', which Sam loved and by which inferiors thought, I suspect, he liked to take the mickey out of us. A serious point is involved: somewhere he points out that naval history written by landsmen is apt to be riddled with errors. Nor would this good stylist confuse the proper use of 'shall' and 'will', 'should' and 'would' any more than on the island: 'The speech of the Mount Deserters was remarkably correct as well as muscular and virile – instinctively they used "shall" and "will", "should" and "would" correctly.'

That is more than even an educated novelist like Louis Auchincloss can do today; to anyone who knows the correct usage, this is a perpetual irritation. But he has the excuse of his Scotch descent, for with Scots and Irish the distinction did not exist – it does not in Yeats, for instance; Oscar Wilde got his friends to look out for these solecisms in his work, for he at least knew that his usage was wobbly. Today, in the obliteration of all standards in demotic society, there is complete confusion; myself, I should be ashamed not to adhere to the correct usage: it is quite easy to learn.

Sam loved the Island people and their lore.

> Your true Mount Deserter disproved the old adage, 'Jack of all trades, master of none'. He could be fisherman, sailor, farmer, lumberman, shipwright and quarryman rolled into one, and master of all . . . I have watched

[4] It is a Truro name, cf. my The Cornish in America, 184.

Wilbur Herrick select a straight hickory tree in the woods, square off a balk about three feet long, split it longitudinally into four sticks of equal size and fashion each into a beautifully fashioned axe-handle. All done with no other tools but an axe and a drawknife.

How much better than third-rate writers of theses!

Sam had the soul of a poet; he appreciated music, but his aesthetic sense was essentially directed towards seascape and landscape. 'It was one of those perfect June days that you often experience in these waters: a light offshore breeze, fleecy clouds rolling up over the land; sky, island and ocean in three deepening shades of blue, and the air filled with the spicy fragrance of early summer in Maine.' He loved the land almost as much.

These rocky shore pastures had a beauty, to my way of thinking, far surpassing the massed groves of spruce and hardwood that the summer people allowed to grow up, after they bought these properties. The close-cropped grass, the purple rhodora and blueberry blossoms in June, the pink sheep-laurel in July, the asters and golden rod in August, had a peculiar charm. Songbirds loved these clearings; one of my earliest recollections is hearing a flock of white-throated sparrows singing their 'Old Sam Peabody! Peabody! Peabody!'

His mastery of all the technical terms of sea-craft, every kind of sailing ship, is still more in evidence. We recall his lyrical description of the most beautiful ships ever made by the hand of man, the New England clippers. All this went into his bigger books from the early *Maritime History of Massachusetts* through his four Columbus volumes, his *History of the United States Naval Operations in World War Two*, in fifteen; to his final works on *The European Discovery of America*, besides naval biographies by the way of Commodore Perry, Champlain and Paul Jones.

It is along this field or, rather, coast that he has our Trevelyan beaten, along with a more popular contact with people, all sorts and conditions of men. Both men were aristocrats, but democrats by conviction; they had the liberalism of the true aristocrat, and supported liberal causes. Sam, when young, actually wanted a woman as President of Harvard, and supported Ada Comstock, head of rival Radcliffe – sporting, but rather provocative. One can't imagine Trevelyan rubbing shoulders with people; he would never describe South Bunkers Ledge, in Mount Desert language, as 'Bunker's Whore', or translate such a bawdy ditty as the Greek one on the brothel-keeper who built a ship out of his profits, and makes the little vessel invite company, ending:

Come, all ye hearty mariners, come mount me by the
    stern;
So long as you can ply an oar, free passage you may earn!

But what a full life Sam had! Responsive to women: he parallels 'a well-built hull with a fair woman's body', and 'the sweet chuckling of water like the laughter of young girls, that you hear outside the hull while lying in a small yacht's bunk'. He read Greek and Latin for pleasure, as well as those other languages, Portuguese and Spanish, French and Italian; he was an excellent connoisseur of food and wine. Some of the menus of those old Boston dinners, and meals on board his yacht, make the mouth water. But one mustn't think of him in terms only of those New England waters; he sailed Columbus' ocean-course in a ship of the same design and specification; he knew the Caribbean and the Pacific; he had sailed the Aegean. One of the best pieces in *Spring Tides* is his account of a summer cruise long ago in the Aegean, and another is his evocative and scholarly essay on 'The Ancients and the Sea'.

What advantages he had! – no wonder people were jealous of him. And if he boasted a bit, isn't that true to an old salt? He would certainly regard it as a greater term of honour to be hailed as an 'old salt' than a professor, and he properly earned his rank of Rear-Admiral. I know academics who refused it to him, friends who would never address him as such – small-minded of them. Sam had been involved in several of the actions in the Pacific with the Japanese, and was proud of having been dive-bombed by *Kamikazi*, Japanese suicide planes. He was a man of spirit and courage, as well as all the rest; a very masculine type for one who was also an intellectual – and rather better at it than the intellectuals.

Oddly enough with someone who became such a good friend, I cannot remember when I first met him – probably in Oxford, for Sam was devoted to Oxford and came over nearly every year. He would give a dinner-party at Christ Church, while I gave a large lunch-party for him at All Souls. On one of these latter occasions I got him to meet Boies Penrose, head of the Philadelphia Penroses – a distinguished clan, most eminent of Cornish-American families[5] – who was scholar and bibliographer, and had written good books on historical geography and Renaissance travellers. On such social occasions one could not have much talk, but we were already exchanging books and letters.

In October 1946 he was acknowledging my little book on *The Use of History*, which he found 'most interesting and stimulating'. He had also been reading my *Poems of a Decade, 1931–1941*; 'I liked particularly "The Stricken Grove". It appeals to me personally because I had the misfortune to lose my beloved wife last year, and the next to the last stanza seems to apply particularly to the house and garden that she built . . . I am back at work at Harvard now, but continuing the Naval History until it is done.' His next letter, 1 March 1947, from the Navy Department in Washington was rather dispirited. He had read my *Poems of Deliverance*,

> which I like *very* much. Especially 'All that was most passionate' which might have been written for me! The death of my wife last year has left me rather played out and discouraged, and I find it difficult to pump up the necessary energy and enthusiasm to carry this Naval History through, but fortunately have some young men working with me; and of course the material conditions

[5] cf. *The Cornish in America*, 97–101.

here, though difficult, are infinitely better than with you, so I really shouldn't complain.

No one would ever think of Morison being discouraged, his achievement was so monumental; but he had his ups and downs. He did not give up – as Trevelyan did; but was given a new lease of life by his marriage, three years later, to a Baltimore cousin, Priscilla Barton. I did not know Sam's first wife, the mother of his children; but I knew Priscilla, who made Sam blissfully happy, and no wonder. She was twenty years younger, a beautiful woman, talented as well as spirited – she had a good voice, and sang, up to almost professional standard. Sam adored her – she appears in many of his later books, in dedications and prefaces, he owed so much to her. The finest thing about her – considering that she was entirely a land-girl, brought up to ride horses, like a good Southern girl – was the way she took to the sea so courageously, making an ideal companion for Sam.

Sam has an exciting account of how, once while she was only a learner, the cable he was throwing out to the yacht under sail just missed, and there was Priscilla in the fairway having to deal with the crisis, the sails taking her out into the ocean. 'But she showed her breeding,' says Sam proudly, 'by keeping her head and using it, just as her grandfather Major Barton, on Stonewall Jackson's staff, had done at Chancellorsville.' (Here's Southern spirit again!) Priscilla, only a novice, was headed straight for Lisbon; she said that, although she loved Lisbon she didn't care to go there right then. Sam was inordinately proud of her, and they were the closest of companions. At 44 Brimmer Street I was amused by the close companionship Priscilla's nightie and Sam's pyjamas kept in their bedroom closet.

I was about the last of my friends to get to America – what with long illness, the war and a relapse in the middle of it, then the currency restrictions: we had no money. At last, in 1951, the Rockefeller Foundation laid on a visit for me to the Huntington Library, so that my acquaintance with the United States came that way round. In the arid, deserty Spanish south-west – New Mexico, Arizona, California – I felt how right that the Spaniards should have colonized country just like Old Spain; while, when I got to New England, the English colonization made sense – just like Old England.

In New England my one contact was Morison, and he very kindly took me under his wing. He invited me to Brimmer Street, gave a lunch party for me to meet academic colleagues. Unfortunately I didn't keep a Journal on this visit, and I remember nothing of it, except one significant episode. For coffee we adjourned upstairs to his grandfather's library, classical busts on top of the crowded bookshelves – all very unchanged, as one can see from the photographs juxtaposed in *One Boy's Boston*. In a moment of silence Sam dropped the remark that he had been down to Washington to see the Great White Chief. There followed an awkward pause; his colleagues affected not to know whom he meant. It was embarrassing for Sam to have to explain that he meant the President – I think President Truman at the time; and they meant to embarrass him.[6] They clearly thought that this was a piece of Sam's hubris – they would, and they were taking him down a peg.

The scene was not lost on the observant young visitor, used to the ways of academics, but whose sympathies were entirely with Sam. Of course, an historian ought to want to meet the President, and it would have been interesting to know what had passed. We never learned, for they stopped Sam dead in his tracks, and shortly the party broke up. Somewhere Sam says that he was glad to have seen every one of the Presidents since his boyhood in the 1890s. Quite right: just the sort of thing an historian should value: Presidents are a part of history.

Sam arranged for me to spend the afternoon with Perry Miller, the guru or high priest of the Puritan Mind, on which he had written several unreadable, coagulated books. I didn't find him at all inspiring or the conversation profitable; I should have been more amused if I had known at the time that his life – in contrast to his life's work – was rather un-

[6] Morison's acquaintance with President Truman paid a further historical dividend: he was able to tell him that the early accounts of pre-Civil War doings in Missouri were all lies. Truman knew.

Puritan. Good for him! That evening I was dined at the Society of Fellows, an attempt to recapitulate the Senior Common Room of an Oxford college, silver candlesticks and all. It was very agreeable, and there I was amused to meet the Bishop of Massachusetts – enough to make the Puritans turn in their graves! Especially when one thinks what rot they uttered, even an educated man like Elbridge Gerry, as late as 1772: 'To plunder America is the plan, and the Bishops will be entitled to their share by the ungodly mode of Tithes.' Before ever the Boston Tea Party he was writing, 'I understand that [British] soldiers are attended to their graves with Mass, and expect that Popery will be soon not only tolerated but established in Boston.' As the result of the American Revolution it is today the dominant religion in Boston.

As with Trevelyan, so with Morison, Puritanism was the one subject on which we disagreed: they found me a heretic from what had been nineteenth century orthodoxy. Sam sent me most of his books; his fascinating essays, *By Land and By Sea*, he inscribed 'for A. L. Rowse – still hoping to educate him about the Puritans!' He certainly made the New England Puritans as attractive as ever they could be made; I still could not like a society without Anglican or Catholic ritual, without the music of the Church, without church-bells, or much secular music; no opera, no theatre; not much in the way of visual arts, no sculpture, nor any real painting – nor even literature, until their dreary addiction to sermonizing broke down. No – Santayana is my cup of tea in these matters, and he detested the Puritan ethos – about which Morison wrote, by the way: *The Intellectual Life of Colonial New England*. We must not forget, when people regard him patronizingly as merely a narrative historian (like Thucydides or Tacitus, Gibbon or Macaulay!) that he made a hefty contribution to intellectual history with four or five volumes on Harvard.

In January 1956 he wrote from the Office of Naval Records and History, of the Department of the Navy: 'I had hoped to see you at Washington, where I hear you gave a very witty speech'. I had been asked by Allan Nevins to speak to a society of historians he had gathered in the hope of improving the academic writing of history – in vain, I fear. This was at the huge American Historical Association – I had never attended such a concourse, such *Kuh-handel* in my life. Morison rarely attended these gatherings, though the profession could not but make him its President one year. To it he gave his address, 'Faith of an Historian', which he summed up in one word: '*Quaero*, I seek to learn'. He did not usually waste time on such gatherings: he once replied when asked what he did when he did attend: 'I raised the glad hand' – not calculated to make him popular with his *chers collègues*. Matey with sea-folk, not with them.

I remember once, when he came to lecture at Oxford, some woman had mugged up a book of his to tell the great man how much she admired his work. On such occasions I let such people off lightly with some rigmarole or other, 'How kind of you'. Not so Sam: he said loudly, 'Which one?', leaving the poor lady stumped, for of course she couldn't remember.

He had read *The Expansion of Elizabethan England* and, a conscientious scholar, sent me a few errata.

> The chapter Oceanic Voyages is very well done indeed. You are right to stress the fact that exploration and colonization were a national enterprise, and the contrast with France, or even with Spain. It has always puzzled me why Spanish painters and sculptors in the sixteenth century never chose an American subject. The Portuguese, however, did to some extent . . . I don't think there is any evidence that Drake raised a monument at Drake's Bay; wasn't it merely an inscription on a brass plate nailed to a tree? I'm glad you do not by implication accept the plate now displayed at Berkeley as genuine. The Capes of the Chesapeake named by Captain Newport are Henry and Charles. Point (not Cape) Comfort is inside the Bay . . . I'm glad you wrote plenty of 'After' to 'The Armada', as most Americans assume that Gloriana captured the trident, definitely, in 1588. The bare-legged portrait of Captain Lee is probably the one I saw

thirty years ago at Ditchley,[7] and always hoped to see reproduced. Too bad Lord Dillon didn't leave it to the National Portrait Gallery.

In November 1956 he wrote from Brimmer Street that, after a long summer, he had now found time to read *The Early Churchills*.

> The idea and execution seem to me to be most admirable. I like your modern, almost staccato, style. The books on distinguished ancestors are few indeed; the only one I know of in this country is one on the Adamses; I do, however, notice a few American Jerome traits in Sir Winston . . . We are going abroad again in mid-April for the Radio Free Europe meeting in Lisbon, but I don't know whether or not we shall be going to England after that . . . it depends on the turn of events. I shall not comment on these now except to say that Priscilla and I see eye to eye with Eden rather than Ike [over Suez] and are seriously contemplating voting for Stevenson tomorrow.

A postscript added, 'Well, we held our noses and voted for Ike; the determining factors being that (1) Dulles can't muck about any more and (2) repudiation of Ike would be used by Russia.'

One would very much like a forthright account by Sam of the insufferable Dulles, who ruined Britain's position in the Middle East, with what consequences for the United States can now be appreciated.

In January 1958 he wrote,

> Priscilla was delighted to get the book and I am equally so to hear that you are to give the Trevelyan Lectures at Cambridge. I see that you are treading in the footsteps of Doyle, and I am sure that you will write more inter-

---

[7] Now emptied of its historic contents, monument to the disgrace of our time.

estingly than that worthy Fellow of All Souls.[8] C. M. Andrews' *Colonial History* is much the best in covering the Elizabethan attempts at colonization that failed. There is also a good recent book, I think in the Home University Library, by Quinn about the Ralegh colony.

Actually, I had recruited him to write it for my *Teach Yourself History* series – he did not respond to my *Ralegh and the Throckmortons*.

Morison, of course, was in marked contrast.

One more fine book of yours to add to my Elizabethan shelf! As I hate to receive acknowledgements of books I send to people along the line 'I know I shall enjoy reading it', I have waited until reading your *Ralegh* to thank you for it. A fascinating book, and the weaving in of the new Throckmorton material is skillfully done. It will hardly please the Americans – especially the Virginians – who have a romantic conception of Ralegh as the pink of chivalry etc, or the New Englanders to whom he was one of the martyrs to Stuart tyranny . . . By a curious chain of circumstances, there is a Raleigh Street in Boston. Although there is a despairing pathos about Ralegh's Guiana adventure which will always appeal to me, Humphry Gilbert was indisputably the better man on every count.

As independent-minded as Morison, I do not think he gets that quite right. Ralegh, though not a nice man, was a man of genius, which puts him into a different class. But it is like Sam's chivalrous nature to have a sentimental feeling for Ralegh's forlorn hope in Guiana; I have none, it was a dubious gamble from the beginning – James I was quite right about it.

Sam wished me to send him a suggested route for a tour of Cornwall; 'having been frustrated last visit for want of time

[8] This was J. A. Doyle, whose books on the Colonial period of American history were authoritative for his time. Morison is a little hard on them. Several Fellows of All Souls made contributions to American history, in action as well as in writing.

we saw nothing of the Duchy. By the way, did you observe that in Birkenhead's *Life of Cherwell* he confesses what I told you (*à propos* Appeasers) that Henlein pulled Lindemann's leg – and Churchill's too'.

On the subject of the second war into which the Germans plunged the world, and the folly of Appeasement – Morison and I were at one. About my *All Souls and Appeasement* he had written to me:

> Thanks ever so much for sending me your little book. Beautifully done![9] Terrifying example for our people now – all the more honour to F.D.R. and Churchill. I spent a few days in Oxford in the fall of 1938, after the Anschluss [annexation of Austria] but before Munich, and found only one don who did not support Chamberlain – he was a Labour man in Exeter College. Even Lindemann, who had just seen Henlein for Chamberlain, was soothing – assured Common Room at Christ Church that Henlein did not want to be annexed because he would lose his importance. I wish the conversations at Cliveden had been 'bugged'.

One sees that Sam was under the impression that conversations at Cliveden were more important than they were.

When I was in Boston in the autumn of 1960 Sam arranged for his friends of the Massachusetts Historical Society to show me some historic treasures. I was conducted down steep Chestnut Street to see No. 50, Parkman's house, with his study in the attic at the top. Then up to the big Otis house – of Sam's family – which has been largely furnished with things Walter Whitehill has collected. A complete room of William Ellery Channing (Unitarian deity of Victorian Boston), furniture, portraits intense and soulful. More moving was Parkman's study; his desk with noctograph – which Prescott used too – when sight was failing, leather sofa behind; a bundle of Indian relics from the Oregon Trail, prints of Blind

[9] A Junior Fellow of All Souls, no more than a journalist, wrote that 'if the story was to be told at all, this was not the way it should be done'. He evidently knew better than a great historian, cf p. 30.

Homer and Blind Belisarius, a fine engraving of Walter Scott in *his* study. Out of the desk came the originals of Parkman's Journals only a few years ago: they had lain there undisturbed during the long reign of his granddaughter, who died a centenarian. There was a print of the lily which Parkman developed after his sight had failed – I never knew he wrote a book about roses.

At the Athenaeum I noticed replicas of three hands: Lincoln's scrawny hand of a rail-splitter; Whitman's, a big longshoreman's; Thackeray's, small and delicate, quite feminine. At the Historical Society more treasures: I had John Winthrop's Journal in my hand, the small vellum-covered volume he started on board the *Arbella*. The second was taken home by an Officer of the Society to work at, and got burned! (Some fool, I suppose, like John Stuart Mill's servant-girl burning the manuscript of Carlyle's *French Revolution* so that he had to write it again.) Volumes of early letters, Winthrop evidently brought his family papers with him: a uniform, small, scholarly hand. Upstairs were the Adams papers, planned to be edited in some forty or sixty volumes. Absurd – like the American giantism in everything; another forty for Jefferson! Ten or a dozen volumes would be ample for each, selecting the best and most important with due sense of proportion, instead of cluttering the things up with the irrelevant and trivial.

Sam corrected my impression that he had been awarded the Nobel Prize – which he certainly should have had.

> My award was not Nobel, but Balzan for history only – G.M.T. would certainly have got it if he had lived. The Balzan was founded to award areas of culture not covered by Nobel. As for the American Academy, it was my fault I wasn't elected earlier. To be elected to Nicholas Miraculous's [the very self-important Nicholas Murray Butler, President of Columbia] Fifty Immortals, one has first to join the National Institute of Arts and Letters. I was elected to it some twenty-five years ago, but as I didn't like the other historians then in it – James Truslow Adams and Beard, I declined. Last year they awarded me

their gold medal, so I *had* to join – and the Academy followed. The only other historian in it is Nevins.

Sam certainly mopped up a whole binful of medals and prizes, Pulitzer Prizes and what not – the more opulent culture of America has wads of these things to dispose of. Again his mopping them up didn't exactly endear him to colleagues.

He next wrote *à propos* of my *William Shakespeare: A Biography*, and the rumpus it caused among the Shakespeare establishment – anyone would have expected them to be grateful for having their problems solved for them and to feed on it in their heart with thanksgiving. Sam wrote now, as Rear-Admiral, USNR (Ret.): 'You certainly have become a famous man, what with being an authority on Shakespeare, Cornwall, pre-war English politics, etc, etc. I don't know whether I acknowledged your Memoir of Richard Pares which appeared in the British Academy, but I greatly appreciated it.' He had previously written to me that he found Pares's work 'disappointing'. I saw what he meant by this, though the question is a more subtle one. Pares had a brilliant mind, and could have written brilliantly, had he chosen to. But he was dogged by the idea that historical writing ought not to be interesting, but academic; it was only in his last two books that he got away from this nonsense. It was then too late, for he died when only in his fifties.

Sam's next letter dealt with some of the troubles he himself had to put up with from the inferior – naturally on the increase in a demotic society where people no longer know their place, and do not even have the sense of humour to realize their rating. I had had an example of this from some miserable instructor at an obscure college in the Mid-West. He couldn't see that Morison was a great historian. I tried patiently to explain to him the elements of greatness, the combination of quantity with quality, the size of the achievement, the original research, the justice and bigness of mind, all expressed in vivid, direct, eloquent writing. The poor young man replied: 'You mean that he is just a good writer.'

At the end of my patience, I said, 'If you were not so third-rate, you'd understand why Samuel Eliot Morison is a first-rate historian.'

And that is the kernel of the matter: I suppose that, if they did understand, it would mean that they were not so third-rate. I know as well as the next man that in a gentlemanly society that had standards, it would not be necessary to say these things. But in a levelling society one may as well tell these people what *we* think of them and it – so far it is still possible to express our opinion of it, as it is not in Soviet Russia. Morison and Trevelyan were alike disquieted at the way things were going, with the people having their way. Even Sam's paradise of Mount Desert suffered from 'rowdy motor tourists who throw trash about, and the ruthless ambition of the Maine Highway Commission to make speedways out of beautiful winding roads'. 'The final era is that of the motel and the Acadia National Park Camp and trailer grounds, which has had the effect of sprinkling many of our beauty spots with empty beer cans, broken bottles and other trash.' Morison and Trevelyan were liberal-minded men. A product of the working people, I have never been a liberal: I know the people too well from the inside to entertain illusions. Morison and Trevelyan were very much concerned for liberty. One can have too much of a good thing: with the people out of control in democratic society, liberty means anarchy. Communists know that: they have no illusions about the people. Said Lenin, when a fellow-traveller thought there was insufficient liberty in Soviet Russia: 'Liberty? What for?'

The situation is not dissimilar in the over-crowded and inferior universities of democracy, where the professors can't write and the students can hardly read – at least they haven't read anything, in my experience of some two hundred American campuses – and modern British education is following in their tracks, when it is only a small proportion of people who are educable up to real university standards. Morison devoted a salutary paper to his seminar at Harvard, some of whom would become professors, 'History as a Literary Art'. 'In the period between the two world wars,' he wrote, 'I became exercised over the bad English used by students of history, especially graduate students, and over the dull, pedantic manner in which many historical monographs were presented.'

The paper contains many valuable reflections impossible to go into in detail here, and useful hints as to how to write. The dominant fact is really a sociological one: there is a complete breach between the productions of the academic history profession and the reading public, which 'for the most part is blissfully ignorant of this vast output'. No wonder, for it is unreadable. Morison points out that the Americans had a good historical tradition of their own: 'Prescott and Motley, Irving and Bancroft, Parkman and Fiske, were great literary craftsmen.' They knew how to write, and in consequence were widely read. As, indeed, with Morison himself. 'There has been a chain reaction of dullness. Professors who have risen to eminence by writing dull, solid, valuable [?] monographs that nobody reads outside the profession, teach graduate students to write dull, solid, valuable [?] monographs like theirs; the road to academic security is that of writing dull, solid, valuable [?] monographs.'

This is the case: I remember a clever graduate student in California who came to me for advice about her thesis on Graham Wallas. She was intelligent and grasped very well how it should be written; she said to me, 'I know you are right; but, if I wrote it like that, I should never get my Ph.D.' I regard this as shocking, but recognize the situation. Morison, himself a master, gives valuable advice as to historical standards, aims and methods. It is all waste of time – I waste none of my time on it: one might as well save one's breath to cool one's porridge, and march ahead alone.

The writing in American historical journals is like the clicking of a thousand typewriters: no music in it, no tone, no rhythm; no rise or fall of inflexion in the prose; no directness or vividness, no concreteness, all lifeless abstractions; no humour, no jokes; all chaff, tasteless, colourless, savourless – so unlike Morison's own writing. These people – like the Shakespeare industry – write for each other, not the intelligent public. Edmund Wilson had a quarrel with the Modern

Languages Association of America as to their over-editing of literary texts, weighing them down with irrelevant footnotes, etc. The issue here was mainly textual, but that of writing was also involved: Edmund Wilson knew how to write, they very largely do not. I happened to say to Garrett Mattingly one day – he was an exception, who wrote well: 'The trouble with these people is that they do not know how to write.' Mattingly answered: 'No: they *do* know how to write; *but they know it all wrong.*'

In 1965 Morison put the coping-stone on his work with a great book, his *History of the American People*, the work of which he was most proud. It is indeed a magnificent book in scope and scale, in justice of mind, understanding of politics and people, feeling for landscape and scene, power of evocation. Look at the setting of the Lincoln-Douglas debates through the summer and autumn of 1858.

> Imagine a parched little prairie town of central Illinois, set in fields of rustling corn; a dusty courthouse square, surrounded by low wooden houses and shops blistering in the August sunshine, decked with flags and party emblems; shirtsleeved farmers and their families in waggons and buggies and on foot, brass bands blaring out 'Hail! Columbia' and 'Oh! Susanna';[10] wooden platform with railing, a perspiring semicircle of local dignitaries in black frockcoats and immense beaver hats.

How it calls up the scene, and how true it is to those little prairie townships – as good as Willa Cather: the historian writes as well.

It is not my purpose to delve into the historian, except for personal traits. But I cannot forbear a professional tribute to the Master. When younger, I did not take to American history, what with the Puritans, the Boston mob and rabble-rousers like Sam Adams, and all. Morison cured me of this:

[10] Cornish folk were close to America and American folklore through constant emigration: my father would sing this song to me as a child, cf. *A Cornish Childhood*.

he made it so fascinating one wanted to read on and on, as with Macaulay. When I read this book I was most impressed by the political judgment – the way he could do justice to both Lincoln and Jefferson Davis, Grant and Robert E. Lee (Churchill's favourite American); perhaps, above all, by the way in which, though a patriot, he was just to the British stand as well as to the American Revolution. My sentiments were Tory: Morison brought me round; no one else could – certainly not Sir George Otto Trevelyan with his partisan Whig and naively pro-American view of it all. Perhaps I might tease Sam, as over the odious John Brown, who brought on the Civil War. Sam describes him, the 'perpetrator of the Potawatomi massacre in Kansas, a belated Puritan who would have found congenial work in Cromwell's invasion of Ireland'. QED.

But we are looking for personal clues, and they are many; for Sam knew instinctively, as real writers do, that the element of personality is what gives a man's work life and keeps it alive. He has a give-away phrase about Senator Charles Sumner, who was friendly with the British ambassador, Sir Charles Vaughan, with whom he stayed at All Souls. (Morison was, characteristically, the one person who researched into Vaughan's voluminous papers there – English historians hadn't bothered to do so, except for Oman, our librarian.) Sam says of Sumner: 'He was one of those fortunately rare and rarely fortunate persons who are not only thick-skinned themselves but assume that everyone else is.'

Sam was not thin-skinned, but he was not thick-skinned either. He was more sensitive than G. M. Trevelyan, who – aristocratic and Olympian – simply didn't notice the yelping of jackals. When Sam's masterly work came out, it was given a disgraceful review in the *Manchester Guardian* – too much regarded in the United States – by the son of a well-known professor of politics who was more of a political journalist than political thinker. I was enraged by it, and when I caught the young offender gave him a piece of my mind. Nothing daunted, he repeated that it was 'a bad book', and was without the sense of humour to see how foolish this was coming from him, who had accomplished nothing and was not likely to. Such are demotic standards all too prevalent.

Sam wrote from his cubicle in the Widener Library, no. 417, where he did so much research:

> I wasn't really put out by — — 's review: it was so typically Left-wing Labour. But I have been somewhat grieved by the reviews here by my academic colleagues, either making picayune faults or praising with faint damns. Reviews by professional critics in the newspapers, etc, have been uniformly favourable and I can't expect anything better.

The book had the nation-wide respect and success it deserved.

Some years before, Sam had written a biography of Paul Jones, the dashing Scotch privateer during the American Revolution, who became a folk-hero to the new nation and entered into their myth. In his usual way Morison had done a lot of original research on this rather elusive subject, had come up with a lot of new facts, and was able to interpret it all with his sailing expertise: he called it *A Sailor's Biography*. In England an article appeared by one Oliver Warner, a writer of no importance, who repeated all the old stuff about Paul Jones without any reference to the new information assembled by the master in the field.

Sam, who had come up with much new information from original research, minded about this, and protested to the historical journal which featured the offending article. He wrote to me, enclosing his protest, 'Why is it that when English historians write on American subjects, they constantly ignore everything written by American historians on those subjects?' I think he was more vexed, and rightly, by the general point than by the off-hand treatment by a third-rater. But, when he got no satisfactory reply, he did drop his subscription to the journal.

He enclosed with this a charming article he had written about his kinsman T. S. Eliot's poem, 'The Dry Salvages and the Thacher Shipwreck'. Sam had discovered that 'he and I are really only seventh cousins, the same relation as Franklin D. and Theodore Roosevelt, but I was very devoted to him'. (Who wasn't that knew him?) 'Cousin Tom' thought that the name the 'Dry Selvages' came from the French *Les Trois Sauvages*. Sam was able to show that 'selvage' meant a strand or edge (cf. OED), in this case, of rock; and that 'dry' meant that it was exposed at low water. Cousin Tom 'came to believe that his first American ancestor was in Anthony Thacher's shipwreck in 1635'. Tom wrote to Sam, 'Did you know that the Reverend Andrew Eliot was in the company with the Reverend Mr Thacher, when they went ashore on Thacher's Island?' The historian had to disillusion the poet: there was no relationship.

But he paid tribute to the poet's knowledge of the coast.

> Tom was not only steeped in the lore of Cape Ann; he became familiar with the encompassing ocean. Cruising in college days with his friend Harold Peters, the Dry Salvages was the last seamark they passed outward bound, and the first they picked up homeward bound. Approaching or departing in a fog, they listened for the mournful moans of the 'groaner', the whistling buoy east of Thacher Island, and the 'wailing warning' of the diaphone on Thacher's itself.

Morison, we have seen, had a fine appreciation of poetry, and was a prose-poet himself.

> Tom remembered the music of Cape Ann – 'the sea howl and the sea yelp':
>
> . . . the whine in the rigging . . .
> The distant rote in the granite teeth,
> And the wailing warning from the approaching headland.
>
> These lines, and indeed all that follow, ring a bell in any sailor's heart. Notice 'the distant rote'. *Rote* or *Rut* is an old English word now seldom heard outside New Eng-

land. It means a distant, continuous roar made by waves dashing on a long rocky coast. Often have I heard a Maine man say, 'Sea's making up. Hear that rote!' T. S. Eliot doubtless listened to the rote from his parents' house, during the windless calm after a storm, or on a 'weather-breeder' day when swells from the eastward begin crashing on the 'granite teeth' of Cape Ann before a storm breaks. These youthful impressions stayed with Eliot for almost twoscore years, producing at last the setting and background of his great poem.

Not even yet was Morison's work complete. In his later seventies he embarked on his vast conclusive work, *The European Discovery of America*. Here also was a culmination of a lifetime's work in research, sailing, exploration. In accordance with his regular habit he travelled to see the places he was writing about: this involved innumerable flights by plane, voyages by sea, as well as research in libraries. He had by now a cohort of helpers, friends all round the world – however he managed to keep in touch with them all, or even remember them, I cannot conceive.

It was a prodigious effort conducted into his eighties; the photographs and maps alone illuminate the enterprise, the ships' courses of his precursors, contemporary views of where they came from – the centre of the Cabots' Bristol, for example – the landfalls, the bays and straits, all round North and South America. There is Sam in cockpit of plane, or at the helm of launch, himself an Admiral of the Ocean Sea, like Columbus whose voyages he had definitively settled in history.

Again, I must restrict myself to the personal. In the first volume, *The Northern Voyages, A.D. 500–1600*, we have a photograph of him, sturdy and upstanding, with his two comrades by their plane 'setting forth to check on Lief Ericsson and John Cabot'. Vast quantities of nonsense have been written about the discovery of America, as about Shakespeare, and Sam had no hesitation in laying about him. For academics –

having been deprived of a classical education, they find
the learning of a foreign language very difficult, and they
dislike getting their feet wet. One cannot do much about
their want of basic Latin; but if only they would take a
cruise in a sailing vessel they might learn something
about the facts of life at sea and not write the nonsense
they do about voyages. The late Eva G. R. Taylor, professor of geography in the University of London, once
laughingly admitted, 'I am absolutely terrified of the
water and would not go on it for anything!' Yet for years
she pontificated about the great navigators of history in
a highly disparaging fashion.

Disparagement of their betters seems to be an occupational
disease of academics; he wrote to me about several of this
professor's navigational errors.

Then for the crackpots – 'the sheer weight of literature on
St Brendan is enormous and most of it is worthless'. (The
same might be said for Shakespeare.) 'The late William B.
Goodwin, an insurance executive of Hartford, Connecticut,
spent a fortune following various archaeological will o' the
wisps, including an alleged pre-Vinland or at least pre-
Columbian "Irish stone" village in North Salem, New Hamp-
shire.' The Harvard archaeologist, Hencken, an authority on
Ireland and Cornwall, investigated and found it to be rubbish
– like the old fool in Philadelphia who spent $2 million
trying to prove that Bacon was Shakespeare. They may spend
as much on trying to disprove that Emilia Lanier was not
Shakespeare's Dark Lady, and get no further; for the answer
is unanswerable.

When Morison came to the southern voyages of discovery,
he found that he had not to deal with so much nonsense as in
the northern voyages; though 'crackpot theories about
Columbus continue to proliferate, and Portuguese historians
still claim that their compatriots were first everywhere . . .
Nobody has yet claimed that Vikings sailed through the great
Strait before Magellan', though one professor insisted that
Africans were in Mexico before Cortés, and a Brandeis pro-

fessor 'has Phoenicians swarming over Brazil even before that', etc.

The first of these final volumes was dedicated to Priscilla, 'who has followed all these Voyages with me in spirit, and some of them in person'; the second 'To the memory of my beloved wife, Priscilla Barton Morison, 1906–1973', with a quotation from Tennyson:

> And o'er the hills, and far away
>   Beyond their utmost purple rim,
> Beyond the night, across the day,
>   Through all the world she followed him.

She was indeed a gallant spirit, a worthy comrade for him. It was a great sorrow to him that, twenty years younger, she died before him. He had written to me of his intended trip to Japan – with her, for his book on Commodore Perry – 'but all such things are now very uncertain'. Priscilla suffered from cancer for some years, putting up the fight one would expect of her. Sam's last book was written

> under the shadow of a great grief, the loss of my beloved Priscilla, still sharing my life as we approached the end of a long literary voyage. She accompanied me almost everywhere by land, sea, and air . . . almost every page of this volume prior to the chapters on Drake I read aloud to her before grievous pain made it impossible for her to pay attention. Her favourite criticism, born of her early experience on charitable boards, was, 'Sam, that sounds like the secretary reading the minutes of the last meeting!'

Any such passage was cast out – little of that remains in Morison's published work.

All things considered and, counting the claims of many British and American historians, I think that Morison was probably the foremost historian in our language in this century. One can think of some who may have had more original minds: Maitland, for example, had genius; Namier had a deeper tragic sense of history – no wonder, with his Jewish background and the wicked suffering inflicted on his seminal people all through history. Morison's was a sane and balanced view of it all, big-minded like the good sailing fellow he was. As a writer, when one considers all that he accomplished and the excellence of his craftsmanship, one must also place him among the great American writers.

6

André Maurois

When I was young, only just ceased to be an undergraduate and become a Fellow of All Souls, I wrote a little book, no more than an essay, *On History*. C. K. Ogden recruited it for his well known *Psyche Miniatures* series, along with celebrities like Bertrand Russell, J. B. S. Haldane, Malinowski, I. A. Richards – and I received all of £15 down.

But André Maurois, in his Clark Lectures at Cambridge, *Aspects de la Biographie*, gave the little book the whole of two pages. This was more than encouraging to a young man commencing author, and I remained always grateful to Maurois for his generous notice. A Celt never forgets kindnesses – or unkindnesses either.

No matter what Maurois said about my essay, which was in effect a summing up of my strenuous experience of reading the History School at Oxford, when I had expected the softer option of reading English Literature. The little book was to be a blue-print of my life's work in history; when I have read it years later, I have had the welcome experience of finding that I still agreed with it (as not with a subsequent book about politics, *Politics and the Younger Generation*. Young people's views on politics are of no value: the subject needs, of all things, experience.) As an undergraduate I was obsessed by the discovery of Marxism and the light it threw on the conflicts, the clashes and movements, of history. But I was determined, in my Marxist enthusiasm, not to go a millimetre beyond what I really thought myself; to subscribe in empirical fashion to what we familiarly called the MCH (the materialist conception of history), without swallowing Marxism whole, certainly not Lenin's Dialectical Materialism – though I struggled through his dogmatic *Dialectical Materialism and Empiriocriticism* and other rebarbative works.

I was quite well read in Marxism, for those days, but retained my own judgment. Paradoxically, when so many of the faithful have regurgitated everything of the Marxism they too uncritically swallowed, I have retained about as much of it as is useful or suggestive for the understanding and writing of history; for example, the decisive importance of classes, class-interest and class-conflict. It is unnecessary to throw out the baby with the bath-water. I had never given my adhesion to Marxism as a complete system of economics and politics, let alone philosophy. The bonus I received from this stubborn working-class independence of mind – as against middle-class parlour Communists (some of them friends, like Ralph Fox and Maurice Dobb) – was that I had nothing to retract. And I can still agree with my little manifesto, *On History*.

Not so much of a novel-reader, I doubt if I read *Les Silences du Colonel Bramble*, with which André Maurois first won attention and some fame. A liaison officer with the British Army in the 1914–18 war, this gave him the insight into the British character upon which he based much of his early work. It provided the foundation of his literary and speaking career – for he was an assiduous lecturer; he became the leading French authority on, and interpreter of, the English, not only to Europe, but to the British themselves and in the United States. It won him a wide public throughout the English-speaking world, honorary degrees and what all.

To tell the truth he had a very good understanding of the British. Half-Jewish himself – his real name was Herzog – this gave him the advantage of a certain ambivalence: his was fundamentally a *sympathetic* mind, I don't think he had any particular bias, as Paul Valéry had towards the Mediterranean, Mauriac towards the South, Montherlant towards Spain and North Africa. Maurois was a marked contrast with André Siegfried, for example, who – for all his being regarded as an authority on the British Empire and his periods of residence at All Souls – was too inflexible a mind to understand the English. I remember how baffled he was when I told him that George Lansbury, socialist Parliamentary leader in the thirties, was an Anglo-Catholic. Anglo-Catholic socialist – impossible! Siegfried, erect as a ramrod, was a Lorrainer – I liked him, dogmatic and rather *raide* as he was; but Maurois and Elie Halévy had a more sympathetic and subtle understanding of the English.

Maurois' earlier books, on which he built up his reputation on the subject, were slighter. Though I do not remember his novels – *Le Discours du Docteur O'Grady, Climats* and so on – I read his *Ariel, ou la Vie de Shelley*, his admiring *La Vie de Disraeli*, and *Edouard VII et son Temps*. His little book, *La Conversation*, was deft and perceptive as always, though it did not have the power of François Mauriac's *La Vie de Province*, which I gave to Edward VII's old mistress, Lady Warwick, a fellow socialist.

As a novelist, Mauriac was much more powerful, obsessive, fundamentally creative, and I did read his novels, every one of them as they came out.

Maurois was much more of a biographer, skilful in attuning himself to his subjects, and he gradually deepened his treatment of them; they became less literary and – dare one say? – superficial, and more historical. His approach became fundamentally historical, and that brought its rewards, in depth, breadth and command. I learned from his *Lyautey*, that great colonial administrator from whom French North Africa, in particular Morocco, gained so much – as Algeria did from the remarkable Cardinal Lavigerie. The civilizing benefit of their work mostly lost today, I suspect.

I recall too a charming *livre de circonstance* that Maurois wrote about Rouen, which he described as a *ville-musée*, which it was, though it had its literary associations too, particularly with Flaubert and Maupassant. Normandy was also Maurois' background, where the family business, a textile firm, was. And, of course, I read his life of Châteaubriand – one of the greatest and most recognizable of Celts – if only, though not only, for its Breton interest.

The second German war and the fall of France made an appalling breach between Britain and France, in which Maurois was caught, much to his detriment. I have always excused it on the grounds of hysteria, near to panic, for what Maurois did was so superfluous – he had only to keep his mouth shut and there would have been no trouble.

The fall of France in 1940 was agonizing for any Frenchman, and many of them – perhaps most – were rendered anti-British by the disaster to their country. I remember four ranking sea officers who, opting for Pétain, passed through All Souls, being rerouted for France. They were all sullen and anti-British. The French Fleet had been brought up to its highest level of strength and efficiency by 1939 – if only the French had continued the struggle with Hitler and Mussolini from North Africa, it would have shortened the war by a couple of years.

When the war was over and France liberated, I happened to call on the chancellor of the Legion of Honour on the Quai d'Orsay. Descended on one side from a family of the *ancien régime* and on the other from a family in Napoleonic service, he virtually broke down and said that he was *ashamed* of France for 1940 and after. I assured him that the catastrophe was more Britain's fault than France's; that British pro-Germanism had been fatal, had gravely weakened France, that Appeasement of Hitler had confused French policy and led straight to 1940.

Maurois fled to England and thence to the United States; but arrived there, he made an attack on Britain. It was so unnecessary and, at that moment dangerous, that I think he must have panicked, and lost not only his nerve but his senses. It was, of course, intensely resented. A fellow Jew publicly assaulted him in the foyer of his New York hotel and struck him twice in the face: '*Un comme juif, et un comme français.*' I will not repeat what Maurois' wife is reported to have said about it, but it occasioned one of Churchill's memorable *mots*: 'We thought we had a friend, but found we had only a client.'

It was years before Maurois recovered respect and something of his old position; there remained always this shadow.

After the liberation of France, he was for years excluded by the British Embassy from its functions; it was not until Queen Elizabeth II's visit to Paris that he was once more received, and peace was restored.

He must have known that I knew what had happened, though it was never mentioned between us. I had never forgotten his early kindness to an unknown young man, and I put down his break in New York simply to sudden nerves – after all, it was unintelligent for a very intelligent man: he had only to keep silent.

In Maurois' later years he wrote a series of splendid literary biographies – research deeper still (aided by his second wife), uncovering new, original material, sympathy lively as ever, judgment mature. This period began, after the war, with his *A la Recherche de Marcel Proust*. It was the first book to reveal the sources of Proust's genius, and may be said to have initiated the subsequent enormous growth of Proust studies. (We now know enough.)

I have always regarded Proust as the most symptomatic, and probably greatest, writer of the twentieth century; in his vast novel he wrote its Paradiso, Purgatorio, and at length Inferno. So I was both grateful for, and immensely impressed by, Maurois' revelation of the Master, and the mystery. Maurois shared with Proust (and Montaigne) the inestimable advantage of being half-Jewish, so that he had the key to both worlds, with the insight and the *souplesse* to render it.

I had written to congratulate Maurois on this most revealing work – he was the first, too, to have permission to draw on the Proust family papers. He replied, 5 April 1951:

> First I must say your letter filled me with joy. Praise from you is praise indeed and what you say is exactly what an author dreams of, but cannot believe he deserves. Your *England of Elizabeth* has arrived and I read it with delight. I always admired those 'spacious times', but never realized so well how much present England owes to them. I could return to you the compliment about the themes delicately woven into the texture of the

book. I always thought that every book – history, biography, novel – should be built as a symphony with recurrent themes. But very few historians realized that. You mention Neale and Trevelyan and they are certainly among the best. Yet from an artistic point of view I prefer your book. Your plan is perfect and the richness of information makes Elizabethan times come alive again.

I had always been clear that a living historical work must be an organic whole, and have beginning, middle and end. It was the trouble with my friend Pares's immensely learned books that they were not – until he learned eventually with *A West India Fortune*; while Namier's books were a succession of brilliant chapters. But the symphonic conception was subtler: I had deliberately interwoven themes to knit together this and the following volumes on the Elizabethan Age as I had observed Proust doing in his great work. There were internal rhythms also, up and down, rise and fall. A writer should learn from all his reading, literary as well as historical, music too; for history includes the whole of life.

Maurois' next book, *Lélia ou la Vie de George Sand*, gave me pure pleasure – or possibly impure, for there are comic episodes like the fiasco when Mérimée failed to come up to scratch with the insatiable woman who had exhausted Chopin. What a woman she was, and what zest for life! What fun they had in the France of Louis Philippe, without the modern shadow upon life – plenty of money and all the entertaining that went on at Nohant. I recall her entertaining Matthew Arnold, when young, athletic and handsome, and the liberating effect she had on his generation, after Rugby and the Oxford of the Tractarians.

Maurois sent me his next biography, *Olympio ou la Vie de Victor Hugo*, with a kind *dédicace* – to me the most valuable of the whole series, for it makes the monster intelligible. Olympio is Hugo's name for himself ('*Tristesse d'Olympio*'): colossal egoist that he was, out of it came his colossal output.

As a part of working his passage back to Britain Maurois was invited to lecture once more at Oxford. Jean Seznec, professor of French Literature, as a Breton a fellow-Celt, was a little nervous of Maurois' reception and asked me to look after him at dinner. He need not have worried on either score. The young men had no knowledge of what had happened during the war, and Maurois received a positive ovation at the end of his lecture. I told him how exceptional this was at Oxford; he was immensely pleased, but it was thoroughly deserved. I couldn't attend the lecture, but he gave me a copy. It was quite extraordinary in its sympathy and understanding for the writing of the generation much younger than his own, with which he could not be expected to be in accord. No wonder the young men had cheered him.

Our next meeting was in New York in November 1960, for which I resort to my American Journals. 'The PEN Club in Washington Square was entertaining André Maurois to dinner. I was very glad to see him again, as he was to see me. I have never held against him his bad break against Britain in 1940 – he must have been unnerved, it was so superfluous . . . When he was at last invited back to Oxford, I did my best, and Maurois was happy and pleased. Isaiah Berlin wouldn't meet him, and Ava Waverley took the trouble to write me a letter of protest, saying that she had heard that I had been very kind to Maurois, that the Paris Embassy did not receive him and people ought not to welcome him, etc. As if I would take my line from her, or anybody else!

'Anyhow, Maurois was visibly pleased to see me at the PEN Club, among all those people he didn't know. I refrained from taking up his time, since I was lunching with him next day; I introduced Leon Edel to him, who had never met him. His speech after dinner was adroit, amusing, perceptive, not at all profound, a wonderful performance for a man of seventy-five. At sixty-five he had declined an American lecture tour on the ground that he was too old. But now it happened to work in with the book he was writing: the American half to a parallel history with Russia – an interesting idea – including interviews with leading Americans in various fields of science, etc.

'In the questions afterwards it was noticeable how doggedly he refused to enter a single note of criticism, and kept consistently to the optimistic line he finds so profitable – and which may genuinely reflect his temperament. (Not mine.) He found cause for a favourable view of the prospects of American culture in the multiplication of paperbacks, the fact that one can buy Plato's *Dialogues* or *Phèdre* at the airport. What does this amount to? I could have put the point to him whether the multiplication of mass-media did not put a premium on all the third-rate purveyors of it. What do popular standards matter where culture is concerned? Is there any increase in first-class achievement? I should have thought a great diminution. [Seznec tells me that the present state of literature in France is appalling compared with before the war. Same in Britain.]

'Maurois was determined to look on the bright side, and of course this pays – though everything is in the balances. Some sense of this was at the back of some people's minds: Robert Halsband said afterwards that the address 'lacked teeth'. But they wouldn't have liked it if Maurois *had* criticized. I understood well enough what the astute old boy was up to. He made one point that appealed to me – the necessity for justice of mind in one people's interpretation of another, the importance of responsible judgments, instead of easy scoring off each other. This should be the historian's attitude.'

Next day, 24 November, Thanksgiving day: 'I went down to Cass Canfield's pretty house on East Side for lunch. Of all the houses in New York this is the one I should like to inhabit: a small, narrow early nineteenth-century house of three storeys, back from the street, with patio, wall and iron gates before it, opened only from the house on ringing. I went early for a business chat with Cass in that downstairs drawing-room, old furniture, flowers, sculpture by Cass's wife. (By contrast with me, I gather that Maurois is an extremely hard bargainer over his books, actually getting 'more than the traffic can afford' . . .)

'The Maurois now arrived. I had never met Madame before, daughter of Anatole France's Egeria, Mme Caillavet, who used to keep his nose to the grindstone and prevent him from falling into indolence. I presented myself with a compliment about her husband's devoting a couple of pages to my first little book – "as if that were not like having one's name inscribed on the dome of St Paul's". After that, no awkwardness, everything went swimmingly. We got on to the subject of Princess Bibesco, and this was not displeasing to Mme Maurois.. She made a point of telling us how pleased she was at being remembered, after fifteen years, by the woman at the shop whence she had sent so many food parcels to Europe during the war. This was a useful line, I registered, in case I knew about the awkwardness.

'What made that still more inexplicable was something that Maurois proceeded to tell us, that he had written the text of the Queen's [now Queen Mother's] speech to the women of France in 1940, and for that she had given him a pair of diamond cuff-links, so valuable that they kept them in the safe at home. In going through the speech with her they came to a phrase like 'tel*s* hommes", which the Queen pronounced without the "s", said that her tutor had taught her that way (he must have been English!), and why was "s" to be pronounced there, in other instances not? etc.

'Maurois had often had his work confused with Mauriac's. The old King of the Belgians said he thought *Le Désert de L'Amour* a good book, wasn't it? When Maurois said, yes, it was a good book, the King looked surprised: he evidently had taken it to be by Maurois.

'I didn't know that they had a country place in the Dordogne, and almost made the mistake of saying "the Mauriac country", through whose books it was familiar to me – but saved myself by saying that they were very near. "Yes, he is in the Gironde – two principalities," Maurois added. Actually he does not *belong*, as Mauriac does. When he was asked at the PEN Club which of his books he most enjoyed writing, two of them were about Jews, Disraeli and Proust, the third about George Sand.

'Cecil Roberts had written me of a visit to the Maurois' house at Neuilly, and the impression of luxury it gave. He must have made a pile of money by his books, and looked after it well. It is obvious that he is a hard worker, and says that he has the best secretary in the world – his wife. She does

much of the research for his books, and all the typing. I liked
her: clever and perceptive, and not in the least overpowering.
She asked me to be sure to let them know when coming to
Paris.

'Their house is next door to the Windsors', whom they
know; they regard him as pathetic, a fish out of water. Wallis
has recently written an article for the Paris press on how the
English people treated her husband – they make a lot of
money by such stuff. She has a terrific anti-English complex.

'Talk was easy and agreeable, mainly historical and literary
– Maurois well informed about American history, upon
which he has written, as upon English. I could not but
admire the vitality of this old couple, who seemed not aged
at all. The lunch was the most delicious, and elegant, I have
had in the States. Cass's beautiful wife runs the house like
clockwork, in addition to being quite a good sculptor. I drew
Madame Maurois' attention to the sculpted pieces about and,
on Cass's behalf, prevailed on his wife to do a head of him.'

In May 1961 I was to be in Paris to give a lecture for the
British Institute at the Sorbonne, and I let Maurois know.
He, however, had to leave for Bordeaux, 'where Chaban-
Delmas, the Mayor of the town, asked us a long time ago'.
Would I still be in Paris for the eleventh or twelfth? – 'Thurs-
day being a holiday we would have to take you to a restau-
rant, whereas Friday we would have the pleasure to receive
you here.'

That summer he was gravely ill with sclerosis of the lungs;
we did not know whether he would recover and I wrote to
his wife for news of him. In September he wrote back himself
in French, his handwriting more minute than ever. '*Mon cher
ami*,' but I will translate into English, 'I reply myself, first
because since my illness my poor wife has been overwhelmed
with work, and further to prove that I am getting much
better. My lungs remain somewhat affected, but I can begin
to work a little. I shall try not to work too much.'

He renewed his invitation to come and see him, 'if M.K.
[Khrushchev] does not intervene: which I don't think, for his
régime would die of it and perhaps himself also. It is a game

of poker, very disagreeable.' I suppose this refers to the Cuban crisis, and the showdown.

Maurois made a marvellous recovery, went on with his work and continued to be productive. I had not cared so much for his book on the Dumas – there were three of them, and this distracted from unity and dissipated the impact. But the life of Balzac which he went on to stands at the summit of his biographical work, not inferior to the *Victor Hugo* and again with fresh material which he brought to light.

In Shakespeare Quatercentenary Year I was again in Paris, to lecture at the Sorbonne for the British Institute, stopping at the Hotel Lutétia. I did not know that under the German Occupation it had been a Gestapo headquarters: I found it highly respectable, '*bon-bourgeois, très familial* and crawling with priests – just the place for me.' I was very busy with lectures and parties, mainly under the wing of Princess Bibesco; but before I left I spent an hour with Maurois, completely recovered and in good spirits, anxious to talk. I resort to my Journal:

'29 April 1964, at 5.30 I duly presented myself at 86 Boulevard Maurice Barrès, the Maurois' opulent but somewhat characterless apartment, looking out on the greenery of the Bois de Boulogne just beginning. A most interesting hour together: he really is a superior man, no nonsense from him about D. H. Lawrence being in the same class with Shakespeare [Leavis nonsense]. He made it clear, without denigrating Anatole France, that he did not regard him as on a level with Kipling.[1] He regarded Saint Exupéry as a kind of minor Kipling. When he had published *Colonel Bramble* he sent a copy to Kipling, who responded generously and asked him to stay with him in Sussex. Which he did – I suppose the book may have been influenced by Kipling's stories of army life.

'When younger Maurois had grown up with the expectation of a large inheritance from the family business; but textiles went down and down, until some years ago the business had closed down – and he had only the money he earned from his books. (He has done immensely well with *them* – no

[1] I do not myself underrate Anatole France.

evidence of want in the luxurious apartment.) He has not left his country place at Essendiéras (near Saint Médard d'Excideuil – how medieval it all sounds), which belongs to his wife; merely parted with the farm, on which he did nothing but lose money on cows. Everybody told him to buy Friesians, since they gave the best yield of milk: with him they ceased to give any milk at all. (I thought how like my literary friends who had put their money into farming, and how much of my savings had gone to the bottom of the sea.)

'We talked for a moment about de Gaulle, who had written me a grand, magistral letter about my Shakespeare biography (Harold Macmillan was even more enthusiastic and warm in its praise, but he was also its publisher). It had been suggested to me that de Gaulle would welcome this attention in Shakespeare Quatercentenary Year, but that the book should be sent to him in both the English and French editions. I was very proud that the great statesman, whom I chiefly admired along with Churchill, should take notice of it: "*C'est avec l'interêt le plus vif que j'ai lu votre oeuvre magistral sur le grand dramaturge élizabethain,*" etc.

'Maurois told me something illuminating about de Gaulle's way of conducting business. He would ask each Minister separately to come and place his views before him, thank him courteously – and that was that. Not waste time in futile Cabinet talky-talky, as revealed in the Crossman Diaries. De Gaulle didn't go in for discussion, he listened to the other's point of view, then made up his own mind. I find this temperamentally, and intellectually, very sympathetic. Never discuss anything with anybody: *il n'y a pas de quoi.* There is nothing to discuss with. The process of decision is a more subtle one than that of mere ratiocination, even if other people are rational – as they rarely are; intuitive choices enter in, subtler than the rationalist accounting of economists, philosophers, theorists in general. Churchill and de Gaulle are my "men of the century", not Bertie Russell.

'The best part of our talk was devoted to Shakespeare and Proust. I explained to him again that the Dedication of the Sonnets to Mr W.H. was the publisher, Thorp's, not Shakespeare's at all; hence the young lord in the Sonnets is *not* Mr

W.H., but the obvious person, Shakespeare's patron, Southampton. But Maurois had already grasped it all, at once – so unlike the bulk of human fools. Veronica, for example, has made an ass of herself falling for Hotson's crackpot William Hatcliffe! The only reputable person to do so, and my old pupil: very poor.'

Maurois, with his perception and literary experience, had grasped that the problems of the Sonnets, except for the identity of the Dark Lady, were now solved, and had allowed my publishers to quote his opinion. Of course, he was not an Elizabethan expert, but he had a great deal more common sense than those who were supposed to be so.

'I said that Proust was perhaps the most Shakespearean writer of the twentieth century – allowing for the immense difference that the twentieth was a prose century. The whole atmosphere of *A la Recherche du Temps Perdu* was poetic – moreover, a musical atmosphere, like Shakespeare's. Maurois at once saw that here was a theme, and that I should write it up. He added that the Baron de Charlus was a Shakespearean creation. (I did not think of comparing him, *ceteris paribus*, with Falstaff: a decadent, outsize twentieth century Falstaff, both comic and tragic.)

'He had no very high opinion of Gide as a writer, even less than mine. He told me of an amusing essay of Rebecca West, starting on a journey to Paris with a high opinion of Gide as a writer, and a batch of his books to read. The first she did not much care for – but still she had a high opinion of Gide as a writer. The second and third did not come up to expectation either; by the time she arrived in Paris and had tried all of them, she found that she had not much opinion of Gide as a writer at all.'

A naughty story. I have given my opinion of Gide in *Homosexuals in History*. In earlier years I was very well read in Gide, and read most of his books as they came out. I regularly subscribed to the *Nouvelle revue française* which he had founded and made into some sort of propaganda vehicle for his literary circle. When he turned up at Oxford he looked, as David Cecil said, a *maître d'école*: he was obviously used to being treated with deference as the Master. His creative inspiration was small – one sees it at its best in *La porte étroite* or *Isabelle* – everything in him turned to autobiography. But his curiosity was insatiable, and he had, in those years, the adventitious attraction of his scandalous interest in homosexuality. Today, nobody would turn a (pubic) hair. Then, he was at his apogee with his Nobel Prize – for his stance was liberal; but Maurois was right about him. He was altogether too literary, in the pejorative sense of the French phrase, '*C'est de la littérature*.'

I was more anxious to learn about Montherlant, who intrigued me greatly: he was the French writer with whom I felt most temperamental affinity – pride, disenchantment, no illusions; realism plus poetry; self-reliance, reliance upon no-one outside oneself; the uttermost exploration of one's own ego, one's own world of the imagination; the sense of history and the drama of human lives; seared by contempt for human folly; hedonist and stoic, a solitary spirit: a dug-out from which to confront the disgrace of the time we live in.

I longed to know more about Montherlant: I was a fool never to have written to him to tell him that here was a kindred spirit. He would have responded, I now know. Maurois could tell me very little about him. He saw him at sessions of the French Academy, where he made his laconic contributions. But he had an iron reserve, and no-one knew him. He had some affection of the throat, and did not go out into society.

'When I made a motion to go, Maurois bade me stay on: he was enjoying the conversation and twice said how pleased he was at my coming to see him. (He has natural courtesy.) He repeated his invitation to stay at Essendiéras. Shall I? – I always forego these chances in the interest of work. But the chance will not come often again – he is nearing eighty, though recovered from his severe illness of two years ago.'

In the event, I did not go – fool that I was, with my genius for missing chances in life, I can hardly explain why: natural deference, not wanting to impose myself on people, not wanting people to impose themselves on me, or even to be in close proximity with them, preferring my own company: a solitary spirit, like Montherlant, not normal and gregarious like Maurois. Now I am sorry: I might have gathered material for something like Barrès' naughty and amusing *Huit Jours chez M. Renan*. But I doubt it – Maurois would have been too aware.

'It was good of *him* to allow me to take up his time, for he was obviously working. *Balzac* would be ready in time in October, he told me to tell Cass Canfield in New York. His admiration for Balzac as a writer was immense, but now that he had made researches into his life he found a number of things that were not admirable. (Was this an unspoken apology for himself?) When I get back to Oxford I will send him a Shakespeare epigraph for his book: "The web of our life is of a mingled yarn, good and ill together." How will he take the textile reference – apply it to himself?

'On my leaving we went up together to the de Laszlo portrait of him, large as life in his Oxford D. Litt. gown, both of us Oxford Doctors of Letters.'

7

Princess Marthe Bibesco

I first met Princess Bibesco with the Abdys at their exotic house of Newton Ferrers in East Cornwall. At least they had made it exotic, with their French taste. The exterior is a rather *gauche* Queen Anne manor-house, but with one spectacular feature: a series of semi-circular granite *perrons*, descending to a forecourt, with a heavy balustrade, big balusters with balls on top. Sir Robert Abdy told me that, in the moonlight under snow, they looked like a regiment of grenadiers. The formal forecourt ended at a gate, which looked down a gorge to the River Lynher (Cornish for long pool).

It was the interior that was exotic, filled with French furniture and rugs, a striking Boldini in sharp perspective, a lovely shadowed Winterhalter of Princess Troubetskaya, an enviable Hubert Robert on the staircase. The library, looking like a Paris *salon* of the time of Louis Philippe, filled with sumptuous bindings, red and gold from his queen's collection, a Houdon bust of Marie Antoinette from St Petersburg (now Leningrad, as if Lenin built it!).

Bertie had got to work on the surroundings: at the back a pool with a big Rodin in the centre; the hillside along the cherried drive he had torn up to install a series of descending fountains and pools, *les Grandes Eaux de* Newton Ferrers. At vast expense: when Diane pointed this out, Bertie replied simply, 'Well, Louis XIV did it at Versailles.' During the war the house was damaged by fire; all the panelling was lost, except for the library wing; the other wing remained a shell, adding to the haunted look of the place.

The place indeed had its ghost, a story only I knew from the documents: of the Coryton son and heir who had killed his father, sometime in the late Elizabethan age – and the Corytons left it in the eighteenth century for Pentillie on the Tamar.

It was, and is, a strangely lost place, a *pays du grand Meaulnes*. One can see the house, lost in its trees and woods, from hardly anywhere. Often as I visited it at intervals I had difficulty in finding it among the long winding lanes; my best bet was to make for the known beauty-spot of Clapper Bridge, two bridges and an island in the stream, and up the valley which Bertie had planted with cherries.

There I met the Princess, with the Abdys whom she had known from their Paris days – if not before; for she was well acquainted with English life. Asquith's daughter, Elizabeth, had married a cousin, Antoine Bibesco; Marthe was a friend of the MacDonalds, through her friend from Roumanian days, Lord Thomson. She was indeed a European figure, with her Roumanian and Greek, French and Italian descents; she had known the Russian Imperial Court in the days of its glory before 1914, and was a friend of the Hohenzollerns. Her literary friendships were even more interesting, for she had known Anatole France and Proust. She was a distinguished writer herself, a member of various academies, and had written several good books.

It was through her friendship with the Abdys that she fell for Cornwall – it reminded her of the Bosphorus – and bought a pretty Regency villa at Perran-ar-worthal (Perran-the-wharf), above the river going down to Restronguet, across from the woods of Carclew, about which I had written my poem, 'How Many Miles to Mylor?' This charming property had already appeared in literature in Kilvert's Diary – Tullimaar, home of young Mrs Hockin, with whom the inflammable curate was enamoured.

The Princess in turn loved Tullimaar – I hear her French pronunciation of it as I write – and set about refashioning and planting with her extraordinary zest and vigour. The dining-room there she repapered to look like a tent, after the room at Malmaison (for she enjoyed an illegitimate descent

from Napoleon). Not much money can have been left from
the confiscation of the Bibesco fortune, but the shelves of the
little library she had gold-leafed, to go with the few fine
eighteenth-century bindings the Communists kindly allowed
her from her palace, which they had taken over.

She had been one of the richest, as well as most beautiful,
women of Europe – and the family had suffered terribly. She
had restored the splendid sixteenth-century palace, designed
by a Venetian architect. When Hitler's hordes invaded Rou-
mania, she managed to get away with the family emeralds,
first to South Africa, I think. She once told me the adventures
of her escape, but unfortunately I did not write it into my
Journals, and have forgotten them. She never once complained of what she had lost, or what they had all suffered –
this was one of the things I most admired about her: courage,
magnanimity, zest for life: she was a *great* woman, besides
being a great lady. Instead of repining and regretting lost
wealth and grandeur, when now she had to earn her living
by her writings, she one day said to me: 'I like this better.' I
thought it wonderful of her.

Her only child, a daughter, Princess Ghika, and her husband had been caught and held by the Nazis in internment
camp for five years. When liberated, they were held by the
Russians for another seven years! No word of complaint from
the daughter either, with a charm and gentleness all her
own – though it had wrecked her and her husband's health
and made invalids of them both. Cornwall was chosen partly
to get away from it all, in the depths of the countryside, to
recuperate physically and mentally, cultivating their garden
at Tullimaar.

It was an honour for Cornwall that she should have chosen
it. It amused me, as well as irritated me, that small-minded
Cornish gentry in their crevices did not appreciate their
acquisition – too ignorant of Europe (they had all been
Appeasers), let alone of European literature. I made the most
of this stroke of fortune in the summers, when we were both
down in the county. She spent most winters in her apartment
in the Bibesco house on the Île St Louis, the old heart of Paris
– is it the house that appears in perhaps the best of her books,

Catherine-Paris? We became playmates, with all Cornwall to explore, with me – her 'Professor' – as guide. She became very patriotic about Cornwall; I promised that when Cornwall was happily cut off at the Tamar from insanely tax-ridden England, she should become *Madame la Présidente de la République Cornouaillaise*.

The first of many letters to me mentions her pleasure at my introducing her to Kilvert and his enchantment with Tulli-maar. The house had more recent associations: General Eisenhower had occupied it during the fortnight before D-Day, 1944, making final preparations with Montgomery nearby. I had met Montgomery at lunch at Trenarren before I came to live there, and had an argument with him about the place of war in history. The Princess wanted to know all about that; fortunately I had recorded it in an article for some magazine at Oxford – it led to a marginal acquaintance with him. Someone here saw the two generals upon whom so much depended – the liberation of Europe – walking out along our headland to the Black Head, in those unforgettable historic days.

The first of our expeditions was to the beautiful seques-tered church of Landulph by the Tamar, where a descendant of the Greek Emperors from Constantinople lies buried – of interest to her, since she was one herself. I can see her now sitting in the aisle, my obedient pupil taking down the inscription which I dictated to her:

> Here lieth the body of Theodore Palaeologus,
> of Pesaro in Italy, descended from the
> Imperial line of the last Christian Emperors
> of Greece; being the son of Camillo, the son
> of Prospero, the son of Theodore, the son of
> John, the son of Thomas, second brother to
> Constantine, Palaeologus, the 8th of that name
> and last of that line that reigned in
> Constantinople, until subdued by the Turks;
> who married with Mary, the daughter of William
> Balls of Hadleigh in Suffolk, gent., and had
> issue five children, Theodore, John,

Ferdinando, Mary, and Dorothy, and departed
this life at Clifton the 21 of January, 1636.[1]

The Princess was always game for an expedition with
something to see at the end of it; nothing deterred her –
certainly not the weather. As at the Rector's Lodgings at
Lincoln College, Oxford, in the days of Mark Pattison and
his highbrow wife, the weather was not to be mentioned; I
was more easily deterrable, the Princess not. I remember a
somewhat damp expedition to Roche, the most extraordinary
natural feature in our vicinity at St Austell: an exciting
upthrust of rocks high up on the moor, on top of which a
hermitage had been built for an anchorite about 1400. Two
storeys of huge shaped stones, living room on the living
rock, with chapel above – he must have had great charisma
to have had that built for him and supplied with food by the
folk around – resident confessor and psychiatrist for all mid-
Cornwall (or, perhaps in still more demotic terms, TV star).

All round, prehistoric country: Hensbarrow (i.e. old bar-
row), the tumulus of some prehistoric chieftain; in the distance, the ridged encampment of Helman (i.e. rocks on the
moor) Tor. In one of the recumbent rocks at Roche, like an
Irish bawn, there was a suggestive deep hole, filled with
water, into which one cast a copper and made one's wish –
such was the folklore. I had often enacted the ritual, and been
televized doing it; the Princess was game, and followed suit.

More frequently we drove round to friendly, more intelligent country-houses, to lunch – most often at Newton Ferrers – with me as chauffeur, the Princess anxious not to go
too fast along Cornish roads and lanes. One trip abroad I
regret that I had not confidence enough in my driving to
undertake – to the grandest of medieval *châteaux* in Brittany,
Josselin, where she was a kinswoman of the La Rochefou-
caulds. Once again my lack of social enterprise meant that I
have never seen Josselin.

However, we met outside Cornwall – at Oxford, where
she came down to lunch with me at All Souls, or in London
at the Ritz where she regularly stayed. On one occasion I

[1] i.e. 1637. I have modernized the spelling.

took her up to the American Embassy to meet the most beautiful ambassadress in London, Evangeline Bruce. There Marthe told us a sensational story of the Comtesse de Noailles, which appalled me. The best woman poet of her time, a self-absorbed egoist, she was the mistress of Maurice Barrès, who ultimately tired of her (I don't wonder). By way of revenge, Anna de Noailles got Barrès' adolescent son to fall in love with her and gave him an assignation at an hotel, I think by the Rhine. When the youth got there, he found no beautiful woman awaiting him; having been made a fool of, he committed suicide. (I have no sympathy for the young ass – typical French fixation on women.) Naturally, a complete breach followed between the father (a writer of genius, underrated today)[2] and his mistress. They did not meet again for years; when they did eventually, by accident, she said precisely how long it had been since: — — years, — — months, — — minutes. She was a fine poet. I thought the story a pretty example of French bitchery.

Marthe had been a close friend of the Crown Prince William, the Kaiser's son and heir. She never told me, but that it was so I judge from the intimate piece of information she once gave me about the Kaiser. His notorious *Daily Telegraph* interview caused a first-class political crisis in Germany; the Kaiser was left exposed by his Chancellor, the treacherous Bülow (what a lot they were!). The Princess told me that during one whole night of despair, the Kaiser thought of abdicating (others have seen a comparison between him and his young cousin, the Herzog von Windsor). He would have been succeeded by the Crown Prince, of whom the Princess had a more favourable view, as a 'normal' man, not unpopular in England before 1914, as his father was. Was the implication that the Kaiser was not 'normal'? He certainly was psychotic, with his schizophrenia about England, his complex about his uncle, Edward VII; his entourage liberally sprinkled with homosexuals, it was probable enough that William was not operative – though that would not have made him any more normal. We did not go any further into the matter, but I drew my own conclusions.

[2] Barrès' *La Sainte Colline* is a classic that will endure.

Once more, at the time of the suicide of the Kaiser's grandson, who drowned himself in the Rhine, it was evident that the Princess was closely concerned. She knew the young man, the most Anglophile of the family, married to a Guinness, ambivalent between Germany and England, torn in two. Marthe said nothing, except – she had a rhetorical way of speaking and writing – that he had heard the 'call of the Rhine-maidens'. She evidently knew the family well, if not too well.

She was a piece of history herself, with a living sense of history: this was a main part of her charm for me and what doubled the fun of going about with her. Her publishers, Plon (who published the French translation of my *William Shakespeare: A Biography*) occupied the house where Talleyrand lived 'when he became *"Ce coquin, le Prince de Bénévent,"* as Louis XVIII used to put it, mildly.' She was able to tell me that the proper family pronunciation of the name omitted the 'y' – Tallerand, but that Napoleon couldn't manage it: he pronounced it 'ey'. The family pronunciation of Montesquieu – of the poet, Robert de Montesquieu – was Montesquiou. Comte Robert, a baroque comic character – the chief original of the Baron de Charlus – was mad with family pride, descended from Charlemagne; at the nadir of depression one day, he sighed, *'Je ne m'intéresse même dans mon propre nom.'* Once in Paris, the Princess pointed out the large mansion that Napoleon's mother had occupied, Madame Mère, and her strong Corsican accent, *'Pourvou que ça doure' (pourvu que ça dure).* I often think of Marthe when looking at the tiny little wildflower so common upon our walls here in Cornwall, ivy-leaved crowfoot – she told me its romantic French name, *'les ruines de Rome'*.

In return for my tutoring her in Cornish matters, she was my tutor in regard to France – and how much I learnt from her. Under the *ancien régime*, for example, people at Court didn't say 'le roi', they said 'le rey'. Her own taste in literature turned to the rhetorical and romantic: her literary hero was Châteaubriand, of whom she could recite whole paragraphs. This was not an English taste – the English have never liked French rhetoric – but Châteaubriand as a Breton had his appeal for me. I once was reading his description of primeval American forest in the *Mémoires d'Outre Tombe* and of the Ohio, as the train was headed for the Mid-West alongside a great river – and found that it was the Ohio. Marthe could tell me of Châteaubriand's Egeria, Madame Récamier, and her close friendship with Madame de Staël – at Coppet are many mementoes of the friendship. We both appreciated the psychological subtlety and ethical refinement of Mme de la Fayette's *La Princesse de Clèves* – that the crux of it was not the renunciation of love, common enough, but the avowal of renunciation, which brought not satisfaction but further unhappiness to both wife and husband.

Marthe and I had plenty to talk about – her first glimpse of young Marcel Proust, for instance, arriving at a country house of her relations who had invited him: all informally dressed in weekend country clothes, for tennis and sport, and the young Proust uncomfortable in black suit and stiff collar. Oddly enough, I do not recall her *Au Bal avec Marcel Proust*. And it was disappointing that she did not know my chief admiration among women writers, Colette. She told me of her strong Bourguignon accent, and thought there was something *'couvie'* about her – surely quite wrong: was that a touch of feminine jealousy for a woman of transcendent gifts as a writer?

The Princess knew de Gaulle – as she knew Churchill, Asquith and Ramsay Macdonald. When de Gaulle was opposed by the intellectuals, she said, he has 40,000 against him, but 40 million French people with him. I remember a well-known academic saying to me, *'Il parle comme ma grand'mère.'* In France the intellectuals had counted for much more than in other countries; they, and what they thought, were taken seriously. De Gaulle, an intellectual himself, but a far better one, showed how little they really mattered and could be disregarded.

What wonder, when so many of them took their cue from a muddle-headed Franco-German like Sartre, who urged that Soviet Russia was the incarnation of human freedom?! And in another outburst of wisdom argued that, to understand a person, one need know nothing of his origins, upbringing, or early development! Completely contrary to all the findings of modern psychology, of history, or even of common sense. No wonder that de Gaulle was able to manoeuvre these Leftists into the Cave of Adullam where they belonged.

Mauriac was worthy of respect – with a record of resistance to the German Occupation, yet anxious that there should be as little revenge as possible against the collaborators, and, with sympathies liberal and humane, doing his best to serve as interpreter between de Gaulle and the people. All the same, it was rather comic to meet Mauriac at Oxford, on his one visit to England and not knowing a word of English, to note his surprise that there were cultivated people in the island who were well read in his books. He gave the impression of thinking that civilization ended at the Channel. I remember his description, in talk with Graham Greene, of Evelyn Waugh: *'Ce n'est pas un romancier: c'est un fantaisiste.'*

Marthe's letter of May 1960 is full of the fuss of launching the first volume of her autobiography, *La Nymphe Europe* – curious title (on the back of what bull did she think she was being carried off? What Zeus?). 'Childbirth is nothing (Valentine my only experience) compared to publishing a book in Paris: 300 inscriptions to invent straight off, *Radio-diffusion* in one's private home, a snake coming through the window and a little group of passers-by in the street busy talking about you with your own *concierge*, swelling with pride.' Then TV, etc. – those were early days, and of course Marthe enjoyed all the fuss and fume around her: she had a way of creating it (I found it the least bit troublesome), and always had been used to it. Sometimes, the most impatient man in the world, I showed my impatience; she never once resented it – it proved her own magnanimity, 'greatness of mind' – as a lesser person would have done. Perhaps it witnessed to an inner sympathy for, like all intelligent persons, she was highly impatient too, never once with me.

On her way to Cornwall in December 1960 she was meeting our Cornish friends at Burlington House 'in the presence of Charles II. How very Continental the King of England looks! No wonder the Restoration did not last' – a very pertinent remark, for the Stuarts had hardly any English blood at all, and Charles II took after his French grandfather Henri IV and the swarthy Medicis. In Paris she had been at some reception to celebrate St Jean Perse's getting the Nobel Prize: there were the Academicians in a row, Mauriac, Lacretelle, Émile Henriot – that old worthy left over from the Third Republic. 'The secret about St Jean Perse getting the prize is that his poems have been translated into Swedish by no less a person than Mr Hammarskjöld.' Perhaps this was a sufficient explanation, when more important writers – Montherlant or Robert Frost, Trevelyan or S. E. Morison – went unrecognized; the liberal Hammarskjöld was always anxious to be in the van with the intellectuals. The state of Africa, for which he sacrificed his life uselessly, might dispel his illusions today. Not Marthe, who sped on to me the *mot* circulating in Paris: a cable from the Congo government to the United Nations – '*Envoyez troupes fraîches – les dernières étaient délicieuses.*'

The oysters at Prunier's made her suggest an expedition to the Duchy oyster-fishery on the Helford. This was not for me: an Oyster Feast there had been one of the least agreeable chores of my candidature for the Penryn and Falmouth constituency. But Marthe had an appetite corresponding to her zest for life. I once faced a lunch at Tullimaar which provided a feast of fresh lobster from Falmouth, and on top of that, out of Cornish patriotism, a proper Cornish pasty. Professor Simmons, when I took him there to lunch, was fascinated by the spectacle of the little parrot – who had had a book written about him, *Le Perroquet vert* – perched on the Princess's head and horrified to see him descend on the table to be fed from her plate.

Invitations to Paris were regular. 'If I wanted to know the situation there, "Come and see" – as Lytton Strachey answered Margot Oxford, when she inquired if he slept at night with his beard outside or inside the blanket.'

On her way to lunch in my vicinity she had brought Prince Charles Murat (with all that history in the name). I was away a great deal in America or at Oxford, so Marthe and the Prince peeped in at my gate to see 'the enchanted view down the valley to blue sea, framed by *walls* of rhododendron in full bloom'. When she came to Trenarren she indulged a fantasy: from the terrace the sea looked as if enclosed in a chalice, with the optical illusion that it was above the level of the terrace. Now she was bringing to Cornwall the holograph letters Proust had written to the Abbé Mugnier, her confessor and the spiritual guide, if not director, of a large circle in Paris. Much of his literary correspondence he left to her, and she made a book out of it.

Her letters of 1962 and 1963 complain increasingly of my absence and her sense of desertion – I was more and more committed to California, where my Shakespeare campaign was unfolding. Not only his biography with the solution of the problems of the Sonnets (except for the Dark Lady – that was an unexpected bonus for getting the answers right: if they had not been correct, I should never have been able to pinpoint her by dating and corroborative circumstances), but following it up with biographies of Southampton and Marlowe. I was up to my eyes with work, and occasionally sent a close friend as messenger to keep touch. From 45 Quai de Bourbon, 24 May 1962: 'Your friend you made mine by one of your magical tricks, Robert Halsband, was *here* – where you ought to be at least from time to time – yesterday.' He would bring me her news – of her election to the Belgian Royal Academy and festivities beginning with a dinner with Proust's niece. Meanwhile, the French translation of my Shakespeare biography was coming out with her publishers, Plon, and the British Institute had arranged a lecture at the Sorbonne to celebrate the Quatercentenary. At last I was going to pay one of my rare visits to Paris.

'28 April 1964. Here I am at the Hotel Lutétia where I have stayed twice before (in earlier years at the Hotel du Quai Voltaire, where Wilde and the poets of the '90s used to stay). My old friend Princess Bibesco has been as good as her word and drummed up a good deal of interest. Last evening I at last penetrated into her apartment, a couple of floors up in the seventeenth-century house on the Île St Louis, right at the prow of the stone ship islanded in the Seine.

'What a situation! Plenty of windows, the room full of

white light: on one side the church of St Gervais, and further up the Tour St Jacques; on the left the towers and *flèche* of Notre Dame, and the spire of the Sainte Chapelle. The heart of ancient French civilization, still beating: the Seine barges going up and down, the greenery along the quays just coming out. She told me that at the angle of the island just beneath, Baudelaire wrote the famous poem beginning:

Sois sage, O ma douleur,
Et tiens-toi plus tranquille.

'Looking out on the scene from the Princess's apartment, my mind flashed back to the impoverished student circling the Île St Louis and looking up eagerly at those historic houses, the Hotel de Lauzun and the rest, with never a hope of penetrating into them.

'I was enchanted by what she had made of the little apartment, the windows banked with flowers from Tullimaar, camellias, rhododendrons, viburnum scenting the room with its subtle incense. On a glass table in front of the sybaritic, invitatory divan was an arrangement of flowers bespeaking her originality: an array of large scent-bottles, an ox-eyed daffodil in each one, a procession of white nuns bowing their heads to Notre Dame. Charming myth, perhaps in the end, it doesn't have to be true.

'Inside the door was a large portrait of the Abbé Mugnier, confidant of many years, with penetrating grey eyes, seeing through everything. A Boldini pencil sketch for the portrait of the Princess, some sketches by Renoir, a large Boucher overdoor in each room – such were relics put together from the palaces she has inhabited before the rape and destruction of our time. The *perroquet vert* was very much at home, crouching in and out of the stalks of vegetation with a nutshell in beak, playing with Blanche (the *femme de chambre*) and talking to her with almost the affability of a kitten: for the first time I saw his charm.

'On our way out to dinner she told me of her early morning walk along the quays with Ramsay Macdonald back from

the Stresa Conference.[3] Macdonald always liked early walks
– and she was young then. She looked back to see that they
were followed by four detectives, two French, two English.
"They must have thought, What are those two doing so early
in the morning?" Ramsay had a *tendresse* for *grandes dames* –
who can blame him? – but was very proper; while power is
incense to *their* nostrils.

'We arrived at the Hotel Vendôme – the square looking
so different from the shabby, squalid days of the Third
Republic – all cleaned, rich cream stone, balconies properly
gilded. Under the German Occupation a guard every night,
au clair de lune, marched up and solemnly saluted the column,
all on his own. (Rather nice, but all the same, so like the
Germans, a goose-stepping ass.)

'Napoleon III in his youth had stayed in this pleasant old-
fashioned hotel, and we dined in a Second Empire apartment
occupied by an American, more French than the French,
widow of a gifted scientist, Le Comte du Nöuy, who wrote
books on science and religion. A woman of strong prejudices, which jangled throughout the evening as her Middle
Eastern turquoises jangled and jarred. She was very argumen-
tative, in the manner of American women, her arguments all
prejudice, though she didn't recognize it: violently anti-
American, pro-French, Gaullist. When in the United States,
I always put the case for the French and for de Gaulle; and it
is true that Roosevelt and the State Department treated them
with appalling arrogance and ignorance. It was bound to
bank up fires of resentment; all the same I am appalled by the
depth of anti-Americanism everywhere in Paris. So I set
myself to try and put the American case – anyway, to explain
it reasonably. Of course, one is always sustained by contempt
for human fools' incapacity to *think*: their thinking is merely
reacting, usually emotional. They can't think (*pace* A. E.
Housman), and that is all there is to it.'

The Princess remained silent while the argument, if that is
the word for it, raged. I hope I did not disgrace her, for I kept
my temper and plodded patiently on. A fourth at table was a

[3] In 1935, at which neither Macdonald nor Simon warned Mussolini of the
consequences of an attack on Abyssinia.

delightful old boy, Raymond Eschollier, author of a book on Delacroix. He was just as enraged with the Americans as the American expatriate, our hostess: they treated us '*comme des singes, comme des singes,*' he repeated – and the Americans had treated the French tactlessly, after all the most distinguished people in Europe, the heart of European civilization.

In the end we came down to the monopoly of nuclear power which the Americans possessed at the time, and were withholding from others. Of course they would, chimed the two anti-Americans: it is in their own interest to do so, they are just looking after themselves. I allowed that this was so – people have to look after themselves; but *all the same* the extension of nuclear power was contrary to the interest of the human race. I went half way to meet them for, after all, I had not approved of the American frustration of the Anglo-French stand over Suez, nor of the Americans' anti-imperialism directed against the French in Algeria. Was it any improvement to civilization when they went?

My statement of an in-between position, sympathetic to both French and Americans, had its effect; for, at the end of it all, I won an accolade from the American expatriate lady, who thanked me for defending her country. I was relieved not to have disgraced Marthe, for they were friends – and I had given them a good run for their dinner. I was more taken with the distinguished old boy, with his *cordon* of the *Légion d'Honneur.*

'He had had an interesting public career, secretary to Briand, of whom he gave a close-up account. A Gaullist, Eschollier was contemptuous of democracy (that was all right with me): on a tour of the South of France, the European statesman had to put up with being told his business by café proprietors, commercial travellers, small town business men: "If I were in your place I should have done this" – knowing nothing whatever of what they were talking about. (Like ordinary folk about Shakespeare: they don't qualify to hold an opinion.) That had finished democracy for him. How right de Gaulle is to cut the cackle, *discuss* nothing: they haven't anything to discuss with.

'And yet – the opinions of superior people, like those at

that dinner-table at the Hotel Vendôme, are not much better than those of the café proprietors or commercial travellers. The only difference is that, in the end, superior people are amenable to reason, or can at least follow it. Inferior people, i.e. the vast majority, not. What then is best? When a great man like de Gaulle, or Churchill, arises let him lead, but with proper constitutional checks on him, not such as to impede or obstruct the process of government itself. Mass-democracies, in large countries, are apt to be ungovernable, even in their own best interest.

'28 April: I went along to collect the Princess early. While I waited I observed the pretty picture of Louis XIV as a child, seated on cushions, holding a large Madonna-lily as a sceptre, order of the Saint Esprit round his neck, a little crown on head, rosy naked feet exposed. The picture had belonged to SAR the Duc de Berry. I looked again at the dark, cinder-coloured sketch done by Carpeaux at the Château de Ménars in 1870, of Valentin de Riquet, Comtesse de Caraman Chimay, Princess Bibesco. Immensely aristocratic, perfect oval of a face, looking downwards, slightly slanted large eyes, aquiline, ribbed nose, controlled lips – all of a Chinese perfection. The ash colour of it accentuated the sense of that disastrous year. Was it painted in the country while the Germans were invading? Had the family left Paris to take refuge in the country? What was her story? When did she die? It is difficult to think of this perfect creature, in such control of herself and life, as dead – the whole thing radiated the sadness of mortal perfection under the threat of time.

' – Like the Princess, my old friend – and Ramsay Macdonald's, Charlie Londonderry's, Mr Asquith's, Lord Thomson's friend – gallant, courageous, in decay. What fun simply going through the streets of Paris with one who has been part of it all her life! Going along the *quais* we passed one fine eighteenth-century *hôtel*, which had been her mother-in-law's, very grand with entrance court, grille, and screen of one-storey buildings looking on the Seine. She knew the seventeenth-century *hôtel* at the bottom of the Boulevard St Germain, of which I possess an attractive painting at home – now, I gathered, the Roumanian (Communist) Embassy.

'In former days, what wealth power meant! – it must have been a chief incentive, almost as important as power in itself. It is obvious *how* it accrued as an accompaniment of acquaintance with the holders of power – the families of kings' mistresses, their descendants, the favourites of Valois and Bourbons, as of Tudors and Stuarts.' But – until the social revolution of today – power and culture went together: the cultivated minority had the power. Today, no longer: whether it is Soviet Russia, or Britain, or the United States, it is the uncultivated who have the power, whether philistine trade union bosses, or lower-middle-class types like Brezhnev or Carter, Harold Wilson or Callaghan. It is to be expected that increasingly the best people, the really superior, will withdraw from politics, leaving the squalid mess to inferior types. Will that be good for society, let alone culture? The really cultivated will withdraw, as with the aristocracy under the Third Republic (except for the army and diplomacy).

'We lunched with the daughter of the Duc de Grammont, in a grander apartment in the Rue Dominique – but no view like the Princess's. We passed St Clothilde, *très frequentée* – naturally in this aristocratic area, for religion has become largely a matter of class. What a contrast with the eighteenth century! The Revolution taught the aristocracy the error of their ways, at least in that respect – they had opened the way to unbelief among the people, with fatal consequences.' So, with the *Restauration* the upper classes recovered religion; the middle classes now took to unbelief, with predictable consequences. Alfred de Vigny, I think, has some illuminating pages on this dialectic.

'I fell for our hostess – she was natural and unaffected, intelligent as well as charming, like an English girl in spontaneity of manner, but more taste and finesse, perfection of breeding. The same was true of my neighbour at lunch, a young Princesse d'Arembert – half Spanish, her father killed in 1940. I remembered the name in the earlier form, Aremberg, grandees in the Spanish Netherlands, who remained with Spain against William the Silent; one of them cropped up in Ralegh's underhand dealings which brought him to book under James I.[4]

'We lunched under a large dominating Nattier of Madame de Vintimille – regular oval, rose-coloured face (or rouge), hand raised in perpetual conscious charm or expostulation – who had been a mistress of Louis XV and had a son. Beneath sat her descendant, the son of the house. How much alive the *ancien* régime still is in these circles! I have always felt that something irreplaceable went out of French life with the monarchy – as Alfred de Vigny, a congenial spirit, thought. At the same time, a devotee of Proust, I reflected that though the Faubourg Saint Germain was impenetrable to outsiders, once one was inside ways were relaxed and easy, spontaneous as with the English aristocracy, rather English in fact.

'One phrase revealed the anti-Americanism, however: our hostess thought the American influence "poisonous" – in so far as it was demotic and populist, it would be disagreeable, Henry Adams or Henry James would agree. The Princess d'Arembert was more open-minded, less emotional; she said that she could well understand foreigners not liking the French. If she were a foreigner she would not like their pride, their self-sufficiency. I did not accept this, and said that any-one who appreciated French history and culture accepted and admired France for herself, and not for something different. I did not say how much I respected the prudent meanness: France had accepted something like £2000 million from the Americans, one way and another, held on to it and made the most of it. So unlike the easy-going English who had got nothing and squandered their resources on others after the war; while it is impossible to respect the wastefulness and extravagance that runs through the American way of life.

'There, all round the apartment were the evidences of French civilization. I have never seen such a superb writing-desk, except the one made by Riesener at Blenheim: this one more simple, rectangular lines, ormolu decorations on the cupboards, opening perfectly with the dull sigh of fine wood. On the desk the leather writing *cahier* had the *poissons* of the

[4] v. my *Ralegh and the Throckmortons.*

Pompadour; another object the arms of Marie Leczinska.[5] In the blue boudoir within were eighteenth-century books that had belonged to the Comtesse Grefulhe, of Proust's adoration, a chief original of the Duchesse de Guermantes.'

In the evening, after a reception at the British Institute, the Director, Francis Scarfe, took me out for a quiet meal before my lecture at the Sorbonne. 'Richelieu's Chapel loomed immensely down as we went up – a very good audience, the Amphithéatre Richelieu three parts full, mostly youngish research students. In the front row sat the Princess with her friends, our hostess's son, the young Comte de Maigret, the Comtesse de Rougemont, her daughter and friend, a young man of immensely old family, de la Falaise.

'Afterwards the Princess gave a small party in her apartment, and I had some pleasant chat with the Rougemont lady, very Anglophile and sympathetic. She told me that the Pompadour, in addition to being beautiful and intelligent, was a kind woman, always doing people good turns, and not so influential politically as people thought. I said the same was true of Mme de Maintenon: she had been blamed for the Revocation of the Edict of Nantes, but the bishops were responsible, not she.

'29 April: lunch with Francis Scarfe in my favourite Place de l'Odéon. Across the street was the Library Benjamin Franklin – all the windows displaying photographs, books, enlargements of MSS of Robert Frost: an effort to impress Paris with American culture. To what effect? At lunch a Cambridge disciple of Leavis expressed the view that D. H. Lawrence was a writer in the same class as Shakespeare. I did not let this Leavis nonsense pass – what bloody fools, humans: they *never* know. Coming back along the Rue Vaugirard, I popped into the church of St Joseph des Carmes, in the crypt of which the September massacres of French aristocrats took place – the people at their fun.

'30 April. I was to take the Princess out to lunch, and made it early, 12.30, to get in good time to the airport. I shopped in the charming little shops of the Île St Louis: a mass of white flowers, gladioli and tulips, to take the place of the

5 Louis XV's Queen.

extinguished daffodils; chocolate-liqueurs for Blanche; nothing for the *perroquet vert*. The Princess was not ready. I read Maurois' *Le Monde de Marcel Proust*, fascinating photographs, but not one of Robert de Montesquiou. Still no sign of the Princess. I should have banged on her bedroom door, perhaps have entered. Instead, I grew furious – the old impatience, the familiar complex from childhood at being frustrated. I marched loudly up and down the creaking parquet; I banged books. No one appeared; no sign of life. Time was getting on. I went outside on the staircase and rang the bell. Blanche appeared from nowhere: No, the Princess was not ready. I told her that it was now too late, I had to get to the airport.

'I began to go downstairs; if the taxi had not been waiting I should have walked out on her. I know myself well enough: I have done it before, when anyone keeps me waiting too long and I start walking away. But the taxi was there; I went back, and there she was descending the staircase, nearly an hour late. This succeeded in spoiling my departure.

'While waiting, Blanche had brought out a curious picture to occupy me: a Jacobite portrait of Charles I as Jesus Christ, with a mysterious inscription about the head having been executed by Lentulus and sent to the Senate. I was so beside myself with impatience that I never gave the matter a moment's consideration, or I should have seen that the reference had something to do with Speaker Lenthall, the execution reported to Parliament.

'We hurried along to lunch at the Espadon, the Ritz restaurant – imagine having to rush through a delicious turbotin, fresh woodland strawberries and cream! The day was ruined, and I had an appalling programme of lectures before me in England.' But I had seen another side to my *chère Princesse* and she of me – she never once seemed to resent it – but wrote asking to be forgiven.

On my return I got a letter: 'My Professor, Immediate is the answer with you, always' – she had got the message – with more information about the mysterious picture. It had come to her from her aunt, the Comtesse Odon de Montesquiou; it had belonged to the Château de Courtanvaux, which her aunt had restored with Bibesco money. The châ-

teau was the original home of Montluc, author of the military *Commentaires* of which I once (before taxation became penal) possessed an original edition. The picture was known as '*Le Jésus mousquetaire*'. Why?

D'Artagnan of Dumas' *Trois Mousquetaires* was a cadet of the Montesquiou family; the Château d'Artagnan was always the seat of a younger son.

In my time Robert de Montesquiou – Proust's Charlus – owned the *château*, whence he wrote his letters to me – and the sonnet about my emeralds which is quoted in *Au Bal avec Marcel Proust:*

> Vous portiez sur la robe en satin d'un vieux rose
> Des émeraudes dont Shakespeare dit l'attrait . . .

But why 'Jésus Mousquetaire'? Everything at Courtanvaux smells of *mousquetaires* – the famous picture of the real D'Artagnan by Philippe de Champagne being on the wall over one of the seventeen staircases. I stayed at Courtanvaux during my honeymoon . . . The picture may have been propaganda for the Stuarts, showing the King as Christ condemned by his own people! . . . All here remember you and wish to see you revisiting Paris very very soon, and often.

Alas, that I did not.

At the end of Shakespeare Year she was writing to her 'dearest Professor' her pleasure at the letter I had received from de Gaulle, for whom she had a fervent admiration and whom she was to meet at a reception for him at the 'Palais Royal facing the Louvre, Mazarin's abode'. She had been a guest at the Académie française at the introduction of Dr Adenauer as honorary member, 'as also when they received *our* beloved Sir Winston, on a very different occasion'. She had been exchanging greetings with him on his ninetieth birthday, and attending the Toulouse-Lautrec Exhibition at the Petit Palais. This had been 'a revelation: I thought I knew, and discovered, as many others did, that I *knew nothing*. What a genius, and from his early boyhood, poor little monster! He had his divine revenge, thank God.' Then, 'bring me back some camellia-seeds from California,' of which she affected to be jealous for taking me away so much. 'P.S. I saw Anouilh's *Richard III*, and to my surprise I loved it. *Your French text is in the program.*'

My Journal records one or two more outings in Cornwall, always best when we were alone. We were to go down to Falmouth, where an All Souls colleague possessed an exquisite Regency house: cream-washed stucco, with two large niches for statues, with a granite colonnade. One of a number of delicious late Georgian houses built round Falmouth for post-captains or officers retired from the Packet Service. Inside, elegant staircase going up to a cupola, honey-coloured mahogany doors brought back from Honduras, drawing room hung with a lovely landscape wallpaper. O the taste of the eighteenth century, and O the horrors of today, the grounds built up with trivia. The stables retained their distinction and were lived in by an Oxford acquaintance, a discriminating bachelor. The Princess used him for chauffeur – she had brought him to lunch at Trenarren – and for company for her daughter when she was away in Paris. The daughter, Princess Ghika, accompanied, submissive, charming, *distraite*, and her taciturn soldier son.

'I drove down the narrow drive of close-planted Cornish elms I used to walk down with my cousins, as children, to Swanpool: the house then belonged to cousins of Charles Henderson. We all infiltrated into the coach-house, which our bachelor friend had made charming: good taste and good china, Sèvres and Chelsea, which he inherited. He keeps house and cooks for himself. He served drinks, but was in no hurry to serve lunch, after twenty minutes in his pretty garden – a fine viburnum, cherry-coloured and rose-red hydrangeas, plenty of pears on the wall.

'The Princess and I chatted together on the sofa, mainly about my little de Gaulle campaign in *The Times* (which much displeased Lord Gladwyn, with whom I had wrangled through lunch with Leola Epstein at Claridge's). With no appearance of, or move towards, lunch, the Princess began to play up. "I am feeling faint . . . I am ill. I must have lunch." She commanded our host to begin lunch at once. I was amused: quite right, it revealed the impatience superior persons feel towards ordinary mortals – a feeling I shared – and perhaps the latent tartar always held in restraint with me. She was in a rage – just like me at being kept waiting in her Paris apartment. Lunch began in an atmosphere of considerable *gêne*, while I worked away papering over the cracks and bringing things round. All went well and lunch ended fairly happily; a crack had, however, appeared.

'After lunch our host took me out into the garden where I learned a few things, more in the car going back with the Princess. She had found a rich wife for him in Italy: he had found her impossible. The lady was a French Singer, who had made a mess of life and reputation, been left by two husbands, and would welcome rehabilitation by a respectable marriage. Very rich, with a villa in Florence and a house in Paris. When he saw the set-up, he decided against. I said, Wouldn't she do for me? Marthe replied, "Too low-brow. Too unintelligent. You would be bored." Then, meditatively but conclusively, "Tous les Singers sont un peu fous."

'This led us on to another of the French Singers, whom we both knew and had taken the measure of – I one weekend at that paradisal house, Compton Beauchamp, under the escarpment of the Berkshire Downs, moat, water-garden, formal forecourt and all. O to live in it – one of the Astor boys subsequently did. Marthe repeated her story of the Singer lady's jealousy at her dancing at a ball with someone she passionately wanted to marry. Off the rebound she had married a cousin of Winston's, a sprig of Blenheim.

'Many stories were told of her – of the handsome young Italian declaring his passion for her, and her saying "Prove it", pointing to the shadowy moat in the twilight. He dived in – it was empty – and the fool smashed his handsome profile against stone. This was the woman who, on the excuse of being in mourning for her husband, killed in the 1914 war, had herself presented at the English Court in black plumes and train, against a forest of white.

'This was the woman who tried to get me to break a public engagement at Bristol to stop a weekend with her to meet Duff Cooper – and would hold up the telephone line to Paris to discuss a chess-game with Duff when ambassador. She did make me break a Codrington rule at All Souls to lend her the *Memoirs* of the Duc Decazes, her great-grandfather and Louis XVIII's boyfriend. People are immoral about books – no sign of her returning it: in the end I made her. With her wonderful taste, exotic and exquisite, she was a full-bloomed specimen of French bitchery. She got no further with me: I expect she found me rather *naïf* and innocent.'

One last Cornish trip, from my Journal: to beautiful Croan, near Wadebridge, a William and Mary manor-house which the taste of an Air-Marshal, Sir John Tremayne, had made still more so. The square farmyard beside the house he had turned into a formal court, rather Italianate, with urns and summer houses. Within, the house was haunted by a Queen Anne lady, Madam Damaris, whose portrait hung in the drawing room; tapestry furniture, *petit-point*, 'the house smells like Hatfield', as one of the Cecils said – that nostalgic fragrance of polished wood, beeswax and wood-smoke which David Cecil describes in his book about Hatfield.

The Princess was working on three books simultaneously, now that she had a full-time secretary: this lady was born a Crèvecoeur, of the 'American Farmer's' family and Sir John had been all the way to Perran-ar-worthal to bring them to lunch. While the joys of family life occupied the conversation, I occupied the French lady, and at intervals observed the golden charm of this Cornish house: three rooms *en suite* all looking across the small forecourt and long lawns to the gate which John had made. I had once observed a striking colour arrangement outside: beds of gold montbretia between the silver boles of the beeches.

'The Princess, troublesome as usual and making a practice of asking for a flower, asked for a magnolia bloom, which necessitated John's going off for long mechanical cutters to get up so high. A trouble – but with his refinement of courtesy he managed with some difficulty to reach two, another for "the pretty French lady", as he had called her in introducing his grandchildren. The demonstration of aristocratic manners was not lost on me; but I was not persuaded by it.

'I drove the ladies back to their lair, since John had brought them. Enough. As we drove into Truro the Princess – another test – wanted to be taken off the road to Alan Bennett's new antique shop. She did not get out of the car: he was summoned to the presence. I took the opportunity for a quick five-minute look round inside. Intensely concentrated on the job, I was subconsciously aware that the unattached widow had taken her opportunity to trail round at my heels – a thing I detest – and corner me. Alone with her on the sofa I had half-registered her pointed inquiries about my house – the Princess must have told her that I was well off and unattached. Having to leave in two or three days, I felt safe and took no notice. Now was the moment: with only five minutes to decide on two Victorian footstools (like those which Nancy Astor had snatched before my eyes), consider a *chaise longue* and exclude a pair of Staffordshire china baskets, the French lady was upon me, forced to call attention to herself. I took no notice of the interruption.

'Going back to the car with my catches, a lot of feminine fuss was made about taking them in and where to stow them away, choc-a-bloc with the ladies' traps. "He travels furthest who travels alone" had always been my motto. Detesting feminine fuss, I crossly stowed one footstool under my feet, rather in the way of the driving, and was tucking the other away at the back of all the impedimenta. But no – the pretty French lady held up the proceedings – she wanted to inspect it: another endeavour to draw attention to herself. By now irritated and impatient – very far from a chivalrous Sir John – I drove them fast home with few words. On taking my leave the French lady gave me only the tips of her fingers for a handshake: she had been shown where she got off, and that evening it gave me, in spite of a little self-reproach, not a few laughs.'

In her last years Marthe had a deal of ill-health – shingles,

which went on for months and months: a nervous ail-
ment, perhaps from overwork and certainly overworry, the
family, family finances, the strain of keeping up Tullimaar.
Gallant old war-horse, she said to me only once, with no
accent of complaint, that it fell to her to be the pillar to
uphold everything and keep it going. She poured out her
books, most of them *livres de circonstance* to make money –
about Churchill, about Queen Elizabeth II – while working
at her serious book, the second volume of *La Nymphe Europe*.
I did what little I could to help, in getting books, small
literary commissions.

In 1972 she was sending me her *Le Confesseur et les Poètes*,
the correspondence of the Abbé Mugnier with commentary.
She had sent her *Échanges avec Claudel* to the French Institute
at Oxford inscribed as a present from me: I don't think she
knew that I was allergic to Claudel as a writer. He repre-
sented what I disliked in French literature – rhetoric, intellectual arrogance, Ultramontane intolerance; his bullying of
Gide was intolerable – a kind of French Belloc (but then
Belloc *was* French). However, to be just, I had been unexpectedly impressed when young by Claudel's *L'Annonce faite
à Marie* at the Odéon.

Now she was writing about 'Le Prince de Galles, le Roi, le
Duc de Windsor'. The Princess had a stalwart, and genuine,
admiration for the royal family in Britain: not just snobbery
or flunkeyism – she was above that – she appreciated what a
tremendous factor the monarchy was in ensuring social sta-
bility, all the more by contrast with the political instability
of France she had lived through. (Miraculously, De Gaulle
had remedied that; and, happily, she did not live to see Britain shabbily, unnecessarily, weakened.)

'May I ask you for one more favour, having received so
many from you?' Would I receive a nephew of hers now at
Oxford, at my old college, Christ Church: Prince Constantin
de Brancovan, 'very dear to me and very near' – another
historic name from the old Eastern Empire. 'Impatiently
waiting for more news of you, I remain, my dearest Professor, your obedient Pupil, regardless of absence and age.'

Her next, from the Île St Louis, May Day 1973, begins:

'Time has no effect on my admiration and affection for you.'
She had missed so much a visit from me last year and hers to
me 'and *that* garden with the sea as drapery, above in the
sky.' She was failing, but lived long enough to hear of my
discovery of the Dark Lady, and asked for my *Shakespeare the
Man* which announced it. 'If you come to lecture in *La Sorbonne* you will find me an hermit in my island until 14 July.'
She went each year for treatment at the baths at Bagnolles sur
l'Orme, and would be in the 'Delectable Duchy' in September. 'I am writing you on *le jour du Muguet, porte-bonheur*, and
enclose one for you.' There is the little fragment of lily-of-
the-valley sticking to the letter still – touching remembrance
from one soon to die.

Fortunately I was able to pay her a visit that summer –

> the memory green of your visit to Tullimaar is with me,
> for ever, every problem solved . . . It was heaven to see
> you, in your Delectable Duchy which has the honour to
> have you as its Poet-Son, and Master as well. Hoping to
> see you in Paris and to hear you again at the Sorbonne,
> I dream of you in your Cornish garden where the sea is
> drapery to the lawn. I say *à toujours, à jamais.*

It was her last letter to me. I see her now, very pale and
frail, having been placed on the sofa in the drawing-room, by
the chimney-piece with the Cousteau horses prancing, afternoon sun filling the room from the western window looking
down the drive. Her voice – it is impossible to recapture it –
low and a little masculine, with a curious crackle in it, giving
it a character all its own.

Gone the old vigour, yet the zest for knowledge, the intelligence, still lit up the dark eyes in the perfect ivory skin. She
never quite lost the dark, black lustre of her hair, ringlets a
little after the fashion of the Regency. I never knew her in the
days of her great beauty – she once, again only once, said a
brave, stoical word about that, the futility of women regretting vanished beauty.

Looking back over this friendship, I have now a sense of
my own inadequacy. I had done my best – or, not quite – my

best within my willed and deliberate limitations. The two great emotional experiences of my life had both come to grief and suffering. Henceforth I was immune. Human beings were always inadequate (hence religion), and my expectations of them were always too high. The Princess was one of those rare beings who do not fail; I have now the obscure and humble feeling that I may have failed her. Could it be expressed in the one word – love? The thought then never occurred to me – I should have thought it presumptuous on my part. There was the difference of age, every sort of difference – and yet, in spite of that, a deeper kinship of spirit than I realized. I regarded her with admiration, deference, a fascination that was partly historic and partly personal. But I did not love her; it never occurred to me that possibly she might have loved me.

All in all, she was the most remarkable woman I have ever known.

8

An Evening with Edmund Wilson

I confess that I have some difficulty in doing justice to Edmund Wilson: he was not one of my favourite American writers. I could construct a list of a score of them – from my favourite in early years, Nathaniel Hawthorne, through Walt Whitman, Henry James, Henry Adams, Santayana, going on to Edith Wharton, Willa Cather, Flannery O'Connor – but Edmund Wilson would not be among them. (My unfavourite American writers would be no less revealing – Dreiser, Carl Sandburg, Sinclair Lewis, Steinbeck and such.)

The fact that Edmund Wilson was something of a mentor to the fashionable Left intellectuals, at Oxford and elsewhere, did not recommend him to me: I had ceased to be a Left intellectual myself in my thirties, with the oncoming of the second German war. Wilson's ambivalence about England was obvious, a kind of quirk – he was full of quirks – rather than a fully-fledged complex. I did not much care for his report on England after all the strain and suffering of the war, 1939 to 1945;[1] actually rationing of food and fuel went on for years. The British people were underfed for some years after the war – not until 1953, coronation year, did things take an upward turn.

Hence, in this perspective, I was still more unfavourably impressed by a remark of his that the high estimation of English literature reflected Britain's ascendancy; with her decline perhaps her literature might be less highly regarded. May be. No doubt about the decline, but literary decline does

[1] In *Europe Without Baedeker*.

not necessarily accompany political decline. France, at the apogee of her power under Napoleon, was rather bare of good literature, while the squalid Third Republic witnessed a marvellous explosion of genius in the creative arts, not only literature, but music and painting.

Wilson's judgment seemed to reflect something of *Schadenfreude*, and his was not an historical mind for all that his best work in literary criticism was historical rather than analytical. The best thing about him was his passion for literature, his ever-questing mind for new work; his unfailing nose for anything good. His literary flair was remarkable, his judgment good in this field, certainly not in the field of politics.

He held on for too long to the old American liberal tradition and democratic illusions – he thought T. S. Eliot's political conservatism 'twaddle', though it stands up to the subsequent tests contemporary society has posed far better than Wilson's Jeffersonian liberalism. He later added a flavouring of Marx and Communist sympathies – even defending Stalin, explaining away the purges, massacres of the faithful; but ended up disillusioned, and confessing himself 'alienated' from all the United States stood for.

Literary people are not very good judges of politics, and Wilson was no exception. No, to do him justice we must judge him on his literary showing, rather than his views on politics or history.

As a writer he was singularly uncreative – his ventures into fiction, *I Thought of Daisy* and *Memoirs of Hecate County*, are really autobiographical. A great egoist, he could never transcend himself. He treasured up every scrap concerning himself, scraping the bottom of the barrel to publish adolescent notes and jottings hardly worthy of print in, for example, *A Prelude: Landscapes, Characters, Conversations from the Earlier Years of My Life*.

On the other hand, his literary curiosity was insatiable – though very odd that he should never have read *Don Quixote*, one of the supreme imaginative experiences of the world. His range of reading was immense, his appetite exceptional, the zest and intellectual vivacity admirable.

No work of his, in my opinion, came up to his first book

of criticism, *Axel's Castle*, which had unity of theme, the then Modern movement in literature: Yeats, Valéry, Eliot, Proust, Joyce, Gertrude Stein (for what she counted), Axel, i.e. Villiers de L'Isle Adam, and Rimbaud. The book was dedicated to Wilson's remarkable preceptor at Princeton, Christian Gauss; the dedication proclaimed what was to be the signature tune of Wilson's best work and his statement of 'what literary criticism ought to be – a history of man's ideas and imaginings in the setting of the conditions which have shaped them'.

I am much more sympathetic to that than to the verbal analytics of I. A. Richards or Empson, or the want of proportion and common sense which accompanied the paranoia of Leavis, the acutely personal bias disguised as objective critical discipline, though the disguise was transparent to anyone with any psychological perception. In other words, Wilson's interest was in the history of literature, the works themselves and the personalities of the writers – something more real than to suppose that you need know nothing of that out of which the work of literature sprang, in the mind and experience of the writer or the conditions in which he wrote.

For all that, Wilson was not interested in history as a branch of literature – in that very characteristic of literary critics in general, and an important loss to them. He had read Gibbon and Macaulay with pleasure, but as literary art only. It is curious that there is not a single mention in his *Letters* of Samuel Eliot Morison, a near neighbour when Wilson went to live in Cambridge (Mass.); I suspect that they did not much approve of each other. Prescott is never mentioned, and Parkman only once indirectly via an essay about him by the literary critic Van Wyck Brooks. And it is amazing that the universal reader had not read that most distinguished and beautiful work of American historical writing, Henry Adams' *Mont St Michel and Chartres*.

One consequence of this was that Edmund Wilson tended to follow the bias of a Leftist historian such as Charles A. Beard – in spite of Morison's devastating exposure of him in

'The Shaving of a Beard'[2] – or a crackpot like Harry Elmer Barnes, who appeared to think that at Pearl Harbour the Americans attacked the Japanese. Wilson subscribed to their absurd interpretation of the event. After this one is the less surprised at his statement that in many ways the United States was closer to other countries than to England. An historian like Morison, Nevins or Mattingly would know that this was nonsense. With Wilson it was his irremediable Scotch-Irish prejudice.

Ambivalence was similarly characteristic of his attitude towards my friend, T. S. Eliot. I do not suppose that his attitude was so simple as that of Carl Sandburg, whom I once heard denounce Henry James for not being sure whether he was a citizen of the United States or a subject of a British monarch. Wilson's judgment was too good to set any store by a Sandburg, whose vast self-identificatory book on Lincoln, Wilson said, was the worst thing that happened to him since Booth shot him.

Wilson's essay on the early (i.e. American) Eliot in *Axel's Castle* is penetrating and just; but, as time went on and Eliot's experience deepened, his thought matured, Wilson became querulous. By 1933 he was writing:

> I heard Eliot read his poems the other night. He did them extremely well – contrary to my expectation. He is an actor and really put on a better show than Shaw . . . He gives you the creeps a little at first because he is such a completely artificial, or rather self-invented, character – speaking English with a most careful English accent as if it were a foreign language which he had learned extremely well.

Virginia Woolf noticed that Eliot was careful also to pronounce French precisely and correctly.

Why? The answer is simple: Eliot was a perfectionist. A master of language, he wished to present a language at its best, in the best way he could. André Maurois noted something psychologically perceptive, that the way a man reads his

[2] In *By Land and By Sea.*

work aloud reveals his ideal conception of himself, the self he has at heart and would be.

By 1957 Wilson was writing to Van Wyck Brooks, 'There is a scoundrel and actor in Eliot. It was the young scoundrel who wrote the good poetry and it is now the old scoundrel who is putting on the public performance.' This is the kind of clever nonsense that intellectuals like to write. Anyone less of a scoundrel than Eliot would be hard to imagine: he was always fastidious, if one wanted to be critical one could say – inclined to be priggish, in the end a good deal of a saint. Still more absurd than Wilson was the view of another literary patriot; he was writing to Van Wyck Brooks, 'I know that you regard him as a more sinister figure.'

Wilson could not understand why in Britain people were so critical of his Irish friend, Cyril Connolly. The answer again is simple: Connolly never fulfilled the talents he had, the 'promise' of *Enemies of Promise*, in any constructive work. Connolly hadn't the character to achieve it; so he became a commentator on other men's work – like Wilson himself. Connolly was a much better stylist; like the Irish (Eugene O'Neill, Scott Fitzgerald, Flannery O'Connor) Connolly had a specific gift for language – there was in him an aborted poet.

The poet, John Hall Wheelock, old-fashioned but authentic, used to make a comparable criticism of Edmund Wilson to me: 'What does it all add up to?' Perhaps we may confront that searching question at the end. Wheelock would compare Wilson unfavourably with Brooks, who – in spite of the disadvantage of having endured years of madness – did in the end accomplish a large constructive work with his successive volumes on the history of American literature.

Altogether, it may be seen that I was rather critical of Wilson, though that was of no importance since I did not enter into his fields of literary criticism or literary journalism. And he would be given no unduly favourable report of me by his informants among the Left intellectuals in Britain. However, when he turned up as a guest of one of them at All Souls – in those days everybody turned up there, sooner or later – I happened to be at the head of the table and did my best to make his evening agreeable. I was able to assure him that he had an elect following in England; this was evidently not disagreeable to him and rather turned his flank.

We got on quite well; he found that I was, though an historian, equally interested in literature, and I promised to send him my *Poems Partly American*, if only because very few English poets had ever responded to the American landscape. When he got back safely to Cape Cod, he wrote to me that he had enjoyed the poems: 'You are good on the American landscape, for which many Europeans have little real feeling.' Then came the reservation. 'But you do run true to type in speaking of "the loneliness that is America". It is natural for a European to get this impression, but, except in the great wilds and waste places, America does not seem lonely to us – especially at East Hampton!' I had experienced this feeling of aching loneliness, not only up in the mountains of California, out on the prairie of Illinois or Nebraska, going through the forests of North Carolina, the deserts of New Mexico and Arizona, but even in Central Park, New York. As for East Hampton, about which I had written a poem (later reprinted for the Music Festival there), there was the loneliness the early settlers had looked out upon in the waste of waters, the ocean that had once broken in and surrounded my friend's house on the coast.

Wilson went on:

> The relation between the people and the country is different from what it is in the closely packed and cultivated countries of Europe. I now live most of the time near the tip of Cape Cod or in a village in the Adirondack foothills, and this seems to me far more normal than living in American cities where I have a good many friends. The difference in this relationship from the European one lies in one's feeling that in order to function – to think, to realize oneself, to do solid work, etc. – one has to *pit oneself against* the country, which at the same time, however, will give one support.

This is very different from England, and – alas! – in both

terms. One does not have to pit oneself against nature, as in America – but one gets precious little support from the country, especially from democratic, popular society, i.e. a society without standards, 'without pride of ancestry, or hope of posterity', in Disraeli's phrase.

Wilson concluded in friendly wise: 'If you should ever be in this part of the world, I hope you will let me return your All Souls dinner.'

So, on my next visit to Boston, in October 1960, I decided to take him at his word, pay him a visit and satisfy my curiosity as to what he was like at home. I find some account of the experience in my Journals.

'As bidden I telephoned Edmund Wilson, and was asked to wait a minute, while I heard the inevitable typewriter clicking. Wilson was hard at it earning his living. The German voice of his young wife – the third (?) – resounded, then the rich, rounded Irish voice came back: would I come to tea at 5.30? I taxied out to 12 Hilliard Street, an ugly house in an old-fashioned street next to famous Brattle Street. In the pleasant lighted room were the sage, his wife and her contemporary, young Mrs Arthur Schlesinger.

'Edmund Wilson sat in his armchair, a generation older, pot-bellied like a Buddha, sipping glass after glass of whiskey. An extraordinary expression of face: inquiring upraised eyebrows, innocent open glassy eyes, marked downward droop of corners of the mouth, querulous, exceedingly irritable. The face of a crotchety, pernickety man, not unkindly. He began bored at the thought of me: I felt for him, and gradually got him completely round. (He *was* innocent, indeed, transparent: no subtlety.)

'We had a fascinating conversation, more or less ignoring the women, who had their own talk. The sage had a low fender of books by him, Angus Wilson's *Zola* uppermost.

'He talked about Compton Mackenzie, whom he wanted to write about – thinks him much underestimated, out of line with London so dominant in our literary affairs. True enough, but less so than had been, I said. He expressed himself interested in the minorities in Britain as opposed to the

English. He has always felt ambivalently about the English, in fact hostile, himself being Scotch-Irish.

'I teased him about this – said that, in spite of his being rather anti-English, there was much admiration for him in England – the English didn't mind. A curiously impervious man, he couldn't resist this line after a little reiteration. He began to melt, in so far as he is capable of melting – 'wilting' would better describe it, or 'blinking'.

'At any rate he warmed, and was complimentary about Cornwall, had been there once and thought it beautiful. Wouldn't I have a whiskey?'

(I declined whiskey, which I abominate; what I longed for was a cup of tea, to which I had been bidden. This was not offered. The ladies were engaged in ardent talk. In England they'd have been making tea.)

'Wilson now said that he wasn't exactly anti-English, but had a love-hate complex, induced by those of his relations who were Oh, so English. And then there were the English Abroad, their official representatives who were – I supplied the word "insufferable", which he grasped eagerly.

'I said that I was completely unEnglish myself, hadn't a drop of English blood, 100 per cent Cornish. But what was wrong with the English? Much as the Celtic minorities complain about them, they like the English better than they do each other. The Scotch and the Irish, for example – look at Ulster! The Cornish and the Irish miners fought like cat and dog in Wisconsin and Montana.[3] The Welsh didn't like the Irish. He was surprised at this last, but agreed that they preferred the English to each other.

'He came back to Compton Mackenzie and these minority themes in his work, and recommended to me the volumes about Greece and his First War experiences. I hadn't read these, or much of Mackenzie, not being much of a novel-reader. But he had been enamoured of Cornwall, blissful as it was in the pre-1914 days; I had gone up to Oxford properly equipped with a reading of *Sinister Street*, and had met Mackenzie once or twice, visited him at his hide-out near Oxford, celebrated in one of the best of his novels, *Guy and Pauline*.

[3] cf. *The Cornish in America.*

'In an intermission with the ladies we talked about the election. This was, like most of Harvard, a Kennedy household – he is "Jack Kennedy" here, a former pupil. I happened to mention old Joe Kennedy's American performance as ambassador in London in 1940, writing an open dispatch to say that we were defeated and had better make the best terms we could. At that – apparently Wilson didn't know the disgraceful episode (I had heard all about it from Winthrop Aldrich) – Wilson's nose wrinkled up, Irish fashion, just like Connolly's, and he tittered. It was an unpleasant surprise: I saw the ineradicable irresponsibility, the malice of the intellectual. I said that it wasn't amusing in 1940, when Britain needed every ounce of its will-power to survive. He said, "No, it wasn't amusing then. But I can't help laffin'."

'That placed him for me. No real judgment about politics, and therefore history. What is good about him is his passion for literature.

'He went on to talk about the Iroquois, and the immense complexity of Indian languages, of which there were something like eight hundred in the New World, with curious criss-cross similarities, likenesses of some Iroquois words to Mayan. I think he said he knew some sixty of them. (Did he expect me to believe that, or was it the whiskey working?) I told him about my Cornish friend, Donald Rickard's acquaintance with Indian life on the last frontier, in northern Ontario, in case he would be any use to Wilson. But, no, he had finished with the subject, and was on with the next.

'That is how he writes his books evidently – gets a craze for a subject, rushes into it, gets a smattering of it, writes a book or an essay or two, and passes on. Something of a sciolist.

'As with his *Dead Sea Scrolls*. He learnt a little Hebrew – brave of him – sploshed into a fearfully technical subject knowing little about it – and with the usual conceit quickly produced a book to catch the market. He is really a highbrow literary journalist – just like so much of the writing that pours out into the literary journals and gains ephemeral attention, tomorrow forgotten: all the Higher Journalism.

'He didn't relish my saying of Isaiah Berlin that, with his

linguistic gifts and Russian background, he should by this time have given us a big solid history of Russian Social Thought, something weighty and significant – indeed three or four of such books.

'He didn't agree (I expect the thought held some reflection upon himself): had I read Isaiah's thing on Moses Hess?

'I had – just a lecture, like his lecture on Inevitability in History, or his essay *The Hare and the Fox*. Mere lectures and essays, nothing of substance.

'Wilson proceeded to be rather illuminating about Berlin: how the core of his mind was essentially, deeply Jewish, with the characteristic passion for justice; how surprised people had been in Israel at his fluency in the language (Isaiah is fluent and inaudible in all languages); that his people had been very important in some movement towards greater strictness in Russian Judaism.

'He, Edmund Wilson, had "gone into the subject". I said that I agreed rather with Isaiah's English empiricism philosophically, his middle-of-the-road position, careful not to commit himself. Wilson didn't much like that, the old ingrained bias peeped out.

'Wouldn't I have some whiskey? (No, I would not have some whiskey; though, a drug-addict, I had given up all hope of tea.)

'*A propos* of history, one could never find out the truth about things anyway. He had "gone into that" too, had been writing history, etc. Now take Churchill's History – he didn't think much of it. He wouldn't, I reflected – and also he wouldn't know. This is a rather A. J. P. Taylor view, I noted – same irresponsibility, same facile dismissal of something that needs thinking about.

'I said I didn't agree. If you took Churchill's life of Marlborough, for example, it was an important contribution to history. The greatest of English soldiers had always been traduced and this tradition fixed by Macaulay: Churchill had corrected all this, and he was right.

'Wilson said he took his view of Marlborough from Swift.

'I said that there was nothing more biased, partisan and

unreliable. I greatly admired Swift as a writer – and had meant to write a biography of him[4] – but not as an historian. Think of his defaming Duchess Sarah by hinting that she was Godolphin's mistress, when everybody knew that Sarah was a prude: nothing but friendship among the three of them. Fancy the obtuseness of Swift, not much more than an unbeliever, the author of the sceptical *Tale of a Tub*, surprised that he wasn't made a bishop! The author of "The Windsor Prophecy", those terrible verses on the Duchess of Somerset, the Queen's friend, implying that she had murdered her husband – and expecting preferment from the Queen! It really was extraordinarily obtuse of him, apart from the irresponsibility as to historical fact – and then hoping to be made Historiographer Royal!

'Wilson was quite excited by all this on my part, at last surfacing. He said that this attitude was just like the English – a very feeble reply – and that Swift was speaking for the Irish minority. (But in these matters he wasn't: it all sprang, understandably, out of furious personal resentment.) I left it at that – perhaps Wilson had had too many whiskies by this time, at least four or five.

'I was getting anxious for a taxi, having promised to be back at my hotel by 7.30 or 8 p.m. Outside there was a downpour. A certain agitation seized on us both: Wilson was plainly fascinated and frightfully anxious to keep me.

' "Won't you stay on for a simple dinner?" he said hospitably, urgent, and to his wife a bit apologetically, "You've got something?" It was rather touching and pathetic, he so much wanted to go on with the conversation. "This is *most* interesting,' he said, all stirred up.

'I was determined to go, to leave at the best possible moment, when he most wanted to go on – having seen, as he had not before or been told by his Oxford informants, what I really was like to talk to. As for Edmund Wilson, I had done my best, and had not liked him – any more than Eliot had. However, I had seen right into him: a smatterer, who had "gone into all this" and that.

'What I respect is the unquestioned vivacity of mind, his

4 Many years later I wrote *Jonathan Swift: Major Prophet*.

genuine love of literature. Even here his judgments are erratic: Mrs Schlesinger much admired Anthony Powell's sense of style. Wilson flatly contradicted her: he had "no style at a'al" (in Irish brogue). Actually Powell's command of words is one of the best things about him; I don't care for his later novels (one of the Left intellectuals finds them "devitalizing"); but he *is* a stylist.

'I saw something of what the women had to put up with from grandpa. He had told me that he much admired Mary McCarthy, but found her intolerable; I dare say she could say the same of him. And so they parted – as the Athanasian creed might, but does not, say: "And yet there are not two Intolerables, but One Intolerable."

'Edmund Wilson is a pernickety, contradictious and rather pathetic ageing man. Isaiah, who had (according to Wilson), "run down" a young Fellow of St Antony's to him, may have given Wilson a picture of me such that the reality came as rather a surprise. I dare say all the intellectuals had given him a pretty unfavourable report. It was comic – the reluctant invitation that morning to tea at 5.30, no tea – and then the urgent desire to keep me on to dinner.

'But I really had had enough; I had satisfied my curiosity. I passed a more pleasurable, if less intellectual, evening at the hotel.'

However, I think that he never forgave me for refusing his pressing invitation and insisting on leaving. He had expressed an interest in Cornwall and the Cornish, among other minorities under the heel of the English; but when I sent him *Tudor Cornwall* there was no reaction from him. Perhaps it was too historical for him.

What then does Edmund Wilson add up to (in John Hall Wheelock's phrase)?

I think that my ultimate judgment of both the writer and the man must be more favourable than my impression of him that evening. He was a gentleman, not a cad; he was warm-hearted and had kindly impulses, on the whole not malicious.

As a writer, his best critical work, *Axel's Castle*, has permanent value. So also has his conspectus of American literature, *The Shock of Recognition*: anyone who wants a chronological guide to American writing can hardly do better than read that – less biased than Van Wyck Brooks after all. I do not wish to underrate *To the Finland Station*. It would seem that Wilson had read Gabriel Monod's *Renan, Taine, Michelet*, though he does not say so; he has a sensible judgment of Taine, less good on Renan – I expect he found him too sceptical. He has too much respect for Marx – he was a Marxist at the time – anyone would think that Marx was the Law and the Prophets. The deification of Marx is one of the most curious phenomena of the twentieth century; John Stuart Mill would make a better mentor, with his emphasis on the freedom of the individual, with a reasoned sympathy for the working classes, co-operation and a democratic socialism.

At the end, Edmund Wilson was as disillusioned at the way his earlier hopes had been betrayed as the rest of us. It was found that for some years he had not kept up with his taxes; the total sum demanded came as a crushing blow. To help to raise some cash and recoup himself – American taxation is nothing like so confiscatory, so killing to all incentive, as in Britain – he wrote a little book describing his predicament. He also described himself as totally 'alienated' from a society which imposed such burdens.

Here I am wholly sympathetic with him. All his life he had had to work hard to earn a living; while in America, as now in Britain, there are many people who have lived into the second generation on social security and never done a day's work.

So much for his earlier democratic illusions; it seems that T. S. Eliot was right about such a society after all.

9

With Beaverbrook in Canada

Beaverbrook, I confess, I was originally prejudiced against. The matter needs no explaining. After all, I was a straight Labour Party man, loyal to Attlee, Bevin and Herbert Morrison. I was not one of the extreme Leftists patronized by Beaverbrook, supported by him or kept by his newspapers – Aneurin Bevan, Michael Foot, Tom Driberg, for whom I had no respect. When Germany was the overwhelming threat in Europe, to Britain as well as to others, I regarded his preaching of Isolationism as dangerous and ignorant.

It was impossible for Britain to isolate herself from what was happening across the Channel a score of miles away. Ostrich-like Isolation would mean that we should wake up and find the whole Continent under the heel of Hitler – as it very nearly was – and our turn would come next. The only security was in a Grand Alliance, the policy that had been the sheet-anchor of Britain's safety and success in the past three centuries. Beaverbrook was too ignorant of history to know that. In so far as millions read his newspapers they were misled – as he came out with his announcement at New year 1939: 'There will be no war this year.' Good for newspaper circulation, no doubt, but irresponsible.

On the other hand, a straight Labour man, I was strongly in favour of the British Empire; I was not an anti-Imperialist like those on the Left who ate out of Beaverbrook's hand. At All Souls I had been very close to the Empire group who believed in the trusteeship of native races, gradually leading them along the way to better things. A great colonial administrator like Lugard, whom I met there, set a model to be proud of over the vast area of Nigeria, where a man could walk in safety unarmed two or three hundred miles. Today, the blacks in Africa have massacred and murdered each other in hundreds of thousands.

The British Empire meant that under its sovereignty, justice for all and the well-being of its subjects were the prime considerations in governing them – not corruption from top to bottom, and barbarous military dictatorship as the prevailing blue-print of African government. The ideal was to lead these peoples gradually, educate them in government as in medicine, health and welfare services – the take-over would have taken decades and have been given a better chance to take root with more time and at a slower pace.

Not the least of the charges against the Germans for what they have been responsible for in the wreck of this century is that they speeded up the processes of history, advanced the date of a nuclear world, apart from everything else for which we have to thank them.

The British Empire has largely been brought to an end: has this been much benefit to the peoples concerned?

Thus, though I regarded Beaverbrook's campaign for Empire Free Trade as the nonsense it was, utterly out of the question of practical possibility, I was not averse to his Empire enthusiasm, as his Leftist employees were.

I could have been one of his employees myself. Towards the end of the war his right-hand man, George Malcolm Thomson, made me an offer to become a reviewer-in-chief – such as I suppose Arnold Bennett had been – with my reviews syndicated throughout the Beaverbrook Press. I never considered it for a moment – any more than my friend Douglas Jay did, when they made him an offer to write on economic affairs. We were not irresponsible Leftists: we had principles.

I was a supporter of Ernest Bevin, a truly great man, the dominant figure in the Labour Movement after the catastrophe of 1931. Bevin detested Beaverbrook, and regarded him with the greatest distrust. Everyone agrees that – whatever his good qualities, and he had some notable ones – he was a mischief-maker. He had an irresistible itch to throw a spanner in the works; he had charm, generosity, kindness (as well as the reverse), he was even courteous – but he was *méchant*, like a mischievous imp. (I saw this side of him on his native heath in New Brunswick.)

Bevin himself told me that, even in the grave crisis of 1940, Beaverbrook was continually trying to get him out of Churchill's government. At that moment of gravest danger to the nation – the sheer irresponsibility of it! That he was irresponsible is the worst thing I shall say against him. All the same, I regard irresponsibility as a bad mark against a man in politics, where the lives of people are in question (cf Aneurin Bevan's campaign for a Second Front long before it was possible, would have cost hundreds of thousands of lives, and might have lost us the war).

By the same token I detest irresponsibility in historians, for history is past politics, similar issues and persons come up for judgment. If one must have irresponsibility (there is a place for it) let it be on the stage, with dramatists and playboys like Bernard Shaw and Oscar Wilde (both Irish, by the way).

Beaverbrook recruited to his service an historian in the shape of A. J. P. Taylor, whose book, *Origins of the Second World War*, put forward the striking thesis that Hitler was hardly more – or not much more – to blame for the war than we were. However, we may regard his biography of Beaverbrook as a fine effort; it provides a mass of information on which we may make up our minds. The book received scathing criticism from a fellow Leftist, Richard Crossman; I am more appreciative – Taylor tries to be objective, to point out occasionally where Beaverbrook was wrong or went wrong. The portrait that emerges is vivid and authentic, and one finishes with more liking for the man that one had expected.

It is a good fault in a biographer to err on the side of too much sympathy for his subject. Mr Taylor tells us that 'this old man was the dearest friend I ever had . . . The joys of his company are beyond description. [I shall try to describe them.] I loved Max Aitken Lord Beaverbrook when he was alive. Now that I have learnt to know him better from his records I love him even more.' Mr Taylor adds modestly that he did not suppose that he was important to Beaverbrook 'except perhaps by appreciating his historical works at their true worth.'

This touching friendship began with a rapturous review by Mr Taylor of one of these historical works, and since the great man 'trembled' for the reception of his writings by the public, he was correspondingly grateful. It led to great things.

However, the historian has to admit that, despite the 'true worth' of Beaverbrook's history, his claims are not always accurate. His record of events in the first German war, 1914–18, was presented to the public several times over as a diary written at the time: 'this Diary, in narrative form, was kept all through these dramatic days.' Mr Taylor has to tell us that actually the story of events was recorded subsequently in 1917: 'no diary has survived, and it is as certain as any negative can be that none every existed.' A candid omission.

With regard to a statement of Beaverbrook about George Barnes, the Labour member of Lloyd George's War Cabinet, Mr Taylor has to append a footnote: 'This is not correct.' We are told that 'later in life Beaverbrook claimed that he ran his newspapers for the sole purpose of promoting Empire Free Trade.' The historian has to add the gloss that 'in this publicity campaign of 1925–27 the cause of Empire Free Trade is not mentioned.' The biographer candidly admits that Beaverbrook attached much importance to the trick of 'balancing', in other words, inventing: 'At a late stage in the process of drafting and redrafting he livened up the narrative, whenever he felt that it was becoming pedestrian, with a vivid phrase or an anecdote, sometimes I fear invented for the purpose.' And Mr Taylor conscientiously provides examples.

The historian gives a more important example of the art of balancing – on a crucial subject, the introduction of the Convoy System, which saved Britain in the first German war. Beaverbrook described vividly how Lloyd George, 'the Prime Minister descended upon the Admiralty and seated himself in the First Lord's chair.' When Mr Taylor tackled his master on the subject, 'I got little satisfaction on my specific point. Beaverbrook, when pressed, said: "I'm sure it happened. I'll ask Churchill when I see him next." Of course he never did. And of course the incident never happened . . . It was another balancing act, inserted for vivid effect at the last moment.'

What then are we to think of the 'true worth' of Beaverbrook as an historian? What are we to think of Mr Taylor as a professional historian 'appreciating his historical works at their true worth'?

The worth of an historian's work must depend on (a) his responsibility of mind towards events and facts and (b) his absolute adherence to the truth about them. Otherwise, it is not reliable history, though it may be drama, or journalism.

I do not entirely dismiss Beaverbrook's work as an historian, but I have a more limited, and more wary appreciation of it. It is useful as material for the real historian, with a critical mind, to make use of. Beaverbrook was a sharp observer of men in politics, and his vignettes of them have their utility. Take his thumb-nail sketch of the enigmatic Milner, the power of whose personality and whose influence are difficult to understand. Beaverbrook gives us the key.

> He was born in Germany, and his father, although descended from an English family, was a German by nationality. Milner's claim to British nationality was derived from his grandfather, who settled in Germany in 1805. He was educated in Germany . . . He admired Bismarck's Zollverein . . . frowning on reductions of taxation, and favouring extensions of social welfare.

Also like Bismarck.

In fact Milner had a completely German mentality; an administrator of the highest order, imposing social welfare from above, an authoritarian, something of a state-socialist. He had no English sense of compromise whatever, and as High Commissioner in South Africa, determined on the elimination of the Boer Republics – he was a Bismarckian Imperialist – he was more responsible for the South African war than anyone else, more than the unyielding Kruger (after all it was his country), or even the disastrous Joe Chamberlain. The South African war was a great disaster for Britain, let alone South Africa.

The second German war naturally brought about a general party *rapprochement*, the danger to Britain was so immeasurable. And when the war was over the fact of living in a nuclear world transformed the human condition, may be said to have revolutionized history, changed the terms. Henceforth the human race would live contingently.

What was the point of party divisions under this universal cloud? In this perspective differences between Labour and Tory, Democrat and Republican, Britain and America, melted away: our affairs were reduced to a question of survival. In Churchill's government of 1940–5, which saved Britain, party differences hardly existed. Churchill became Prime Minister through the support of the Labour Party; the twin poles of that historic government were Churchill and Ernest Bevin. For the first time, after years of frustration, exasperation and growing anguish, I was politically content; I ceased to be a party man.

Friendships were made across party fences – I always had been friendly to anti-Chamberlain Tories, L. S. Amery, the Cecils, Eden, Macmillan: anything to get rid of that Old Man of the Sea. At Oxford I even made peace with 'the Prof', Lindemann, now Lord Cherwell (from the view from his rooms looking over Christ Church Meadows to the river), united in our admiration of Bevin.

It was my acquaintance with Churchill that brought me that of Beaverbrook. On 6 May 1958 he wrote to me: 'I have been reading your book *The Later Churchills*. It is a delightful narrative and, if I may say so, a magnificent work. Particularly, I enjoyed your material on Churchill, with which I so heartily agree. Will you let me know, please, when you publish?' He must have seen a proof-copy, or perhaps Winston lent him his.

He sent me a couple of invitations to dine or lunch with him in London, and eventually I lunched with him alone in his penthouse flat at the top of Arlington House. As I waited

for the great man I had time to reflect on the historic associations of that street, Arlington Street. Sir Robert Walpole
had lived there and, I think, Lord Salisbury when he was
Prime Minister. At any rate Beaverbrook was virtually a
nextdoor neighbour of the Cecils, while on the other side his
flat looked across St James's Park to Buckingham Palace.

He must have found the proximity provoking, for he carried on a feud with the Cecils, with whom I agreed over
Appeasement and was actually a 'friend of the family' (as
Bobbety Salisbury wrote to me in his last letter). So I did not
approve of Beaverbrook's sniping at the most distinguished
of our historic families, any more than at snide remarks about
the royal family, in particular the Princess Margaret at that
time. After all, they couldn't answer back. I reflected as I
waited that what provoked him was something that he
couldn't *buy*. He had bought a peerage, so to say; very well,
he should accept the conditions and abide by the rules of the
game. At any rate, he couldn't buy *me*; I was all prepared to
sup with him at the end of a very long spoon.

The moment he appeared the situation was transformed by
a comic episode. Ah! Rowse – Cornwall. 'But I own a place
in Cornwall.' I had never heard of it, never knew that he had
any association with Cornwall or had ever been there – and I
thought I knew everything about Cornwall. 'But I do own a
place in Cornwall. What is the name of it?' Of course I didn't
know, and he couldn't remember the name.

I was tickled by the situation – fancy being so rich as to
own a place you didn't know the name of. He rang for his
manservant. 'What is the name of that place down in Cornwall?' Apparently his daughter lived there during the war.
Happily the man knew: it was Treverbyn Vean; but I had
never heard of it, not the Treverbyn near St Austell which I
had known from childhood, but a large modern house standing out on its bluff in woodland, one sees it well from the
railway line approaching Liskeard.

The *contretemps* bridged the gap – anyway there were few
gaps in talk with Beaverbrook, and I at once felt amused and
at home with him. Two significant things I remember from
that talk. He told me that over India Churchill had at last

come round to Attlee's point of view, and accepted the take-over. Apparently Attlee had persuaded him – this wasn't known at the time, if it is since. One can understand Churchill's holding out to the last: he had always realized that India was the heart of the British Empire; if India went, the Empire went; and India opting out meant a strategic vacuum. (Did the Americans appreciate that when they were so anxious to see the British out of India – and the Russians in both Afghanistan and the Indian Ocean?)

Beaverbrook was appalled. Never in history, he said, had an empire come to an end so rapidly. That was something we agreed about, and in deploring its consequences. He went on to launch an attack on the Americans, which I did not hold with. I had always regarded the anti-Americanism of his papers as dangerous. I thought, mistakenly, that this was conceived for purposes of circulation, but found that it was genuine conviction – all the more deleterious. So I stood up to him and said, Look, with Russia and Eastern Europe all Communist, with Communist China a people of eight hundred million, the only hope for us is for the English-speaking peoples to pull together.

To my surprise he wouldn't accept the argument, which I considered unanswerable – as it is.

Angrily he burst out: '*Lousy* people – wanted to push us out of India', and so on; a flood of emotional invective. I wasn't going to give up, and tried another tack. I said, 'Well, by the end of the century, Canada will be a Great Power in her own right. She will be able to confront the United States on her own level, and perhaps mediate between us.' Whether this was right or not, he saw that I wasn't going to subscribe to his anti-Americanism, though I no more approved of the American attitude towards the British Empire than he did. It was not long after Suez, and the collapse of the British position in the Middle East – largely owing to Eisenhower and the appalling Dulles – with all the consequences for the United States that followed. I hope they appreciate them.

Sometime after this he invited me to come to Canada as his guest, stay with him at Fredericton, and give a few lectures at the university of New Brunswick, of which he was

Chancellor. I gladly accepted for the autumn of 1960, and had a fascinating time of it. Nancy Astor professed to be shocked: 'I am surprised you took anything from the person you did. In fact, it shocks me to the quick! However, I am glad you are having a good time. Let me know when you come back.' Little love was lost between those great newspaper owners; however, that didn't affect me. It was a duty for an historian to see something of Canada, especially under such an aegis, and to observe an historic figure on his native heath, see what he was really like at home. In the event, I saw him at his best.

So far I had had only a brief glimpse of Canada. One year on my way to the United States I decided to go via Canada, by the Canadian Pacific steamship *Britannic* – a beautiful white motor-vessel – which took one up the St Lawrence at the height of the autumn foliage, all aflame with scarlet, crimson, gold. The arrival in the pool opposite Quebec was spectacular, the sun a glowing red plate sinking into the river, the Heights of Abraham – and at that moment the bells began clanging for vespers as in a city in Old France. I felt much at home, and had the good luck that Vincent Massey, loyal Balliol man, was in residence at the Citadel, who showed me round it, historic relics of Wolfe and Montcalm and all.

Thence I paid a brief visit to Montreal, where later I was to give the Bailey Lectures at McGill (still unpublished, so remiss have I been!) On the way to New York that night I had a pleasant encounter with an historically-minded conductor on the train. Crossing the frontier, he inspected my passport; noticing my name, he said, 'Do you know we are just passing Rouse's Point?', apparently some strategic position along the route in the American War of Independence. Rouse had fought on the wrong side – I leave the reader to his own taste as to which that was.

I wished to see more of Canada (I still haven't seen much, neither Toronto nor Ottawa, nor even British Columbia, where part of my family lives). I am always keenest to see what is historic, and the Maritime Provinces were part of old Canada, of more interest to me than any amount of the Mid-West. My Journal brings me close to my experience of it, and of the dynamic figure to which it had given birth – now entered into its history in turn.

12 October 1960. 'A good flight in beautiful clear New England weather from New York to Boston; but the horrid accident last week just outside the Boston airport – near sixty lives lost on an Electra, the type I was in – made me apprehensive. The left swerve from the airport, which gave me a beautiful view of the land – lakes, woods, rivers, seashore, blue, dun, green, no sign of wreckage – at an angle of 33°, gave me no pleasure at all. At Boston I waited two hours, and came on in a Viscount to St John, flying across the Bay of Fundy at 15,000 ft., to Yarmouth in Nova Scotia for Customs, then across to St John.

'Here I was met by a nice Scot, Galloway, Professor of English Literature. We halted in the centre of St John to look at the American Loyalists' burying ground (people who didn't accept the Revolution and wouldn't live under the Stars and Stripes). I noted the names of someone designated an Esquire, from Staten Island in the United States, others from Philadelphia. Most names were of Scots, but one was from the West Country, a master-mariner from Bideford. It was a touching scene – these headstones in the clear sunlight and nippy autumn air of Canada. The atmosphere was Canadian: what makes the difference?

'Oct. 15. After half a week in which to observe, I am in a better position to say. For one thing everything happens later here: in US they get up and go to bed earlier. Then this part of Canada is old-fashioned, a quiet backwater: it is like stepping back, except for motor cars, into the world of before 1914. Fredericton is an agreeable place for a university town, a good deal of charm, trees everywhere, on the slope of the hill with this grand river and the two bridges laid out below. Everything is slower and quieter, people slower on the uptake, slower to move – waitresses in restaurants, boy-pages in hotels, ordinary people in the streets. It is nicer that way.

'I have run up against the old United Empire Loyalist sentiment against the United States. A Loyalist historian, Highlander MacNutt, is quite shocked by my pro-Americanism. Revealing of Beaverbrook: I perceive his roots, he is an unreconstructed United Empire Loyalist. I give MacNutt the reason I gave Beaverbrook why, in a nuclear world, with Russia and China massed under Communism, the English-speaking peoples *must* pull together. MacNutt was displeased by my saying in a lecture that the American Revolution was a very English phenomenon – the determination to have self-government when arrived at the maturity to take over. He said that this cut at the roots of Canada's nationhood, the foundation upon which Canada had been built. To which I replied that *both* the Republican Milton and the Royalist Clarendon were good Englishmen.

'The drive up along the St John River was very fine: clear, golden autumnal sun lighting up the colours of the woods, flaming maples and birches, dark greens of pines and coni-fers. At one point the river opened out splendidly to make Grand Bay – what a scene in sailing ship days, when the river was the main artery of communication: New Brunswick grew up along it.

'Galloway took me home to dine – an excellent meal, though I was so tired, I'd rather have gone to bed. The house a delightful one of about 1815, roomy, with a fine view of the lights of the town below. Already late, at 10 p.m. we went on to the President's party for new members of the faculty: another Scot, Colin Mackay, a lean greyhound of a young man, already greying, able, successful, overworking – hungry for what? Power, I think. I diagnose that he would make a good Prime Minister of Canada, another bachelor Scot, like Mackenzie King.

'At lunch in the Lord Beaverbrook hotel, I was recognized by two Rhodes Scholars, who took me for a drive further up the river. The scenery became more rugged and Scottish, colours all delicate golds and flushed scarlets, the great river placid, sweet and summery. A Fenimore Cooper world – I could imagine the Indians still in possession, their canoes darting down. What a vast dispossession of peoples North America has witnessed! They exist only in holes and corners of their own land, now static and mission children, living by potato picking. We passed a so-called "Reserve" – really only a dozen houses with a church by the roadside. How extraor-

dinary it would be to be able to look into *their* consciousness
of the great Dispossession!

'14 October: Dean Alfred Goldsworthy Bailey drove me
round the town, a rather prissy character of some distinction,
has written two volumes of verse, comes from Virginian and
New England stocks going back to the 1630s, with a 1780s
admixture of Cornish: from Richard Goldsworthy of
Redruth, builder and surveyor, master of the King's works at
Quebec, where his house still stands. Dean Bailey has several
volumes of this old Cornishman's books – tables of measure-
ments and accounting, with the usual theological junk.

'A master of local lore, Bailey took me to see the house
where Bliss Carman had lived, and Charles Roberts not far
away. Carman had lived many years *à trois* with a friend and
his wife – people said that he was the wife's lover. I suggested that it was all platonic, and Bliss not one for married
bliss. Bailey agreed. Carman had told Bailey's people that
he had been writing all his life and not made enough to buy
a ham sandwich from his poetry, warning young Alfred
against it.

'We went up to Forest Hill cemetery to pay our tribute to
him: a beautiful graveyard, trees in colour in full view of the
blue river, a scarlet maple planted beside the grave. I thought
of Q. (Quiller-Couch, who put a poem of Carman's into the
Oxford Book of English Verse) – they were contemporaries. Q.
born in 1864, the other in 1861. His was a tall granite tomb,
with an open book and all the Loyalists around him. Not far
away was his cousin Charles Roberts, also a poet, but whose
children's and animal stories were better.

'We crossed the bridge to the north side, flat water
meadows, more English except for the immense size of the
river. For the first time I saw a huge log-jam, men working
on the logs in the river, the trunks packed together like sar-
dines silver in the sun. All the property of Mr Irving, Beaverbrook's millionaire buddy down at St John. (All to be
consumed, in faithless, ephemeral newsprint?)

'We went on to Majorville and the first settlers' church,
even before the Loyalists: a Congregational one, where President Mackay's ancestors are buried. So he's deeply rooted

here, going back to the very beginning. A nice young fellow
on the road wanted a lift. But Dean Bailey never picks anyone up. Once, when motoring in Wisconsin he was just
behind a judge, who had given someone a lift and been shot
dead. Never give anyone a lift in the New World.

'That evening I had to make a speech at a dinner of historians, English Literature people, librarians, from New Brunswick, Mount Allison and Acadia Universities. Next morning
a symposium at which information was exchanged as to the
resources of the various libraries for scholarship. I did my
best to make useful suggestions. In the evening, after the dinner Galloway had given, followed a party at which I talked to
everybody, hearing about the young men's subjects, etc.
while consoling myself on a sofa by holding the charming
Galloway cat, Troilus (thinking sadly of Peter at home at
Trenarren). Not getting to bed until 2 a.m., when I like to
be in bed before 10 p.m., I was so tired that I spent the
afternoon in bed.

'At 6.30 p.m. was called for by a nice Scot, offshoot of
the Camerons, and taken home to dinner: a family affair
with pretty, dark Scots lassie for wife, and two children
aged two and one: I came through the ordeal, and so did
they, rather better than expected. After dinner people came
in, including a Scotch-Australian widow. Lots of laughing
and chaffing, which I enjoyed – and on to the next party at
the Baileys.

'A different atmosphere: this was upper-class, childless,
select, elderly, tasteful. A handsome Jugo-Slav, who had had
fearsome adventures in the war, was unfortunately fearful, as
a newcomer, of monopolising my attention. I suffered hor-
ribly from the heat: *all* the heating on, plus a wood fire on
the hearth. I skirted round the company, keeping as clear of
the fire as I could. Talked to a middle-aged silvery head of a
Woman's Hall, who adored the pure thin cold air of Canada
in the snow in winter, came back from Switzerland longing
for it, etc. etc.

'I moved on to agreeable banter and argument, chiefly
politics, with the men. Toole, Vice-President, beautiful
manners of an Irish gentleman, chemist, Catholic become

rationalist, reads the *New Statesman*, but of a Left doctrinaire
with some of the illusions. I talked too much, but felt that
that was what I was there for. Came up against MacNutt's
Loyalist anti-Americanism again; then hot coffee – at that
hour and in that heat! – the wide eyes of the big Jugo-Slav
constantly on me.'

In the intervals of all this I had been reading steadily and
neither got in touch with nor been summoned by Beaverbrook. I rather enjoyed the Kafka *Castle*-like atmosphere.
There we were both in the Lord Beaverbrook, somewhere
on another floor this dynamo of energy, people coming and
going: I wanted a day or two's intermission before catching
up with him. And was rather surprised to find that I was
given it, left to find my own feet. No summons. One sunny
morning I saw the little black dynamo stepping out along
the river bank with his grand-daughter. There were
rumours that 'Lady Jean' was up here with him. Who was
Lady Jean?

On the third day I went along to the Art Gallery, where
he also has a flat, to announce my arrival. Like Winston,
who must have had a strong influence on Beaverbrook's
ways, particularly in collecting paintings and founding a
gallery, he was in a whirl of energetic direction. People were
coming and going carrying pictures for him to look at and
away again; he was talking into a dictaphone and/or long-
distance telephone, was dictating to a woman secretary, col-
loguing with the velvet-coated Director of his Gallery, and
yet was prepared to receive me in the midst of this whirl-
pool.

'He really is a phenomenon – the speed of his mind, the
quite abnormal memory, the pounce, and at eighty-two! Not
a faculty is impaired: he is like a man of fifty-two or forty-
two. At once he was *au fait* with my movements and, getting
off the telephone and the dictation, cleared himself a space of
fifteen minutes to take me into the vault and have the Hilliard
miniature of Elizabeth I brought out for "the Doctor". I
inspected it carefully: it looked to me like her in the later
1570s, rather young-looking. (She must have looked young
until later middle age.)

'With all these acquisitions around him – some of the modern caricatures he had bought off his own bat I did not much relish – he said, provokingly: "I make my money in Britain, I spend it over here." But he had made a Canadian fortune – all by fixing and company mergers – before he came to Britain, where he made another.

'Walking out into the Gallery, I was no less impressed by his phenomenal memory for people: one young man among the visitors he addressed by name and knew all about him. This too was rather Churchillian, for I noticed the natural courtesy with which he greeted people going round; and then the magnetism of the man who had called it all into existence and made it live. Here he was – on his home-ground.

'Sunday, 16 October, I dined with him in the Gallery flat. Toole was there, and a New Brunswicker from the West who is a Senator; last came Lady Jean Campbell. "Guess who this is! Who is she?" He was as merry as a cricket. "She's my grand-da'ter. Isn't she exactly like me?" Actually a good-looking girl, black hair, grey-blue eyes, pretty figure all in black plus pearls.

'Beaverbrook was in the gayest mood. Stories flowed. Asquith had said: "Some men think while they talk (i.e. Lloyd George); some men think while they write (i.e. himself); some men think both while they talk and while they write, and they are the salt of the earth." We were to guess whom he meant by this, but were floored. I thought of Arthur Balfour; but I might have guessed, from Beaverbrook's own predilections, it would be Birkenhead.

'He thought Horatio Bottomley [popular orator, fraud and cheat] and Tim Healey [Irish Nationalist] the best wits he had known. Bottomley, M.P., protesting against a new kind of Parliamentary veto. "What is a veto? It is a new kind of vegetable." When aristocratic disapproval was expressed, of the way he exploited the credulity of the people – they wanted to be cheated by him – he threatened to follow the Cholmondeley example and call himself Bumley. Beaverbrook enjoyed having the rogue to dinner – much to Bonar Law's disapproval [incomprehensibly, Beaverbrook's hero – a dull man], who thought it disgraceful. Beaverbrook chuckled impishly at this: one saw the *gamin* coming out. One evening he had Beerbohm Tree to dinner, who monopolized the conversation and had no intention of letting Bottomley score. Tree got the conversation round to the most beautiful woman he had ever seen. It transpired that it was the actress, Lottie Collins. Nothing daunted, Bottomley jumped in with "My Aunt", and won.

'Next came the story of Bottomley in gaol: he was eventually run down by the Astors for cheating thousands of poor people of their savings. Visited by an acquaintance, Bottomley was engaged in sewing bags. "What are you doing – sewing?" "No, reaping," said the old renegade, who had mesmerized so many audiences with his "Prince of Peace" peroration. He would estimate what the audience was good for: if over £1000 they should have the "Prince of Peace"; if not, not.

'Then Healey. When Beaverbrook was Minister of Information in the first German war, he got into some serious Parliamentary trouble; Bonar Law wouldn't come to the rescue, and advised him to try Tim Healey. Beaverbrook got him on the phone; Healey said he would cross from Ireland by the Sunday boat after Mass. Beaverbrook hoped that Mass wouldn't last too long and would meet him for dinner. After dinner Tim was too tired to listen to Beaverbrook's case, or decide on any line of defence; next day at lunch he wouldn't think about it. When the debate came on that day in the House of Commons, Healey began: "This Minister of Information isn't so bad. The Minister before him was Carson" – and went over to the wrongs of Ireland. From that moment nothing more was heard of Beaverbrook in the debate. (I was not amused: I registered inwardly – what idiots.)

'So it went on, all popping like the champagne served. (Beaverbrook on his reviewer, Arnold Bennett: "How I loved Arnold, and how he loved my champagne." He would not be able to say that of this teetotaller. But the dinner was excellent, the fish brought up fresh from St Andrew's, artichokes in leaf (too much trouble), butter sauce, meringues, brandy.

'I was placed by the granddaughter, who politely professed

herself an admirer of my *Churchills*. Beaverbrook sang the praises of A. J. P. Taylor, whom I had known since he was an undergraduate. "Your favourite historian," I said as a challenge. At once: "No; you're my favourite historian. But I like Taylor. He's a brave man." I didn't comment on this, though much might be said of their "elective affinities", in Goethe's phrase.

'The young woman was very engaging, spontaneity and charm under the sophistication of the society she frequents. She adores New York, where she lives up on 94th Street among the Porto Ricans, has a job as *Daily Express* correspondent of the United Nations. Also adores Mr Khrushchev – he has such a funny face, is a first-class comic and makes such fun of the solemn Americans and *their* UN. I recognized the family anti-Americanism or, as she put it, a love-hate complex.

'How like her grandfather's impish irresponsibility! I had been in New York at the time of Khrushchev's visit to the UN Assembly, specifically for the purpose of bringing it into derision, taking off his shoe to beat on his desk with it, uncouth brute. Beaverbrook longed to bring him up to Fredericton to shock Canada. "O that 'twere possible": the idea vastly tickled him; he and his granddaughter chuckled at the jolt it would give to Fredericton's old-fashioned respectability.

'We had a subject in common to mull over – a mutual lawyer acquaintance who had been consulted over the Argyll case – "my family has been much before the courts lately." She was wearing a prehistoric gold bangle, treasure-trove from Inverary, I supposed. [All the talk we had about our well-known lawyer friend can wait till we're all dead . . .] So too with her information about the able, attractive President, whom she had been "studying for years". I was naturally much interested. Apparently he was her grandfather's choice, who knew he was the right man, not the Faculty's; though all agreed now how successful he was, all his celibate energy devoted to building up the university.

'Once or twice I noticed her smiling at my shyness or slowness, or just my old-fashioned manner (a teetotaller, I

don't think she observed my observing). Unasked, she gave
me her address and telephone in New York, swore me to get
in touch, and kindly promised to show me the UN Building,
about which she was quite lyrical. [I never did; I had no
interest in the UN Building.] Beaverbrook is obviously fond
of the girl: "Doesn't she know that she's my favourite
gran'child!" etc.

'The brandy circulated. She had two goes, and wanted a
third. Grandfather refused. "But who taught me to drink,
grandpa?"

'Talk circulated about newspapers and their proprietors.
Beaverbrook claimed proudly that only three newspaper
groups had been *created* in the last thirty years, all by sons of
the Presbyterian manse: the *Express* group, the Henry Luce
group, and the Readers' Digest group created by Wallace. On
religions, Beaverbrook described himself as a Presbyterian
Pagan, Toole said that he was a Catholic Pagan; I refrained
from saying that I was an Anglican Pagan.

'At 10.30 we broke up. No more late night sessions as with
Winston in old days. The President says that the old man
"watches himself like a ha'k." Beaverbrook told me that Birkenhead, dying at sixty-two, had expected to live another
twenty years. (The fool, brilliantly gifted as he was, killed
himself with drink.)

'17 October: I had my heaviest chore, addressing the student
body in a large ecclesiastical-looking hall with a gallery and
difficult acoustics. My theme was "The Use of History in
Modern Society" (John Wesley recorded his sermon texts:
why shouldn't I?).

'The President took me to lunch, and then I got *his* perspective on grandfather and granddaughter. [That also can
wait . . .] Rather comically he told me his own experience
with the Beaver, whose house looking on to the river he had
donated for the use of the President of the University. First
year the Beaver had spent two weeks in it; the second, two
months; the third threatened to be more than the President
could stand, it added two or three hours to his work a day.
So, during the seven weeks of vacation he had himself run up

the odd little bungalow he occupies on the campus. The Beaver had lost his caretaker, and took to staying in the Lord Beaverbrook hotel, with a flat in the Gallery as a hide-out. The President thought of himself as a sort of Catherine Parr to Henry VIII and sometimes wondered whether he would survive him . . .

'He had the Beaver well weighed up, good qualities as well as intolerable ones. There had been several changes of President; at one time when there was none Beaverbrook stepped in and practically ran the place, keeping some continuity in the administration. At another time *he* had resigned as Chancellor, to be persuaded back as Honorary Chancellor next year. There was his ceaseless interest on their behalf, in addition to all his benefactions – Library, Art Gallery, a vast Skating Rink for the town – and his interferences. Above all was his loneliness: Mackay would get a telephone call from him any time to come down to New York to talk business. It was just that he wanted company.

'19 October. Beautiful day, took an early class for Galloway up the hill. After early lunch togged myself up for Convocation, and up to the familiar gathering, quite impressive. In the robing room – beautiful Mrs Ross, wife of the Lieutenant-Governor of British Columbia, a powerful economic administrator; Monsignor Lussier, fine figure of a man, Rector of the big University of Montreal. Then the vigorous young Premier of New Brunswick, the first Frenchman to be so. We were the four to receive honorary degrees – the others Doctors of Laws, I a DCL.

'The local grandees assembled: the Lieutenant-Governor O'Brien; the Commander in military red, members of the Senate, the Roman Catholic Bishop of Bathurst in purple, skull cap, silk cloak, ribbons and all. Monsignor Lussier swiftly, proficiently kissed his ring; I complimented him, and said how nice it was to see the purple. "It is my uniform," he said and pointed out the Anglican Bishop of Fredericton also in purple and scarlet.

'The long procession gathered and crocodiled brilliantly downhill in the afternoon sun. As we entered the immense Lady Beaverbrook Skating Rink the audience rose, the band

played – and I realized that I had just picked up a pebble in
my shoe. We mounted the platform, I in a strategic position
on the extreme left. For a moment I was touched thinking of
the long way I had come from my Cornish village to this,
and then laughed to myself at the thought of Hardy's worst
line.

Where are we? and why are we where we are?

'The so familiar academic ceremony unrolled itself, the
graduates coming up to be capped by the Chancellor – one
saw him in a new rôle, *en grand seigneur*. The Public Orator,
with his Welsh background, was so eloquent in presenting
Mrs Ross, an improbably elegant dictator of fats and oils
during the war, that I was quite carried away and forgot my
turn. Monsignor Lussier signalled me up, to stand there and
receive some flowery compliments on my work – with which
I fear the Public Orator was not at all acquainted (he is a
devotee of Howard Spring). Capped by his lordship, I
received a friendly grin and grasp of the hand, with a large
vellum roll to carry about. The Chancellor seemed to enjoy
it, a wide boyish grin on his frog-face.

'Out in a huddle into the cold sun, I having a chat in
French with the Roman bishop, who turned out to be of
Breton stock. Then uphill to the opening of Thomas Car-
leton Hall, after the early Governor who had set aside an
endowment of 6000 acres for the College. "We now have
3000," said the Chancellor; "I recommend the University to
ask the government what has become of the other 3000."
This for the benefit of the new Premier, who had urged
more money for education, etc. Shrewd old Beaver, never
missing a point!

'We went in to tea, where a geologist told me that
Bathurst had had a colony of Cornish miners, who had now
gone over to farming. [Why doesn't someone follow up my
book, *The Cornish in America*, with one on the Cornish in
Canada?]

'The Chancellor gave a large dinner-party for us all that
evening. Before it I had some cosy chat with Lady Dunn, the

widow of Beaverbrook's multi-millionaire friend, Sir James Dunn. When he died, she shut herself up and retired from the world; Beaverbrook has now brought her out into the world, got her interested in things again, to give money and pictures to the Art Gallery, scholarships to the University. I was not allowed to get off with her: I was placed as far away as possible, between two boring men, the Lieutenant-Governor and another. Beaverbrook put her carefully between himself and the Bishop. I did not have a chance of speaking to her again. [Later, Beaverbrook married her: a proper cure for his obsessive loneliness.]

'Next morning, before leaving, I had a consoling visit from a young Cornishman, whose family, a familiar name to me, had lived at Killiganoon, near Truro. Good-looking and *simpatico*, he told me his and his family story: *nihil Cornubiense alienum a me puto*. Over here studying forestry, but with a turn and the looks for acting: a Hollywood actor is taken with his talent and is coaching him in a university production. Left Charterhouse at sixteen to go to Dartmouth, where the Navy was cutting down and offered no prospects, he decided on forestry for an outdoor life and worked his passage over to New Brunswick – worked as a waiter in vacation to pay his way.

'Here was the enterprise of a younger generation, but I wonder what will happen to him? How the Cornish do get about the world!

'Next day kind David Galloway drove me to the airport, after my strenuous visit and varied entertainment. The golden autumn over, there was an inch deep of rain on the cement at the airport, and the same at St John. However, I arrived in Boston without disturbance, had my dinner on board, and even enjoyed the spectacle of the lights of the city spread out below, outlining the bay, the harbour front, quays running out into the water where the ghastly disaster to the plane had occurred ten days before.'

I trace only one more slight contact with Beaverbrook, and since it shows him wise, considerate and courteous, I give it – all the more remarkable in the last months of his life.

As I have said, I think that my brief acquaintance with him sprang out of my interest in Churchill and my two books about the family, particularly *The Later Churchills*. When my *William Shakespeare: A Biography* came out in 1963, it was treated to a disgraceful attack by that exemplar of Christian charity, Malcolm Muggeridge. I know quite well that one is not supposed to take any notice of reviews by people who do not qualify to hold a serious opinion on the subject. Very few people do qualify to hold an opinion on Elizabethan subjects, certainly not glib, superficial journalists.

But if people make trouble for a Celt, a Celt is apt to make trouble for them; and I wrote privately to Beaverbrook to protest. He had read the snide review, and consoled me by saying that

> just about the same time I read an attack on myself by the same author, published in a Canadian magazine. On the whole, I have more right to complain than you . . . I was not warned of the Muggeridge review, but I certainly would be warned of a review of any book on Churchill. Now if you decide to instruct Macmillans not to send any of your books for review by the *Standard*, I will make no complaint. But that sort of situation never works out. It is never any good for the author and it does the *Standard* no harm. But it will not be regarded by me as an unfriendly action on your part. I saw the editor of the *Evening Standard* last evening and told him not to submit any of your books to Muggeridge for review. If any of your work comes to the *Standard* in future, Muggeridge will certainly not be the reviewer. It is a great disappointment to me to have to write this letter. I would much rather have read a joyous and happy review of which you would have no reason to complain.

I call that extraordinarily good and generous of him; it shows him in a most favourable light, and yet true to him. As we know, he was exceptionally sensitive about the reception of his own work and deeply appreciative of understanding. I too was sad that my happy acquaintance with him should end on this note – it shows the damage that inferior people, with little sense of responsibility, can do.

However, I hope that, though for many years on the opposite side of the fence, indeed a strong supporter of Ernest Bevin, inveterately hostile to Beaverbrook, I have not given an unjust depiction of this very remarkable, if controversial, figure who made such a mark in our time.

The Poet Auden

My relationship with W. H. Auden was a curious one, but not without some significance. It began promisingly, and then was bitten off by a characteristic (in retrospect, comic) *contretemps*. After that, our relations were for a long time rather cool, somewhat sketchy, though we never completely lost touch. When he came over to Oxford after the war I used to see him at All Souls, and we used to meet when I was in New York. When he came back finally to Oxford he spent his first month in All Souls, until our old college, Christ Church, got his cottage ready for him there. I determined to make it up to him for my earlier gaffe and took him under my wing again, as more than forty years before. For, after all, I was his Oxford senior: he was a whole undergraduate generation – three years – my junior, and when we were young that had made all the difference.

I can hardly claim that he was my *protégé* – as he was Nevill Coghill's, who was his sympathetic and very understanding tutor. But the young Wystan used to come round to All Souls and read me his poems: from the very first I had no doubt of his genius, his astonishing originality in one so young, his challenging verbal sophistication.

It is a good thing that I have kept diaries and retained calendars all my life – very properly for a historian – or I might get my facts wrong: mere memory is a shaping instrument. (So much for the third-rate reviewer in the *London Magazine*, who couldn't imagine that there might well be a

Rowse industry *à la* Boswell in the next century from the mass of papers the historian has accumulated.)

Wystan and I, as House-men, had friends in common at Christ Church; but, without my calendar, I should not have known that it was my junior who invited me to lunch with him there in October 1926, or again in October 1927, for I have no memory of these occasions. I well remember his rooms in Peck – Peckwater Quad – and my calendar gives me the number, Staircase V, number 5 (for the benefit of those who wish to venerate). Next term, in February 1928 I had him to lunch with me to meet my friends, the historian K. B. McFarlane and Richard Best, whose father was Lord Chancellor of Northern Ireland.

Apparently Wystan refused John Betjeman's invitations to meet obvious grandees, peers and such; mine were not social, but by way of being propaganda for Wystan's poetry. In July, after his Schools, he came to Sunday dinner at All Souls; in spite of his usually appalling clothes, he must have donned a dinner-jacket for the occasion – in those days we were rather particular about that. Next day he came again to tea.

Perhaps he thought terms were getting warmer, for that week occurred the absurd *contretemps* which Charles Osborne partially relates in his truthful biography. After reading his poems to me in the hot July quad, Auden suggested that we adjourn to his rooms. When we got there I was a little surprised at his 'sporting the oak' (i.e. locking the outer door), pulling down the blinds and shutting the shutters. I didn't know about his odd line against sunlight.

Turning on his ugly green-shaded lamp – I can see it now – instead of reading more poems he proceeded to read me long extracts from a friend of his in Mexico, with the Mexican Eagle Oil Company, all about his goings-on with the boys. I sank further and further back into my armchair, wondering what next. I remember registering to myself (God help me), 'Fellows of All Souls don't do that sort of thing.' (Little did I know.) Fortunately, at that moment I heard the bell of Great Tom booming through the quad and, with 'That's four o'clock! I am always in the Common Room at

All Souls for tea at 4 o'clock,' I managed my escape from the awkward situation.

How inept I was! The fact was that I was rather a prig, but, even more, I had none of the sophistication of these Public School boys, years ahead of me in knowledge of the facts of life. What would have happened if I had had their training and Wystan been a handsome young Adonis I tremble to think . . . But he was singularly unappetizing with his nico-tined, nail-bitten fingers, his chain-smoking or pipe-sucking, unwashed, his uncombed tow-hair, dirty collars, etc. I was something of a political fanatic in those days, preserving myself for great endeavours and expectations; I was also a good deal of an aesthete, which Wystan never was. In fact he was neither; at this time he had not opened a newspaper. Our sole bond was poetry.

Though three years his senior, I was years behind in *savoir-faire*. I suppose I was precocious intellectually, and hard-working, and winning a prize Fellowship at All Souls in those days, when it was the blue-ribbon of an Oxford career, had given me an elevated idea of my station, certainly of its responsibilities. No doubt my attitude was a bit patronizing; for that I must be forgiven, for I was his senior and a don, and also I was out to do my best for him.

When Stephen Spender printed a small number of Wystan's first little book of *Poems*, in its orange wrappers, I subscribed for a copy and got E. F. Jacob to subscribe too. (It cannot be that all copies were given away, as Osborne says.) Now an item of the utmost rarity – a copy fetched £1750 after Wystan's death – like a fool, I lent mine to an unappreciative young friend who disappeared in the limbo of the war and never saw it again.

Wystan was always a bit careful and cagey with me after that episode; anyway in 1928 he went down and was away from the Oxford scene for years, while I plodded on as a part-time teaching don, part-time researcher, more and more caught up in the anxieties of politics in the thirties – but practically, as a Labour candidate during those despairing years, and getting more and more ill.

Anyway Wystan had got a bad Third in his Schools. I

could not be expected, as a don, to approve of that, and it did
make me discount him intellectually. This was not donnish
snobbery on my part, though, after a frightful struggle I had
had in getting to Oxford, as a working-class man I did dis-
approve of these bourgeois young men, who had had all the
chances, wasting their precious time at Oxford. There they
were, having had their wonderful time, going down like
ninepins: my exact contemporaries, the most heralded and
brilliant of them all, Cyril Connolly with his Third, Peter
Quennell sent down, Graham Greene and Evelyn Waugh
with their Thirds (Evelyn admitted that his tutor (my friend
Cruttwell) scored with 'It is a mistake to go through life with
an inappropriate label'); John Betjeman sent down; I don't
know what happened to Harold Acton and Stephen Spender
– Fourths, I expect.

For all the dismissive face he put upon it, Wystan knew
that he had been wrong. 'Beneath the fun I was always conscious of a dull, persistent, gnawing anxiety. To begin with,
I felt guilty at being so idle. I knew very well what sort of
degree I was going to get and what a bitter disappointment
this was going to be to my parents.' I also knew what sort of
prospect there would have been for me if I hadn't worked
hard to get one of the best Firsts of my year and then a prize
Fellowship at All Souls. No such cushy job on the *Architec-
tural Review* such as Maurice Bowra landed for Betjeman;
Connolly got the job of companion to old Logan Pearsall
Smith, while Desmond MacCarthy took him under his wing
on *The New Statesman*. And so on.

But there is a far deeper reason for my disapproval (Connolly regarded me as 'censorious'). It is this: those decisive
undergraduate years afforded a precious time, such as would
never recur, for one's intellectual development, and one's
training – above all, to think. One way and another, what I
have noticed about these contemporaries is that, gifted as
they were, and they mostly fulfilled their gifts, they were not
trained thinkers: they were not intellectually disciplined (as
Eliot certainly was). Cyril Connolly, for example, had been
a History Scholar at Balliol; but when he wrote about history
subsequently, it was always uncertain and wobbling.

Similarly with Wystan's criticism and thinking: full of good insights (like Connolly's), but untrained and undisciplined, marred by unreasoned prejudices and flaws. It would have done him good to have worked seriously during those three years at Oxford and emerged with a trained intellectual outfit.

However, his poetry was the thing to him. I continued faithfully to support it, not only buying each volume as it came out (he was always prolific), but putting it across others – my historian friends, for example: Richard Pares, Bruce McFarlane, Charles Henderson, and my German friend, Adam von Trott. Maurice Bowra was inconvertible: he used for years to call Wystan the Martin Tupper of the age – and that put his followers off, like John Sparrow, who wrote a very unsympathetic little book about these contemporary poets. That would have no influence with me. I find from my calendar, what I had forgotten, that in February 1936 I was lending Veronica Wedgwood *The Dog beneath the Skin*, and that that month I saw it in London. I also faithfully went to see *The Ascent of F6*, I forget where.

Even as an undergraduate Wystan was extraordinarily self-confident, would regularly lay down the law like a *Partei-Führer* to his followers. He would then reverse himself, and say to Stephen Spender who took everything solemnly, 'Why do you take everything I say so seriously?' Wystan said a lot of things simply *pour faire effet*. He never did that with me, for he knew it wouldn't be any good. An historian – and Wystan hadn't much historical sense – is interested only in the truth.

His exchange with Eliot about Tennyson, for example, is held up for admiration. Wystan said – and not once only, but wrote it in a Preface – that Tennyson was the stupidest of our poets. Eliot scored by saying that that showed Wystan was no scholar, or he would have been able to think of still stupider poets. I don't think much of their joke, if it was one. Anyone who really knows what Tennyson was like – as revealed by Sir Charles Tennyson, from out under the whited sepulchre of the son's official biography – will know that Tennyson was an utterly independent and original thinker for himself, with an extraordinary range of unexpected and curious reading.

Though continuing to be interested in and to support the work of my immediate juniors, I did not share their German *schwärmerei*. I had had my German phase before them and continued to have my own private line through Adam von Trott. I thought that all that German *Expressionismus* was bad for them, and that it would have been better for them if they had gone to Paris instead of ugly Berlin, or Rügen Island and all that – undergone the influence of French civilization and literature, always good for uncultivated, undisciplined Teutons and Anglo-Americans.

There again I was with Eliot, not with them (and, though Eliot published them and always recognized Wystan's genius, he did not really like their poetry. He once allowed that mine was closer to his – as it was, in its defeatism and despair. He got out of that eventually through religion; I never did: I had no inner beliefs or hopes, and the world grew worse.) Wystan's attitude to everything French was simply childish: 'Italian and English are the language of Heaven. "Frog" is the language of Hell.' How silly, how uncouth! When French is the best-bred of all European languages – the language of Rimbaud and Verlaine, and in Wystan's time of Valéry and Gide, Cocteau and Montherlant, or of a kindred spirit like Radiguet, if they had heard of him: their exact contemporary, and a perfect artist, where they were so flawed and imperfect.

That was just like Wystan: to take up a terrific pose and then with sublime insensibility to adhere to it (he was not the most sensitive of men, unlike Eliot). I never cared for his oracular statements laid down in verse, the rhetoric that made him popular in the thirties. Real poetry is a more subtle and secret affair; I am sure it does damage to a poet's inspiration to create a persona for himself, and then act up to it. This can be proved, or at any rate shown: Wystan's best poetry was written when he was being direct and simple, not fabricating it out of his clever brain with all his verbal and metrical virtuosity (verbosity, too), but writing autobiographically:

> Fish in the unruffled lakes
> The swarming colours wear,
> Swans in the winter air
> A white perfection have . . .
>
> Sighs for folly said and done
> Twist our narrow days;
> But I must bless, I must praise
> That you, my swan, who have
> All gifts that to the swan
> Impulsive Nature gave,
> The majesty and pride,
> Last night should add
> Your voluntary love.

That volume, *Look, Stranger!* of 1936, contains some of his finest poems, precisely *because* – contrary to his perverse theory – they are direct and autobiographical.

My purpose is not literary criticism, but notes written at the end of that volume show just what one was thinking *at the time*, which is relevant.

> Isherwood has told us of the influences entering into the making of Auden's poetry – the unfashionable admiration for Bridges and Housman: he shares ships with the former and soldiers with the latter. Note the impression the depressed areas, the Northern industrial districts have made; in the Malvern Hills he thinks of the chimneys of Lancashire. The theme of rebuilding has brought them [his group] into definite political associations: comradeship and sympathy with the working classes follow from this attitude, consistent and natural, though slightly forced in expression. He has the makings of a great patriotic poet in time – in the Shakespearean tradition, not Roy Campbell. [Whom I had fed on as a poet to Eliot, who thereupon published *Adamastor*. Campbell became a Fascist, though I continued to admire his poetry.] An extraordinary eye for English countryside,

particularly the North – fells, mountains, dales – which I as a Westerner, an extreme Westerner, don't know. It makes me jealous for the West – I wish we had some share in his affections. But he has recently described Dover, nobody better, and 'the wide and feminine valleys of the South'. [I always used to think of this line when passing through Winchester in the train.] Wystan a rhetorical poet, not afraid of rhetoric – appropriate vehicle for expression of feelings about 'this island'.

Came the Spanish Civil War, which was rather particularly their war – the war of the Left intellectuals – and they all went off to serve the Republican cause in various capacities. It didn't make much difference to the result: the Spanish Republic was ruined by its own incompetence, the idiot people riven from top to bottom by their own factions. Such people deserved to lose out. I was already thoroughly disillusioned, eating my heart out with 'the sickness of hope deferred'. Wystan wrote some propagandist verses about Spain – which they all did – and which I did not bother to keep.

And Wystan was shortly as disillusioned with it all as I was – but very fly in keeping it quiet. This leads me to a significant point about him: for all the originality of his stance, his independence of mind, the courage of his convictions, he was in a curious way rather prudent and tactful. He never entered into controversy with people: he let them go their own way, as he went his. This was rather clever of him from a literary point of view: he did not get into trouble; he had enemies, but he did not *make* them. Also he was a gentleman (Eliot a great gentleman, almost a saint); Wystan was a good man, with high standards, in spite of external appearances.

It really was astonishingly courageous of him, independent as well as sophisticated, to come to terms with his own nature as a boy of sixteen at school, accept it and go forward on that basis. He simply saw no reason for not accepting the facts of life as they were. (I was in continual revolt, and on every front, private as well as public – not good for duodenal ulcer, exacerbated it until it nearly killed me.) Wystan was rational about all this; I remember how impressed I was when David

Cecil told me that Wystan could always make a pick-up on the train from Oxford before it reached Paddington. And – a tribute of another kind to Wystan's early *réclame* – when a culture-vulture of a lady found that David's sister, the Duchess of Devonshire, had not read Auden, she pushed the point home with 'I suppose you have never read *Alice in Wonderland*!'

The second German war, to which everything in the thirties had been leading, proved the great divide. Wystan was already in the United States when it started, and he stayed there. An appalling attack on him was unleashed by a good many people, some of them former friends; this must have wounded him, though he maintained an extraordinary self-control, never replied, and just went forward on his own way, as he always did.

I never dared to raise the subject with him; and naturally I never joined in the attack – I thought it beneath me. Privately, I realized the situation: Wystan was so physically unattractive that when, at last, he found someone to love him, that was it.

> Lay your sleeping head, my love,
> Human on my faithless arm;
> Time and fevers burn away
> Individual beauty from
> Thoughtful children, and the grave
> Proves the child ephemeral:
> But in my arms till break of day
> Let the living creature lie,
> Mortal, guilty, but to me
> The entirely beautiful.

This is poetry, not rhetoric.

On the public side, Wystan had arrived at the same degree of disillusionment with men and their affairs as I had myself. He wrote: 'To be forced to be political is to be forced to lead a dual life.' This was what had almost done me in: incessant illness, operations, it took me years to recover. To have survived at all was my only triumph. He went on, wisely – and it spoke for me: 'Perhaps this would not matter if one could consciously keep them apart and know which was the real one. But to succeed at anything, one must believe in it, and only too often the false public life absorbs and destroys the genuine private life.' It had nearly killed me; how wise of Wystan it was to diagnose it and eschew it. Resignedly he wrote, 'Artists and politicians would get along better in a time of crisis like the present, if the latter would only realize that the political history of the world would have been the same if not a poem had been written, not a picture painted, nor a bar of music composed.'

So much for all the political writing of the thirties, his own included. Mine too – I have never allowed mine, e.g. *Politics and the Younger Generation* (which Eliot so carefully wet-nursed through the press for me) to be republished; only the essays in *The End of an Epoch*, for the historical record.

So Wystan settled for America.

My attitude to the great divide in his life was entirely different: I have always believed that his own poetry, and our literature in consequence, were the losers by his not being in the country to share the endurance, and the inspiration, of the last heroic period in our history, those wonderful years 1940–5, when the country's exceptional and happy insular history came to an end fighting the battle for civilization.

It will have been seen that I had already perceived that Auden had the makings of a fine patriotic poet in him. He had already derived such inspiration from the landscapes of England:

O love, the interest itself in thoughtless Heaven,
Make simpler daily the beating of man's heart; within
There in the ring where name and image meet,

Inspire them with such a longing as will make his
    thought
Alive like patterns a murmuration of starlings,
Rising in joy over wolds unwittingly weave;

Here too on our little reef display your power,

This fortress perched on the edge of the Atlantic scarp,
The mole between all Europe and the exile-crowded sea;

And make us as Newton was, who in his garden
    watching
The apple falling towards England, became aware
Between himself and her of an eternal tie . . .

In spite of the uncertainty of the syntax, it is a splendid poem; and there are several fine poems which show his love for England and its landscapes. It is indeed a dangerous thing for a poet to break that eternal tie, to sever oneself from the roots that nourish the imagination. Robert Lowell once said to me in New York that, in some way, the atmosphere of the United States (perhaps the prosiness of so much American life), was not propitious to English poets. And I believe this to be true: very few English poets have been able to write poetry in America. Wystan was prodigiously successful in America, but it was not good for his poetry – at any rate, he missed the undying inspiration of the war years here, and it was bad for him in other ways.

Wystan had the warmest of welcomes over there; he made friends everywhere – he was naturally gregarious, he chain-smoked and drank, far too much. He took jobs in universities; he gave poetry readings all over the country, for large fees; he made money – and, though he was generous, he was prudent about money. And America made him internationally famous – if that was good for him.

I refuse to go into the literary malice that accompanied his return to Europe with the end of the war, unabashed, an American citizen in uniform, or the mischievous reporting of it by such as Edmund Wilson. When he occasionally turned up at All Souls, he was a bit wary of me – understandably, in spite of my baiting him with a camp-joke about 'spectacled sailors' (American of course).

When I was in New York we would meet. He would come up for a drink (always a Bloody Mary) to my modest hotel, the Wellington, which was Edmund Wilson's usual refuge, always hard-up. I wasn't hard-up, by then, but of course we had no dollars. Our talk was usually about old Oxford days and our friends at the House. He put my name into one of his ephemeral poems, because he wanted a rhyme for our old College; and, always a gentleman, asked my permission when he needn't have done. But I noticed that he never asked me back to his flat down in Greenwich Village – still on the defensive with me. I wouldn't have fitted in, though I knew rather more of the goings-on there than perhaps he suspected. Once the young men of *Time* magazine gave me lunch; they very much wanted to do a profile of Wystan – until they found that the domestic life down at Cornela would hardly be suitable for the great heart of the public. How Wystan got away with it all is really surprising – generally respected and, in some quarters, rather revered.

I remember unwontedly attending a literary party given by my kind, discerning agent down in the Village, when Wystan, recognizing my 'limey accent', came across the room to talk to me. By this time he had adopted his American accent – all part of the pose, I suppose – though the short a's were the same as in the North Country, or, for that matter, my original West Country.

Wystan made up to me – rather condescendingly, I thought, he was now so famous (*Ich nicht!*) – with talk about Cornwall, Cornish mining, the old beam-engines and installations – very much his thing, he said. I didn't need to be told about all that. I responded by asking him about the Pennines and Sedbergh. At that, something of the pathos of his situation came through: 'I could never go back,' he said; 'that was Paradise.' Here was the home-sickness that lies behind one of the better poems written in America, 'In Praise of Limestone':

If it form the one landscape that we the inconstant ones
    Are consistently homesick for, this is chiefly
Because it dissolves in water. Mark these rounded slopes
    With their surface fragrance of thyme and beneath
A secret system of caves and conduits; hear these
    springs
    That spurt out everywhere with a chuckle

> Each filling a private pool for its fish and carving
>   Its own little ravine whose cliffs entertain
> The butterfly and the lizard . . .

Then the poem goes off into Auden caricaturing himself (as Eliot was apt to do) with talk about 'Mother', and 'the nude young male against a rock displaying his dildo'. However, the poem recovers itself and ends,

> but, when I try to imagine a faultless love
>   Or the life to come, what I hear is the murmur
> Of underground streams, what I see is a limestone
>   landscape.

On one of these talks in New York Wystan suddenly inter-jected, 'Of course, I've always been an Anglican.' What was the purpose of his telling me that, I wondered, slightly put off, when I knew perfectly well what the situation was, and he must have known that I knew. I don't think religion meant very much to him – as it deeply did to Eliot, and even affected me more than it did Wystan. He may have been coming back to Mother, but all the same it had its utility; he knew very well which side his bread was buttered, and this helped him to work his passage back and rendered him respectable. Fancy preaching in St Giles's Cathedral, Edinburgh, of all places! – breaking his false teeth on the Sunday, and having to have them cobbled up, after a fashion, just in time. (He was never very audible, and read his poems badly – again, unlike Eliot, who was a perfectionist.) Preaching later in Westminster Abbey tickled Wystan, for in that he had 'beaten Eliot'. (It was like Edith Sitwell, who became a Roman Catholic to beat Eliot, who was only an Anglo-Cath-olic. All rather childish.)

What rehabilitated Wystan in England was his election as Professor of Poetry at Oxford; I faithfully supported him – Maurice Bowra not – but was not in on it, for by this time I was a great deal away in America myself, only in Oxford for the summer. So I saw little of Wystan in those years; he was immensely famous (like Eliot) and, sensitive as ever, I did not wish to intrude. I think I a little resented it, having no *réclame* myself, for all my life of achieved hard work, partly I suppose from my secretive way of life. Though Eliot was encouraging and published my poetry, it had little recognition: I was categorized as a historian – and one could not be a historian *and* a poet. Eliot and Betjeman thought well of my poetry but, cagey as ever, I never mentioned the subject to Wystan. They were full-time professional poets.

In my view professional poets are apt to write too much – look at Bridges or Browning; Byron or Shelley or Wordsworth; even Tennyson. And certainly Wystan wrote far too much. A great deal of his later poetry is really prose cut up into metrical form.

In this period fell Shakespeare's Quatercentenary year, 1964, for which I wrote my standard biography, which solved the problems of the Sonnets, though it was some years before I discovered the identity of the Dark Lady. There was nothing surprising about the leading authority on the Elizabethan Age proceeding to write the biography of its leading writer, but it was much resented by the Shakespeare industry. The BBC typically called on Wystan to pontificate on the subject, not me who had written the biography.

The don was immediately shocked by a crass howler Wystan made – worthy of a Third in the Schools – in referring to the young man of the Sonnets' 'exclusive interest in women'. The exact opposite is the case: the whole point of the earlier Sonnets was to try to persuade the young man to take an interest in women. Everybody knows that the young man was ambivalent and as yet unresponsive to women. Shakespeare himself tells us so:

> A woman's face, with Nature's own hand painted,
> Hast thou . . .
> And for a woman wert thou first created;
> Till Nature, as she wrought thee, fell a-doting . . .
> By adding one thing to my purpose nothing.

That is, Nature added a prick, which defeated Shakespeare, who was very heterosexual. The situation is perfectly clear, fundamental to understanding the Sonnets; Wystan got it wrong, and never put it right.

He was blinded by the dogma which C. S. Lewis laid down – and with Ulster dogmatism labelled the converse the 'personal heresy', namely that it is quite unimportant to know the personal facts in question. Wystan repeats the dogma: 'What I object to is the illusion that if the identity of the Friend, the Dark Lady, the Rival Poet, etc, could be established beyond doubt, this would in any way illuminate our understanding of the Sonnets themselves.'

This is rank nonsense: of course it would and does; in fact, one cannot understand the Sonnets fully and intelligibly without that knowledge.

What C. S. Lewis (and Eliot too) meant in extruding the personal and biographical from consideration was that the critical judgment of poetry as poetry is an aesthetic one, and that is unexceptionable, indeed obvious. But, beyond that, to understand a poet's work, or his works, whatever one can find out about him or them helps our understanding of it. Eliot and Wystan both had reasons for wanting not too much known about their personal lives, but anyone who cares about knowledge wants to know all he can. It all has a bearing.

Wystan goes on and on repeating this nonsense, and not only in this essay. 'Even the biography of an artist is permissible,' he says condescendingly, 'provided that the biographer and his readers realize that such an account throws no light whatsoever upon the artist's work.'

A better-trained mind would realize with more discrimination that the importance of biographical knowledge varies very much with the writer: it is immensely important in the cases of Milton and Byron, say, whose egos were so important to their work and whose lives were so much bound up with the events of their time. We might say, less important in the cases of Shakespeare and Dryden, as dramatists – and yet illuminating all the same. As a matter of fact, Wystan contradicts himself in the very next essay. With a bow to the dogma, 'it is not often that knowledge of an artist's life sheds any significant light upon his work, but in the case of Pope I think it does.'

I should have thought it less significant with Pope than with, say, Dr Johnson. Wystan is intellectually rather confused on the subject. Never mind: it is rather amusing to find him subscribing so loyally to the dogma of the Eng. Lit. School at Oxford in which he had done so badly.

There were other ways in which America was bad for him: he became something of a sage, a guru, could lay down the law about anything and everything, and get away with it, with an insufficiently critical audience with real standards. So his later books are filled out with prosy platitudes, if cut up into verse form:

> The Road of Excess
> leads, more often than not, to
> The Slough of Despond.

> Gossip-Columnists I can forgive for they make no
>   pretences,
>   not Biographers who claim it's for Scholarship's sake.
> Autobiographers, please don't tell me the tale of your
>   love-life:
>   much as it mattered to you, nothing could marvel me
>   less.

Both these thoughts are plain silly: biographies and autobiographies have provided some of the great books of the world. What about Boswell's Johnson or Lockhart's life of Scott; the *confessions* of Rousseau or St Augustine? Wystan's own autobiography would have made a marvellous book, if he could have written it; I quite understand that he did not want the tale of his love-life told – but much autobiography is, of course, in his poems.

At length he became lonely in New York – there are poems of loneliness – and he longed to return to the Paradise of those early days, as if one can ever return along the path one has trodden! Christ Church – the House – was remarkably agreeable and allotted him a cottage on the premises, with membership of the Senior Common Room etc., such as E. M. Forster had enjoyed at King's, Cambridge.

Wystan came back and spent his first month with us at All Souls, where I was his oldest friend in residence. I welcomed him warmly, took him under my wing, resumed the old relationship of nearly fifty years before, the senior and junior.

His very first night in College he was burgled of all he had in his wallet, and came to tell me next morning. I said, 'Did you sport your oak?' No, he hadn't; he had gone to bed early and left his outer door unlocked. I said, 'You cannot do that. You must realize that Oxford has completely changed since our young days.' In those days we never thought of locking a door; today, in our filthy society, everything has to be kept locked. Even in the fortress of All Souls, I have had valuable rugs stolen, and lately a box of books and papers.

Someone had read in the paper of this famous man's return to Oxford and came to him with a sob-stuff tale about needing money for wife and child. Wystan, as a Christian (a lot of Christians have been had in Oxford that way – not me!), at once wrote out a cheque. That night someone entered his rooms and took all the money in his wallet. We all knew who it was, but the proof could not be brought home. Another characteristic trait of our delightful society.

Wystan and I resumed our talks, warmer, friendlier than before: I felt that he was sad and lonely, he confessed to me that he did not want to go on living. He told me that he was the runner-up for the Nobel Prize: I don't know who the successful candidate was – some second-rater, I suspect, like Steinbeck or Faulkner, instead of Robert Frost or Samuel Eliot Morison. I dare say Wystan would have got it if Hammarskjöld had lived – he was rather on his wavelength (absolutely not on mine: liberal-minded, universal do-gooder, no friend to this country).

In one of our talks Wystan restated his view of the unimportance of the biographical in the understanding of a writer's work – but gently, almost tentatively. I didn't bother to argue the matter, merely gave him my view. Nor did I take him up on Shakespeare. To what point? I have come to

Henry James's point of view and make it my motto: 'Nobody ever understands *any*thing', and leave it at that. All I care about, as a historian, is the truth of the matter in and for itself, no matter what anybody else thinks, or misthinks.

I was rather touched when Wystan gave me his last book, *Epistle to a Godson*, with the inscription 'With love from Wystan'; I wrote beside it, 'How nice, after all the years!' Reading it, I saw how nearly we had come to approximate in our view of the time we had lived through:

> Housman was perfectly right.
> Our world rapidly worsens:
> Nothing now is so horrid
> Or silly it can't occur.

> We all ask, but I doubt if anyone
> Can really say why all age-groups should find our
> Age quite so repulsive.

> Alienation from the Collective is always a duty:
>   Every state is the Beast who is Estrangement itself.

This is the way we had set out on together, and after such differing courses in life – yet keeping some touch – had reached the same conclusion. When I was young, I tied myself in knots to make some rational sense of the concept of Equality. Now, towards the end of our course Wystan – altogether more tactful than I – had not hesitated to say that there was immeasurably more inequality between men, in their gifts and abilities and potentialities, than is to be seen anywhere else in the animal kingdom. Think of the difference between a marvellous brain surgeon like Hugh Cairns in our time at Oxford, a physiologist of genius like Sherrington or a physicist like Rutherford at Cambridge, a Newton or an Einstein, and – shall we say – an average shop-steward! Now Wystan was saying:

> My family ghosts I fought and routed;
> Their values, though, I never doubted:

I thought their Protestant Work-Ethic
Both practical and sympathetic.

Then Speech was mannerly, an Art,
Like learning not to belch or fart . . .

Dare any call Permissiveness
An educational success?
Saner those class-rooms which I sat in,
Compelled to study Greek and Latin.

In short Wystan and I adhered to the old Oxford values we
had been brought up in – which he had briefly played truant
from earlier – and both believed in. He ended by asking:

Is it Progress when TV's children know all the names
Of politicians, but no longer play children's games?

I see that my note on that reads: 'Loss of innocence goes with
loss of imagination, quality, joy.'
    When he died, he left a message in a posthumous volume:

No summer sun will ever
dismantle the global gloom
cast by the Daily Papers,
vomiting in slipshod prose
the facts of filth and violence
that we're too dumb to prevent.

We were at one; and when this light – that had accompanied
me, nearer or farther, all my life – had gone out, dear Wystan, I found, somewhat to my surprise, that I had been rather
fond of him.